Engaging Departments

Engaging Departments

*Moving Faculty Culture From Private
to Public, Individual to Collective Focus
for the Common Good*

Kevin Kecskes
Portland State University

Editor

 ANKER PUBLISHING COMPANY, INC.

Published by Jossey-Bass
A Wiley Imprint
989 Market Street, San Francisco, CA 94103-1741   www.josseybass.com

Jossey-Bass books and products are available through most bookstores. To contact Jossey-Bass directly call our Customer Care Department within the U.S. at 800-956-7739, outside the U.S. at 317-572-3986, or fax 317-572-4002.

Jossey-Bass also publishes its books in a variety of electronic formats. Some content that appears in print may not be available in electronic books.

Library of Congress Cataloging-in-Publication Data

Engaging departments : moving faculty culture from private to public, individual to collective focus for the common good / Kevin Kecskes, editor.
        p. cm.
    Includes bibliographical references and index.
    ISBN-13: 978-1933371-02-3
    ISBN-10: 1-933371-02-1
    1. Universities and colleges—United States—Public services. 2. Universities and colleges—United States—Departments. 3. Education, Higher—Aims and objectives—United States. I. Kecskes, Kevin.
LB2331.44.E54 2006
378.1'2—dc22   2006009879

Printed in the United States of America
FIRST EDITION
HB Printing   10 9 8 7 6 5 4 3 2 1

To Sophia and Nico and all young people who bring hope for the future.

Table of Contents

About the Editor.. xi

Foreword.. xiii

Preface.. xvii

Acknowledgments.. xxiii

Part I ▪ A Broad Perspective

1 Big Questions for Engaging Departments 1
   Kevin Kecskes

2 Civic Engagement: A Broad Perspective................ 11
   Richard Battistoni

3 Characteristics of an Engaged Department:
   Design and Assessment 27
   John Saltmarsh, Sherril Gelmon

Part II ▪ Departmental Approaches: National Exemplars
Large-Scale Change

4 From Rogue Program to Poster Child:
   A Department's Shaping of a University's Agenda 45
   Paula T. Silver, John E. Poulin, Stephen C. Wilhite
   Center for Social Work Education at Widener University

5 Samford University's Communication Studies:
   Seizing an Opportunity 63
   Charlotte Brammer, Rhonda Parker
   Department of Communication at Samford University

6 Geology, Children, and Institutional Change
   in Southern California 76
   Jay R. Yett
   Department of Geology at Orange Coast College

Long-Term Commitment

7 Engagement in the Arts: Commitment
   to an Urban Experience............................. 89
   Susan Agre-Kippenhan, Elisabeth Charman
   Department of Art at Portland State University

 8   Sustaining a Service-Learning Program:
     An English Department's Commitment to Service 108
     Marybeth Mason, Pam Davenport
     Department of English at Chandler-Gilbert
     Community College
 9   The Spelman College Total Person Commits
     to Positive Social Change 125
     Cynthia Neal Spence, Daryl White
     Department of Sociology and Anthropology
     at Spelman College
10   Nursing Excellence: Community Engagement
     Through Service-Learning. 139
     Georgia Narsavage, Evelyn Duffy, Deborah Lindell,
     Marilyn J. Lotas, Carol Savrin, Yea-Jyh Chen
     Frances Payne Bolton School of Nursing at Case
     Western Reserve University
11   Community Service-Learning, Research,
     and the Public Intellectual. 159
     Leda Cooks, Erica Scharrer, Michael Morgan
     Department of Communication at the University
     of Massachusetts, Amherst

Mission Alignment
12   Fostering Engagement for Social Justice:
     The Social Justice Analysis Concentration
     in Sociology at Georgetown University 172
     Sam Marullo, Kathleen Maas Weigert, Joseph Palacios
     Department of Sociology at Georgetown University
13   "UCLA in LA": The Engaging Department
     of Chicana and Chicano Studies 192
     Reynaldo F. Macías, Kathy O'Byrne
     Department of Chicana and Chicano Studies
     at the University of California, Los Angeles

14 From Engagement to Marriage: A Systems
    Perspective With Formal and Durable
    Commitments to Service-Learning 205
    *Michael G. Laurent, Judith J. McIntosh, Rie
    Rogers Mitchell
    Department of Educational Psychology and Counseling
    at California State University, Northridge*

Part III ▪ Meta-Level Strategies
15 Continuums of Engagement at Portland State
    University: An Institution-Wide Initiative to Support
    Departmental Collaboration for the Common Good ... 219
    Kevin Kecskes, Amy Spring
16 A Journey of System-Wide Engagement 243
    Season Eckardt, Erika F. Randall, Lori J. Vogelgesang
17 Engaged Disciplines: How National Disciplinary
    Societies Support the Scholarship of Engagement 264
    Sherwyn P. Morreale, James L. Applegate

Part IV ▪ An Emerging Vision
18 The Engaged Department in the Context
    of Academic Change 278
    Edward Zlotkowski, John Saltmarsh

Appendix A: Engaged Department Strategic
             Planning Matrix 291
Appendix B: Connective Pathways
             for Engaged Departments 292
Appendix C: Engaged Department Resources 293

Index 295

About the Editor

Kevin Kecskes is director of Community-University Partnerships at Portland State University (PSU). Since 2002, Kevin has been charged with helping campus and community constituents live the university motto: "Let Knowledge Serve the City." From 1997–2002, Kevin was director of service-learning at Washington Campus Compact and program director of the Western Region Campus Compact Consortium. He served three years in leadership and program development positions with AmeriCorps* National Civilian Community Corps. Kevin cofounded the Boston College International Volunteer Program and spent 12 years working, serving, and studying in the developing world, primarily in Latin America and Asia. He has run his own small business and has taught in both secondary and higher education. Kevin studied biology, philosophy, education, and public administration and policy at Boston College, Harvard University, and Portland State University. His recent publications focus on the nexus between cultural theory and community-campus partnerships, ethics and community-based research, faculty and institutional development for civic engagement, student leadership development, and service-learning impacts on community partners. He lives in Portland, Oregon, with his wife and two children.

Foreword

Early in 2006, the Johnson Foundation convened one of its agenda-setting Wingspread conferences on "Engagement in Higher Education: Building a Federation for Action." The concern was not whether community-campus partnerships should be formed to address the critical social issues of our time or whether service-learning had finally emerged as a national movement. The central purpose was to launch a major federation of the multitude of associations, collaborations, universities, colleges, and community-based organizations that already had established initiatives aimed at effective academic and civic engagement. The intent was to collaborate on advancing the field, deepening understanding, and laying the groundwork for the advocacy of a common cause.

This book appears at a particularly critical time and is a part of this larger, advanced initiative. University-community collaborations are proliferating, service-learning is here to stay, the power of community-based research cannot be denied, and the importance of intellectual capital in a knowledge-based global society is a dominant theme in the popular media worldwide. The importance of the engaged campus is broadly recognized, but the infrastructure required to move this endeavor from the periphery of the college and university to the center has yet to be established. *Engaging Departments* addresses this critical need.

Every provost, dean, and department chair needs to read this book. It provides intelligent guidance for those considering taking the challenges of building a genuinely engaged campus seriously. The importance of focusing on the role of the department is made clear, and strategies for change—too often neglected in addressing higher education issues—are given thoughtful consideration.

The call for the engaged department is placed effectively within its historical and cultural context. Concrete examples of departments in which faculty have made the difficult cultural transition from focusing on "my work" to "our work" are described in helpful detail. Moving stories are told of how departments that have learned to work collaboratively then reach out into communities and learn to build relationships that are mutually beneficial. The chapters of this book give the reader a sense of the transformative experiences that can come to the students, faculty, and community partners who take the work of the engaged department seriously. Readers will find in this book an extraordinary combination of pragmatic strategy and genuine inspiration.

It is important to note that the editor of this volume, Kevin Kecskes, is director of Community-University Partnerships at Portland State University (PSU). As an award-winning engaged campus, PSU has provided national leadership as it has steadily encouraged campus and community constituents to live out the university motto: "Let Knowledge Serve the City." The several chapters that build on PSU's rich experience are particularly instructive.

Among the many contributors to this book are the names of leaders who have fundamentally shaped the public engagement agenda of higher education. To be able to tap the recent thinking of Edward Zlotkowski, John Saltmarsh, Sherril Gelmon, Sam Marullo, Sherwyn Morreale, James Applegate, and other mainstays is a privilege—the quality of their work and their faithful stewardship have made the advances represented by the publication of this book possible. I do not recognize some of the names of the contributors and am encouraged to see that there is a new generation of leaders emerging and cultivating fresh perspectives on the many facets of the engaged campus—especially the engaged department.

As one who contributed to the publication of the Carnegie report *Scholarship Reconsidered* in 1990, and as one who has been deeply interested in fostering the growth of the scholarship of engagement in subsequent years, I am delighted with the intellectual quality of the essays found in this book. Most of them are discipline-based and are rooted in the substance of their fields. They are examples of serious scholarship that bring together research and organizational practice, content and process, and theory and experience, and they focus on relating academic and civic knowledge, as well as academic and civic needs.

At the heart of this book is an epistemological challenge to the disconnection of the university from the larger purposes and deepest needs of local communities, regions, states, and nations. The walls of the university and college are becoming more permeable; the old knowledge boundaries no longer apply; reaching out can no longer be seen as a service, but as a necessity. *Engaging Departments* takes us into new territory—new ways of knowing, learning, and relating.

R. Eugene Rice, Senior Scholar
Association of American Colleges and Universities
Washington, DC

Preface

The service-learning movement in higher education, indeed higher education itself, is at a crossroads. Adding their voices to those of the prescient social critics preceding them, former associate director of the National Communication Association, Sherwyn P. Morreale, and past president James L. Applegate suggest that "Society appropriately is asking that we justify the huge investment made in research and teaching institutions in higher education. Campuses configured as ivory towers and disciplines huddled in silos where members communicate only with one another are no longer acceptable. The academy is responding to this public mandate" (Chapter 17).

Since the early 1990s, service-learning and a broader focus on civic engagement have challenged and helped change the culture of the academy. What started as a student movement in the 1970s and 1980s inspired by a desire for greater social justice morphed into a course-connected pedagogical initiative. Service-learning initially attracted faculty partly because of the social resonance it shared with educators trained in the 1960s. Surprising traditionalists, service-learning expanded quickly due in part to its proven positive impact on student learning (Astin & Sax, 1998). In 2005, the Corporation for National and Community Service calculated that 33% of America's students experience service-learning during their education.

A call for institutional renewal emerged that posed broad questions about the role of "universities as citizens" simultaneous with the expansion of service-learning in the 1990s classroom. In the late 1990s, hundreds of institutions declared their commitment to community engagement in one form or another. However, many institutions, especially those with large research portfolios, remained anchored in the post–World War II traditions of basic research and publication; most national disciplinary associations supported narrow, traditional definitions of scholarship and promotion criteria.

In 2006, the service-learning and civic engagement movement stands at a crossroads between marginalized success and the transformation of academic culture. Edward Zlotkowski and John Saltmarsh write in the concluding chapter of this volume, "It is our belief, a belief strongly reinforced by the cases in this book, that the ability of service-learning to contribute to the renewal of American higher education will depend on it becoming an integral part of the core work of academic departments."

In the late 1990s, National Campus Compact acted on this logic and initiated Engaged Department Institutes; a team of departmental and campus leaders from Portland State University (PSU) participated in the 2001 institute in Portland, Oregon. Subsequent to the gathering, PSU's Center for Academic Excellence prioritized a department-focused organizational development initiative and launched an Engaged Department Program. Over the past five years, PSU has intentionally worked with 20 departments, and these efforts have deepened the institutional commitment to community engagement. My colleague Amy Spring and I write about some of the surprises we encountered and lessons we learned from marshalling this institutional approach to departmental engagement in Chapter 15.

My overarching motivation for editing this book is to help ensure that service-learning contributes to the renewal of higher education. After witnessing many transformations in departments at PSU and hearing about the successes of academic units across the country, it became apparent that collecting the stories of service-learning exemplars and sharing them would have wide utility. Despite the diversity of departments (e.g., geology, art, nursing) and institutional types (two-year, four-year, public, private, comprehensive, land-grant, and research), two common, meta-level themes emerged in nearly all of the 11 case studies: 1) context matters, including institutional, departmental, and disciplinary context, and 2) having skilled change agents as part of the team can make a big difference. Recognizing how engaged departments were able to capitalize on changing unit or institutional environments suggests alignment with Kingdon's (1995) "multiple streams" theoretical policy development model. Kingdon posits that at critical points in time "policy windows" open that make it possible for a successful "policy entrepreneur" to implement change.

Audience

The primary audience for this book is current and emerging academic leaders. However, students of higher education and service-learning staff and faculty practitioners will discover useful information in the early chapters regarding definitions and frameworks and in the later chapters concerning the scholarship of engagement and academic reform. Engaged faculty in general, and specifically those associated with the disciplines highlighted in the case studies, will find inspiration in those chapters as well as several practical implementation strategies. Individuals with an interest in organizational or policy change and implementation will find the collective work of the departments illuminating.

Content Overview
Part I ▪ A Broad Perspective

Chapter 1. Kevin Kecskes sets a larger context for departmental engagement by inviting readers to consider questions about the purposes of community engagement.

Chapter 2. Richard Battistoni offers a broad perspective on civic engagement and provides diverse disciplinary frameworks for consideration. He challenges us to differentiate between civic engagement and civic learning and focuses on the distinctions between civic knowledge, skills, and values. This chapter concludes by offering several curricular integration methods and strategies.

Chapter 3. John Saltmarsh and Sherril Gelmon explore characteristics of engaged departments and discuss design and assessment topics. They outline four imperatives for engagement: mission, pedagogy, epistemology, and assessment. This chapter concludes with a discussion of evaluation strategies to align civic goals, assessment methods, and outcome measurement.

Part II ▪ Departmental Approaches: National Exemplars

Comprised of three subsections—large-scale change, long-term commitment, and mission alignment—the academic units in Part II were selected and invited to submit chapters from an initial list of more than 100 possible candidates. The chair of each department was involved in writing the chapters, and all authors followed a prescribed chapter structure to facilitate ease of reading, comparison among departments, and analysis: 1) short vignette; 2) demographics (institutional and departmental); 3) processes (leading to collective thinking, planning, and action); 4) analysis (including events and leadership); 5) impact; 6) lessons (successes, barriers, and key strategies); and 7) vision for the future. Although much of the collaborative work of creating an engaged department is quiet and unglamorous, several departments demonstrate how their work has led to large-scale organizational change. For example, in Orange County, California, thousands of K–12 students and their parents annually participate in Community Science Night. This gathering, sponsored by the Department of Geology at Orange Coast College, has precipitated district-wide change in the K–12 system, especially around the delivery of science curriculum in schools. At Widener University, located in one of the poorest counties in the United States, the collaborative efforts of faculty in the Department of Social Work Education have helped to unlock doors that previously isolated the institution from the surrounding neighborhood. There is much to learn from each of the case studies in this volume.

Part III ▪ Meta-Level Strategies

Chapter 15. Kevin Kecskes and Amy Spring summarize a five-year, institution-wide effort to support 20 engaged departments at Portland State University. This chapter offers evaluation results based on formative and summative assessment of this developmental work.

Chapter 16. Season Eckardt, Erika F. Randall, and Lori J. Vogelgesang describe the California State University (CSU) system-wide Engaged Department Initiative. Innovative and bold in scope, this initiative is housed in the CSU Office of the Chancellor and endeavors to create large-scale synergy among departments within the 23-university system. This chapter also presents evaluation results from an assessment conducted by staff at the University of California, Los Angeles Higher Education Research Institute.

Chapter 17. Sherwyn P. Morreale and James L. Applegate discuss the role of national disciplinary associations in support of this work. They argue that "continued funding for higher education's research efforts will in large part depend on reconceptualizing research, both basic and applied, as engaged." This chapter demonstrates how the scholarship of engagement and "use-inspired basic research" is being promoted at other national disciplinary associations, including the American Historical Association, the Association of American Law Schools, the American Sociological Association, and the American Political Science Association.

Part IV ▪ An Emerging Vision

Chapter 18. Edward Zlotkowski and John Saltmarsh offer an emerging vision of academic change by suggesting that "the task of creating engaged departments is one of the most important and one of the most challenging facing the service-learning movement." They confirm that service-learning is at the crossroads suggested earlier: "Whether one focuses on the integrity, the sustainability, or the impact of academy-community partnerships, it is difficult to see how the national service-learning movement can realize its potential—or even reach the next logical step in its development—without the leadership of engaged departments."

Kevin Kecskes
Portland State University
Portland, Oregon
January 2006

References

Astin, A. W., & Sax, L. J. (1998, May-June). How undergraduates are affected by service participation. *Journal of College Student Development, 39*(3), 251–263.

Kingdon, J. W. (1995). *Agendas, alternatives, and public policies* (2nd ed.). New York, NY: Longman.

Acknowledgments

This book could not have been written were it not for each authors' daily commitment to academic reform, deep learning, and the creation of a more socially just world. Their work brings hope, and to them I am indebted.

I would like to thank the creators of the Campus Compact Engaged Department Institute—Rick Battistoni, Sherril Gelmon, John Saltmarsh, Jon Wergin, and Edward Zlotkowski—for their steadfast national leadership in the service-learning movement. Among these tireless leaders, I especially thank my long-time friend Edward Zlotkowski for his faith in my abilities and for the inspiration he continues to bring to thousands of students, faculty, and higher education administrators across the globe.

Much appreciation goes to Carolyn Dumore, managing editor at Anker Publishing, for her continual patience and good nature, and to Jim Anker for his visionary leadership in higher education publishing.

I thank the dedicated staff at Portland State University's Center for Academic Excellence for their support through this writing effort, especially Abbey Lawrence and Martin Patail for their help with critical organizational tasks, Kelle Lawrence for her superb and timely editing skills, and Amy Spring for her friendship and enduring commitment to excellence and positive community change.

Finally, with abundant gratitude and love, I thank my wonderful wife Beth and children Sophia and Nico for their grace, understanding, and willingness to share me with this project.

1

Big Questions for Engaging Departments

Kevin Kecskes

Higher education in the United States is in swift transition. Near the heart of this transition is a contest of competing stories. These central narratives offer divergent visions for the future of higher education. While academic freedom is of central importance to both, one story advocates for a focused definition of disciplinary research and learning emblematic of the years following World War II. This view values the creation of pure knowledge unencumbered by the vicissitudes of society. An opposing impulse suggests we embrace the ambiguity and rapid cultural change representative of globalization. This approach seeks out and engages those societal vicissitudes, especially in the public sphere. Caught in this dialectic struggle are students and junior faculty who must daily find their way in potentially autocratic classrooms and departments.

Taxpayers, students, and parents are becoming increasingly anxious about the future costs of education. Citizens are registering their concerns and voting with their wallets to cut funding for education at the ballot box. Embedded in American society's response to this dichotomy, evidenced by the clearly decreasing trend of public financial support for higher education, is a provincial question: What's in it for me? However, there is a second, quieter, and more powerful question undergirding taxpayers' concerns: Education for what? Unless higher education intentionally and publicly responds to that second question, then anything goes and the public will continue to answer both questions however they wish.

Higher education is not the only institution in transition. Shellenberger and Nordhaus (2004) recommend that environmentalists take an urgent step backward before taking two necessary steps forward. They advocate for a decreased focus on issues and a radical concentration on "myth-making" based on a collective response to deep soul-searching for core beliefs, principles, and values. Only then, they contend, can a more comprehensive approach begin to emerge to create durable change. To map Shellenberger and Nordhaus's prescient thinking to higher education, we could begin taking that urgent step back by considering not only the important question *Education for what?* but also a more values-laden question that approaches the core of who we are as educators: What is the public purpose of a college or university? Or finally, apropos of this book, we might ask, How can my discipline contribute to the common good, and how does that look in *my* department?

Faculty Culture

For faculty in an academic unit to begin to respond to these questions they have to collaborate. Yet as Battistoni, Gelmon, Saltmarsh, Wergin, and Zlotkowski (2003) point out, "Faculty culture is highly privatized; as a faculty member, my teaching, research, and service are *my* work" (p. 3). Placing individualistic academicians together in a privatized unit may inspire healthy debate and rigorous research; however, competition rather than collaboration generally describes the environment. Indeed, this aligns with the findings of departmental scholar Jon Wergin (2003) when he asks,

> Why is it that when you talk about departmental collaboration people treat it as an oxymoron? Why is it that, even though I wrote *The Collaborative Department* (Wergin, 1995)…ten years ago, I continue to be kidded by colleagues who say that it was the only book of pure fantasy

ever published by the AAHE [American Association for Higher Education]? (p. 42)

The individualized nature of faculty work is not a new phenomenon. More than 40 years ago, Kerr (1963) observed that the university had become more of a bureaucracy than a community—"a mechanism held together by administrative rules and powered by money...a series of individual faculty entrepreneurs held together by a common grievance over parking" (p. 20).

Deep Soul-Searching

What, then, will it take for faculty to think collectively on a regular basis and for departments to truly collaborate? Wergin (2003) suggests that "members must address two matters they rarely address: the shared values upon which the work of the department rests, and the kind of evidence that will help them make the most useful judgments of quality" (p. 64). Regarding values, Wallack (2005) seconds Shellenberger and Nordhaus's call for deep soul-searching. He builds on Lakoff's (2004) work to identify three levels of analysis that can stimulate lasting social change. Level 1 involves big ideas and universal values; Level 2 involves how we classify issue types; and Level 3 involves specific policies or programs that might be developed to remedy the problems. Wallack concludes,

> the task we face...[is] to think about an overall "progressive story" that creates a context for programs and policies that can make a difference. We need to have...stories rooted in...Level 1 values and principles that can be the context for an elaboration of social policies and programs (Level 3) that are fairer, provide more opportunity...and advance the larger cause of a socially just society.

We need to hold close the big questions regarding the purposes of higher education, and by association the public purposes of disciplines, and grapple with our answers. Education for what? Effective pedagogies and transformative practices that align with the socially responsible world we hope to create must emerge from our responses.

While this book is largely focused on Level-3 type questions about pedagogies and collective practices—how members of specific disciplines housed in distinct departments engage with one another and with local and global communities—what provides meaning and can lead to personal, departmental, and institutional transformation is our ability to ask and to answer the big, Level-1 question of why transformation is important. National Campus Compact responded with its historic *Presidents' Declaration on the Civic Responsibility of Higher Education* (Ehrlich & Hollander, 2000). The result is that there are now nearly 1,000 colleges and universities that have taken on the challenge of paying particular attention to the public purposes of higher education. The American Association of State Colleges and Universities grappled with this question in 2003, and initiated the American Democracy Project (ADP). In 2006, there are more than 200 ADP schools that are attempting to respond to the big questions about the role of higher education to (re)create and sustain democracy in America.

Since 1990, several higher education leaders and scholars have called for institutional change by exploring the question of values (Boyer, 1990; Leslie & Fretwell, 1996; Plater, 1999; Rice & Richlin, 1993; Schön, 1995). Higher education practitioners and theorists have also attempted to establish a sense of institutional urgency, calling especially for a reexamination of the "relevancy" of disciplines in society (Bok, 1982; Halliburton, 1997; Lynton, 1995). Educational systems across the nation, and increasingly across the globe, have responded with a renewed commitment to public engagement, especially to the practices of service-learning, community-campus partnership building, and community-based research (Ehrlich, 2000).

Is Engagement Durable?

Kotter (1996) suggests an eight-step process for creating lasting change: 1) establishing a sense of urgency, 2) creating the guiding coalition, 3) developing a vision and strategy, 4) communicating the change vision, 5) empowering broad-based action, 6) generating short-term wins, 7) consolidating gains and producing more change, and 8) anchoring new approaches in the culture. Indeed, new collaborative approaches must be anchored in faculty and department culture if they are to endure. To this point, in Chapter 18 Zlotkowski and Saltmarsh ask an essential question: "Will individual faculty interest [in service-learning] seeping up from below and administrative encouragement [for civic engagement] trickling down from above finally reach each other at the level of departmental culture or will they instead encounter an impermeable membrane?" Portland State University's (PSU) intentional work with more than 20 departments since 2001 demonstrates that many of the membranes *are* permeable. Moreover, the 11 departmental exemplars highlighted in this book, along with many other academic units yet unknown beyond the faculty that comprise them, reveal that the kinds of healthy collaborations that Wergin (1995) envisioned are alive. National disciplinary associations—the intellectual gatekeepers for faculty and their departments—are prioritizing engaged pedagogies and beginning to encourage and value the scholarship of engagement (see Chapter 17). Therefore, if we have reached the tipping point (Gladwell, 2000), then what questions should we ask? What academic unit characteristics should we look for to begin answering Wergin's (2003) second question about the kind of evidence departments will need to help them make judgments of quality?

An Emerging Rubric
for Departmental Engagement

Informed by participation in one of National Campus Compact's Engaged Department Institutes and the excellent work of Wergin (2003) and Battistoni et al. (2003), the Center for Academic

Figure 1.1.   Characteristics of Engaged Departments:
Four Perspectives

Unit Perspective
Mission: The academic unit has a mission statement that includes civic engagement as a goal.
Leadership: The chair or other faculty leaders in the unit provide advocacy and support for engagement activities.
Visibility: The department publicly displays the collective commitment to civic engagement (on web sites, in promotional brochures, etc.).
Collaboration: The unit plans collectively and shares best practices.
Resource development: The unit pursues external resources to fulfill collectively determined, community-based, or civic engagement goals.
Inventory: The unit maintains an inventory of faculty members' community-based research and service-learning teaching activities.
Assessment: The unit tracks students' civic learning outcomes.
Faculty Perspective
Common understanding: Faculty in the unit individually and collectively understand why the department is involved in community-based activities.
Rewards: Faculty in the unit are rewarded for their civic engagement efforts.
Research: Faculty in the unit are encouraged to pursue research initiatives that are applied or that have a clearly defined application in a community setting.
Articulation to student/community partners: Faculty in the unit regularly articulate to students (in courses, catalogues, and during advising) and to community partners why the department is involved in community-based activities.

Excellence at Portland State University implemented an Engaged Department Program in 2001. Based on insights gained from the reflective experience of working with 20 PSU departments on collaborative engagement initiatives within their units (in addition to those learned from the literature and the 11 exemplars showcased in this volume), we have outlined an initial list of key

Figure 1.1. *Continued*

Student Perspective
Common understanding: Students in the major understand why the faculty/unit is involved in community-based work or other engagement activities.
Clarity of purpose: Students in the major understand why they are involved in community-based work and other civic or political engagement activities.
Inclusion: Students in the major have (some) regular and structured opportunities for providing input into unit-related decisions (e.g., faculty/staff hiring, curricular changes, etc.).
Leadership: Students in the major have multiple formal and informal opportunities (e.g., service-learning courses and community-based research) to develop civic leadership skills.
Community Perspective
Common understanding: Community partners understand why the faculty/unit is involved in community-based activities.
Clear expectations: Community partners understand their role in relation to this academic unit.
Interaction: Community partners interact with the unit by visiting classes, serving as adjunct faculty members, and so on.
Connection: Community partners attend departmental meetings.
Collaborative planning and action: Community-based projects, including service-learning courses and community-based research efforts, are designed with community partner input.

Note. Adapted from Battistoni et al., 2003; Kecskes, Gelmon, & Spring, 2006; Wergin, 2003.

characteristics of an engaged department. No department represented in this book or at PSU consistently and simultaneously demonstrates *all* of these characteristics; however, the rubric shown in Figure 1.1 can inform dialogue at the unit level and provide discussion prompts from four main perspectives: unit, faculty, student, and community partner. If departments periodically evaluate their regular weekly/monthly/yearly activities using these perspectives, this evaluation can help inform practitioners about the level of engagement in the unit and illuminate areas of excellence as well as topics for possible enhancement.

The Challenge of "Permeability"

In 1995, Astin asked the following Level-1 type question of university presidents:

> We [higher education] educate a large proportion of the citizens who bother to vote, not to mention most of the politicians, journalists, and news commentators. We also educate all the school administrators and teachers, who in turn educate everyone at the pre-college level. And we do much to shape the pre-college curriculum through what we require of our college applicants. In short, not only have we helped to create the problems that plague American democracy, but we also are in a position to begin doing something about them. If higher education doesn't start giving citizenship and democracy much greater priority, who will? (p. B2)

Although he did not use the word *moral,* Astin is talking about morality, about "big ideas and universal values" (Wallack, 2005). Kotter's (1996) sense of urgency permeates higher education today, and a period of rapid transition has arrived. The authors, institutions, and departments highlighted in this volume represent part of the vanguard of 21st-century durable change in higher education. They keep asking, and answering, the big-picture questions and intentionally continue to ensure that the "membranes" separating their departments—from individual faculty engagement as well as institutional inspiration—remain "permeable." To rephrase Astin, if academic departments and the disciplinary associations that guide them don't start giving citizenship, public problem solving, and democracy much greater priority, who will?

References

Astin, A. W. (1995, October 6). What higher education can do in the cause of citizenship. *The Chronicle of Higher Education*, p. B1.

Battistoni, R. M., Gelmon, S. B., Saltmarsh, J. A., Wergin, J. F., & Zlotkowski, E. (2003). *The engaged department toolkit.* Providence, RI: Campus Compact.

Bok, D. (1982). *Beyond the ivory tower: Social responsibilities of the modern university.* Cambridge, MA: Harvard University Press.

Boyer, E. L. (1990). *Scholarship reconsidered: Priorities of professoriate.* Princeton, NJ: Carnegie Foundation for the Advancement of Teaching.

Ehrlich, T. (Ed.). (2000). *Civic responsibility and higher education.* Phoenix, AZ: ACE/Oryx Press.

Ehrlich, T., & Hollander, E. (2000). *Presidents' declaration on the civic responsibility of higher education.* Providence, RI: Campus Compact.

Gladwell, M. (2000). *The tipping point: How little things can make a big difference.* New York, NY: Little, Brown.

Halliburton, D. (1997, January/February). John Dewey—A voice that still speaks to us. *Change, 29*(1), 24–29.

Kecskes, K. J., Gelmon, S. B., & Spring A. (2006). Creating engaged departments: A program for organizational and faculty development. In S. Chadwick-Blossey & D. R. Robertson (Eds.), *To improve the academy: Vol. 24. Resources for faculty, instructional, and organizational development* (pp. 147–165). Bolton, MA: Anker.

Kerr, C. (1963). *The uses of the university.* Cambridge, MA: Harvard University Press.

Kotter, J. P. (1996). *Leading change.* Boston, MA: Harvard Business School Press.

Lakoff, G. (2004). *Don't think of an elephant! Know your values and frame the debate.* White River Junction, VT: Chelsea Green Publishing.

Leslie, D. W., & Fretwell, E. K., Jr. (1996). *Wise moves in hard times: Creating and managing resilient colleges and universities.* San Francisco, CA: Jossey-Bass.

Lynton, E. A. (1995). *Making the case for professional service.* Washington, DC: American Association for Higher Education.

Plater, W. (1999). Habits of living: Engaging the campus as citizen one scholar at a time. In R. G. Bringle & E. A. Malloy (Eds.), *Colleges and universities as citizens* (pp. 141–172). Needham Heights, MA: Allyn & Bacon.

Rice, R. E., & Richlin, L. (1993). Broadening the conception of scholarship in the professions. In L. Curry, J. F. Wergin, & Associates, *Educating professionals: Responding to new expectations for competence and accountability* (pp. 279–315). San Francisco, CA: Jossey-Bass.

Schön, D. A. (1995, November/December). The new scholarship requires a new epistemology. *Change, 27*(6), 27–34.

Shellenberger, M., & Nordhaus, T. (2004). *The death of environmentalism: Global warming politics in a post-environmental world.* Retrieved March 15, 2006, from the Breakthrough Institute web site: www.thebreak through.org/images/Death_of_Environmentalism.pdf

Wallack, L. (2005). *Framing: More than a message.* Retrieved March 15, 2006, from the Longview Institute web site: www.longviewinstitute .org/research/wallack/levels

Wergin, J. F. (1995). *The collaborative department: How five campuses are inching toward cultures of collective responsibility.* Washington, DC: American Association for Higher Education.

Wergin, J. F. (2003). *Departments that work: Building and sustaining cultures of excellence in academic programs.* Bolton, MA: Anker.

About the Author

Kevin Kecskes is director of Community-University Partnerships at Portland State University. He oversees faculty and departmental development for community engagement as well as institutional civic engagement initiatives and events. His research and scholarship interests include community-university partnership development, faculty development for service-learning and civic engagement, and institutional transformation in higher education.

2

Civic Engagement: A Broad Perspective

Richard Battistoni

Before discussing the rationale for and examples of departmental engagement, it is helpful to define what is meant by engagement—more specifically, *civic engagement*, which is the underlying conceptual framework for this volume. One of the earliest expressions of the engagement agenda in higher education is found in the Campus Compact *Presidents' Declaration on the Civic Responsibility of Higher Education*, endorsed by more than 400 college and university presidents (Ehrlich & Hollander, 2000). In this document, campus leaders committed themselves "to renew our role as agents of our democracy, [to] catalyze and lead a national movement to reinvigorate the public purposes and civic mission of higher education" (pp. 3–4). The declaration reflects a major change in the way campuses view their civic mission and the role of service in this mission. The ultimate aim has shifted from promoting community service to institutionalizing service-learning, and now to fostering student civic engagement in a diverse democracy.

Why Civic Engagement?

There has been great concern about citizen disengagement from public life and anxiety over the decline in the social capital necessary for the survival of a vibrant democracy (Galston, 2001; Keeter, Zukin, Andolina, & Jenkins, 2002; Putnam, 2000). With mounting evidence of disengagement from American politics and public life, especially among young people, there is an ever-deepening feeling that our educational institutions are leaving students unprepared for a life of engaged, democratic citizenship.

Higher education in particular seems concerned about this civic disengagement, and is sensitive about its own failings in involving students as active citizens in their democracy. In the early 1990s, a report by the Kettering Foundation charged that higher education "appears to leave students without concepts or language to explore what is political about their lives" (Harwood Group, 1993, p. xii). When the National Commission on Civic Renewal reported on the state of civic disengagement in 1998, it seemed to offer no role for higher education in providing solutions. Once again, academia was subjected to the charge of being irrelevant to public problems and unresponsive to public needs. Bok (1990) put it this way: "Communities have problems, universities have departments" (p. 4). Campus Compact's recent efforts, as exemplified in the *Presidents' Declaration,* can be seen as a response to this charge of civic deficiency on the part of higher education.

A common strategy for meeting the challenge of stemming the tide of civic disengagement has been to connect work in service- and community-based learning to the campus's civic outcomes. The idea behind these efforts has been to capitalize on the well-documented involvement of students in community service to advance the mission of civic engagement. This strategy assumes that a clear relationship can be developed between acts of service and citizenship, which depends on how concretely campuses and their academic departments can define the civic engagement outcomes for students.

What Is Civic Engagement in the Context of Higher Education?

The emphasis on engaged departments is part of a broader agenda to comprehensively promote civic engagement across the curriculum, to get each academic unit to define their civic goals.

In 2002, I tried to make a comparison to previous higher education initiatives involving writing across the curriculum. The movement for writing across the curriculum was based on the premise that whatever a student's major or future aspiration, he or she needed to be proficient at written communication to be effective. Similarly, the current movement toward civic engagement assumes that just as we want students to be good writers, we want them to be good citizens. Whatever the student's major, career, or life goals, he or she will be a member of some community, and for our democracy to continue and to flourish, we need people who will effectively exercise their civic rights and responsibilities. All faculty need to be enlisted in this effort to improve civic education.

Although we might like to draw a parallel between civic engagement across the curriculum and writing across the curriculum, there is an immediate difference. Those in higher education who advocate civic engagement across the curriculum face an immediate disadvantage not confronted by their counterparts who launched writing across the curriculum. While there may be some disagreements, especially around the margins (no pun intended) about quality writing, there seems to be basic consensus around the question "What is good writing?" The question of what constitutes good citizenship, however, is highly controversial and contested. And the controversy surrounding definitions of good citizenship stems in part from the way citizenship language is used. I can think of three areas where citizenship language actually serves as a barrier to positive conversations in the academy about education for civic engagement. First, citizenship is a legal status, a status not shared by all in our educational institutions or in the communities of which they are a part. Language around citizenship can be a real barrier when working with immigrant populations. This extends to the academy itself, where admonitions to faculty to be good departmental citizens overlook the differential status between senior and junior, full- and part-time faculty members.

Second, the language of citizenship is ideological. More liberal faculty complain that citizenship education tends to convey images of patriotic flag-waving, while more conservative faculty see the language of civic engagement masking a leftist, activist agenda. Either way, the goal of civic engagement seems to lack objective, academic substance.

Third, the language of citizenship and civic engagement conjures up a childhood past that many faculty would just as soon forget, or at least would not endorse as characteristic of democratic life in a diverse society. Some of us remember our grade school "civics" courses as pedestrian and/or downright boring. For me, growing up in California, public schools gave "citizenship" grades on report cards based on a student's silence in the classroom, neatness, politeness, and passive obedience to school rules (I am told this still occurs in some school districts across the country). When citizenship is tied to exclusive legal identities, ideologically charged language and symbols, or conformity to institutional norms, it is bound to raise suspicions, especially in the minds of academics.

Moreover, civic engagement language tends to be somewhat amorphous, meaning different things to different people. This, of course, is its strength, as it can be attached to a number of issues—community development, student leadership, service-learning as a pedagogical strategy, mission reclamation and the public perceptions of higher education, and more (Saltmarsh, 2004). But civic engagement language tends to lack concreteness or clarity, especially when it comes to learning goals for students.

Civic Engagement and Civic Learning

Perhaps a better way to conceive of civic engagement, in the context of higher education, is to ask ourselves which student learning outcomes should be associated with a civic engagement perspective. Newman (1985) argued for this approach:

> The most critical demand is to restore to higher education its original purpose of preparing graduates for a life of

involved and committed citizenship.... The advancement of *civic learning* [italics added], therefore, must become higher education's most central goal. (p. xiv)

More recent studies have begun to emphasize the civic learning outcomes we should seek for our students (Colby, Ehrlich, Beaumont, & Stephens, 2003; Saltmarsh, 2005; Torney-Purta & Vermeer, 2004). Howard (2001) offers a definition of civic learning in particular that begins to capture what could be a common framework to inform any academic department.

We conceive of "civic learning" as any learning that contributes to student preparation for community or public involvement in a diverse democratic society. A loose interpretation of civic learning would lead one to believe that education in general prepares one for citizenship in our democracy. And it certainly does. However, we have in mind here a strict interpretation of civic learning— knowledge, skills, and values that make an *explicitly direct and purposeful contribution* to the preparation of students for active civic participation. (p. 38)

Under this definition, the focus should be on what types of knowledge, skills, and values we seek to foster in students to better enable them to actively participate in the public life of our diverse democratic society. Each disciplinary department or interdisciplinary program can, in turn, determine how it will contribute to the civic learning of students on its campus and what primary pathway—knowledge, skills, or values—it will pursue to make this contribution. Some examples follow.

Civic Knowledge

When defining civic knowledge, past educators tended to focus on the purely academic forms that this knowledge takes: dates and places of important civic events, knowledge of the different conceptions of citizenship in a democracy, knowledge about the institutions and operations of our democratic government. Indicators of civic knowledge once included the ability to answer questions about how a bill becomes a law, the names of your congressional representatives, and how many justices sit on the U.S. Supreme Court. But we have learned from students engaged in community-based experiences that civic knowledge is much broader than this and comes from multiple sources, including community members. It involves a deeper knowledge of issues, or what some might call the root causes of public problems, and an understanding of how different community stakeholders perceive the issues. An understanding of "place" and the community history that provides a context for service and public problem solving—including learning about how individuals and community groups have effected change in their communities—is another key element of civic knowledge. An added benefit to defining civic knowledge in this broad manner is that students and community members become cocreators of knowledge, rather than simply relying on "expert" texts or professors.

Most important to a discussion about the engaged *department,* civic knowledge can be defined in terms of the distinct perspectives that different disciplines bring to questions of democracy and public life. There are several different conceptual frameworks of civic engagement that have been developed, in particular, by political and social theorists (Battistoni, 2002). These frameworks share some common themes, but are also distinct in their specific views of citizenship, understanding of civic education, and associated civic skills. These frameworks and the disciplinary affinities for each are illustrated in Table 2.1.

Rich conceptual frameworks also exist outside the social sciences and can be used by disciplinary departments to ground their understanding of engagement. Conversations with 13 national educational disciplinary associations as part of the Engaged Disciplines Project conducted by National Campus Compact with

Table 2.1. Conceptual Frameworks From the Social Sciences

Conceptual Framework	Citizenship	Civic Knowledge	Civic Skills	Disciplinary Affinities
Constitutional citizenship (Rawls, 1971)	• Rights-bearing individual • Voter	Knowledge of government institutions, laws, elections	• Political knowledge • Critical thinking	• Political science • Law • Policy studies (health, education)
Communitarianism (Etzioni, 1993)	• "Good neighbor" • Duty to fulfill common good	Knowledge of community values and civic responsibilities	• Civic judgment • Community building	• Philosophy • Religious studies • Social work • Public health
Participatory democracy (Barber, 1984, 1992)	Active participant in public life	Knowledge of democratic participation processes	• Communication skills • Collective action • Civic imagination	• Political science • Education • Public health
Public work (Boyte, 2000; Boyte & Kari, 1996)	Cocreator of things of public value	Knowledge (through projects) of the skills, habits, and values of working with others on public tasks	• Public problem solving • Coalition building	• Political science • Public administration • Health administration • Professional disciplines
Social capital (Putnam, 2000)	Membership in associations of civil society	Knowledge of social connections and institutions	• Communication skills • Organizational analysis	• Sociology • Nonprofit management

support from The Pew Charitable Trusts identified a list of terms from each discipline that were summarized into seven conceptual frameworks connected to civic engagement (Battistoni, 2002). These frameworks are summarized in Table 2.2, along with their different answers to questions of citizenship, the nature of civic education, and the associated civic skills needed for effective public life. Also included is each framework's disciplinary affinities.

Civic Skills

In *Civic Engagement Across the Curriculum* (Battistoni, 2002) I have detailed a set of civic skills that educators from different disciplines and/or parts of campus life should try to instill in students when preparing them for active participation in democratic public life. This set of civic skills includes critical thinking; communication and deliberation (speaking and listening); public problem solving; civic judgment; civic imagination and creativity; teamwork, coalition building, and collective action; community organizing; and organizational analysis. That work also contains exercises and assignments intended to develop these skills in students who are involved in community-based service and research connected to the curriculum.

In many ways, these civic skills have traditionally been defined as part of a liberal education. More recently, they have been associated with the "employability" or workforce development literature (see Battistoni & Longo, 2005). Still, the research suggests that many service-learning programs do not achieve their desired civic impact because they have not sufficiently addressed the development of fundamental civic skills (Kirlin, 2002).

Civic Values

Here I think we can run into trouble, mostly in the reticence of higher educators to broach the subject of civic values. This may be why some proponents of civic engagement use the seemingly more neutral terms of *attitudes* or *dispositions* to describe this area of civic-learning outcomes (see Colby et al., 2003; Torney-Purta & Vermeer, 2004). Values are an important dimension of civic learning, and I think we can have a conversation about what values are appropriate to democratic public life, even though there may be strong disagreement over them. Saltmarsh (2005) presents the "key democratic values" (p. 55) as participation, justice, and inclusion, values he believes "can be widely agreed upon and shared" (p. 55). Faculty from different disciplinary perspectives or frameworks will frame the question of civic values differently. For example, the framework of *civic professionalism* understands civic values as the way a professional's technical expertise "discovers its human meaning" (Sullivan, 2004, p. xix). This perspective thus allows students to bring their own public values to the work they are doing, in the classroom and in the community.

Additionally, civic values might be framed by the values expressed in the institutional mission of the university. The University of Minnesota, for example, has an "institutional commitment to public purposes and responsibilities intended to strengthen a democratic way of life in the rapidly changing Information Age of the 21st century" (Bruininks, 2005). Portland State University (2006) uses the following value-laden definition: "Civic engagement aims to improve society, enhance the public good, and promote social justice." These are just two examples of ways in which a public institution of higher education might define its civic values. Faith-based institutions may define civic values through a different lens. For example, at many Catholic colleges and universities, dialogue about civic values comes through concepts such as dignity of the human person, the preferential option for the poor, solidarity, and subsidiarity.

Methods and Strategies

While a department's conception of civic knowledge, skills, and values provides the pathway to engagement, a department's curriculum provides the primary resource for building the student's

Table 2.2. Conceptual Frameworks From a Range of Disciplines

Conceptual Framework	Citizenship	Civic Knowledge	Civic Skills	Disciplinary Affinities
Civic professionalism (Sullivan, 2004)	Professional work with a civic purpose	Knowledge of the civic traditions and values of the professions	• Public problem solving • Civic judgment	• Professional disciplines • Management • Law • Public administration
Social responsibility	Responsibility to the larger society	Knowledge of public problems most closely associated with chosen field of work	• Political knowledge of issues • Organizational analysis	• Health professions • Business disciplines • Computer science • Public health
Social justice (Hollenbach, 1988)	Bringing one's spiritual values to bear on social problems	Knowledge of the principles of social justice and their application to public life	• Civic judgment • Collective action	• Philosophy • Religious studies
Connected knowing; ethics of care (Gilligan, 1982)	Caring for the future of our public world	Knowledge of others and their perspectives on the world	• Critical thinking • Coalition building	• Women's studies • Nursing • Psychology
Public leadership (Greenleaf, 1996)	Citizen as "servant-leader"	Knowledge of the arts of collaborative leadership	• Community building • Communication	• Literature • Visual and performing arts

Table 2.2. *Continued*

Conceptual Framework	Citizenship	Civic Knowledge	Civic Skills	Disciplinary Affinities
Public intellectual (Jacoby, 1987)	Thinkers who contribute to the public discourse	Knowledge of the traditions of writers and artists who have served as public intellectuals	• Civic imagination • Creativity	• Literature • Visual and performing arts
Engaged/public scholarship (Boyer, 1996)	Participatory action researcher	Knowledge of how scholarly research might contribute to the needs and values of the community	• Organizational analysis • Public problem solving	• Journalism • Communications • Professional disciplines

Note. See Battistoni (2002) for a more detailed discussion of each of these frameworks.

road to civic learning. Several methods and strategies are available for integrating civic learning into a department's curriculum, and a department may deploy them at different stages in students' academic (and professional) development (Gelmon & Battistoni, in press). These include course-based service-learning, field-based experiences and internships, capstones, community-based research projects, cocurricular activities and organizations, and professional development activities.

Many of these strategies are illustrated in the specific case studies included in this book. All have demonstrated impact as mechanisms for promoting civic learning and can be deployed depending on the level of curricular or student development, the orientation and training of faculty, and existing relationships or opportunities with community partners. Regardless of the methods chosen, research suggests that effective civic engagement strategies share the following common characteristics (Battistoni & Longo, 2005; Eyler & Giles, 1999).

Placement Quality and Curriculum Applications

Student learning is strongest when the service and work students do in the community is intentionally connected to civic development outcomes in the classroom. Colleges and their faculty need to be intentional in designing service-learning courses and projects, ensuring that the community experience is meaningful and ongoing and can be harvested for the civic outcomes they seek. In particular, it is important to incorporate the civic perspective and skill development necessary for effective public life into the curriculum itself.

Critical Reflection

Although reflection has almost become a mantra in the service-learning field, the research clearly demonstrates that reflection "transforms experience into learning" (Bringle & Hatcher, 1999, p. 180), and that it matters greatly in terms of maximizing student impact. The quantity and quality of reflection has been consistently associated with academic learning outcomes, so engaged department faculty need to be intentional about incorporating civic reflection into their courses. Practitioners are also beginning to understand that reflection can take many forms, and it is most successful when faculty use a variety of reflection methods.

Community Voice

Successful service-learning programs have long understood the importance of reciprocity in their community partnerships. This begins with a commitment to work collaboratively with the community to establish projects and activities that meet community-identified needs. But it also goes well beyond that to seeing the community as a crucial partner in learning rather than merely as a "placement site." Community partnerships for learning imply strong, long-term relationships that students have the chance to experience fully. In particular, if we are to recognize the importance of place and public problem solving in educating students for civic development, we need to involve students in understanding the different stakeholders' interests in the community and in mapping the assets and resources that exist in a given neighborhood.

Student Voice

Research and practice in service-learning has established the importance of giving students a voice in the design of community-based projects connected to the curriculum and in the resulting discussions/reflections that accompany the community-based experience. But we are also finding that student voice means enabling students to be involved in public problem solving connected to the issues that *they* determine to be important. A quality program allows students to develop projects and activities connected to their interests and ideas about what could be improved in their communities.

Departments looking to engage students as active citizens in the lives of their communities have a number of pathways and strategies available to them. The important thing to remember is that civic engagement does not happen automatically; it must be nurtured through close attention to departmentally appropriate definitions of engagement and the intentional connection of these definitions to the curriculum and to corresponding community-based experiences.

References

Barber, B. (1984). *Strong democracy: Participatory politics for a new age.* Berkeley, CA: University of California Press.

Barber, B. R. (1992). *An aristocracy of everyone: The politics of education and the future of America.* New York, NY: Ballantine.

Battistoni, R. (2002). *Civic engagement across the curriculum: A resource book for service-learning faculty in all disciplines.* Providence, RI: Campus Compact.

Battistoni, R., & Longo, N. (2005). *Connecting workforce development and civic engagement: Higher education as public good and private gain.* Lynn, MA: North Shore Community College Policy Institute.

Bok, D. (1990). *Universities and the future of America.* Durham, NC: Duke University Press.

Boyer, E. L. (1996, Spring). The scholarship of engagement. *Journal of Public Service and Outreach, 1*(1), 11–20.

Boyte, H. C. (2000). Civic education as a craft, not a program. In S. Mann & J. Patrick (Eds.), *Education for civic engagement in democracy: Service-learning and other promising practices* (pp. 61–72). Bloomington, IN: ERIC Clearinghouse for Social Studies.

Boyte, H. C., & Kari, N. N. (1996). *Building America: The democratic promise of public work.* Philadelphia, PA: Temple University Press.

Bringle, R. G., & Hatcher, J. A. (1999, Summer). Reflection in service-learning: Making meaning of experience. *Educational Horizons, 77*(4), 179–185.

Bruininks, R. (2005). *About public engagement*. Retrieved March 16, 2006, from the University of Minnesota web site: www.umn.edu/civic/about/index.html

Colby, A., Ehrlich, T., Beaumont, E., & Stephens, J. (2003). *Educating citizens: Preparing America's undergraduates for lives of moral and civic responsibility*. San Francisco, CA: Jossey-Bass.

Ehrlich, T., & Hollander, E. (2000). *Presidents' declaration on the civic responsibility of higher education*. Providence, RI: Campus Compact.

Etzioni, A. (1993). *The spirit of community: Rights, responsibilities, and the communitarian agenda*. New York, NY: Crown.

Eyler, J., & Giles, D. E., Jr. (1999). *Where's the learning in service-learning?* San Francisco, CA: Jossey-Bass.

Galston, W. A. (2001, June). Political knowledge, political engagement, and civic education. *Annual Review of Political Science, 4*(1), 217–234.

Gelmon, S., & Battistoni, R. (in press). Civic engagement: Conceptual frameworks. In M. Stefl, S. Gelmon, & A. Hewitt, *Civic engagement in health administration education*. Arlington, VA: Association of University Programs in Health Administration.

Gilligan, C. (1982). *In a different voice: Psychological theory and women's development*. Cambridge, MA: Harvard University Press.

Greenleaf, R. K. (1996). *On becoming a servant leader: The private writings of Robert K. Greenleaf* (D. M. Frick & L. C. Spears, Eds.). San Francisco, CA: Jossey-Bass.

Harwood Group. (1993). *College students talk politics*. Dayton, OH: Kettering Foundation.

Hollenbach, D. (1988). *Justice, peace, and human rights: American catholic social ethics in a pluralistic context*. New York, NY: Crossroad.

Howard, J. (Ed.). (2001). *Service-learning course design workbook*. Ann Arbor, MI: University of Michigan OSCL Press.

Jacoby, R. (1987). *The last intellectuals: American culture in the age of academe*. New York, NY: Basic Books.

Keeter, S., Zukin, C., Andolina, M., & Jenkins, K. (2002). *The civic and political health of the nation: A generational portrait.* College Park, MD: Center for Information and Research on Civic Learning and Engagement.

Kirlin, M. (2002, September). Civic skill building: The missing component in service programs? *PS: Political Science and Politics, 35*(3), 571–575.

Newman, F. (1985). *Higher education and the American resurgence.* Princeton, NJ: Carnegie Foundation for the Advancement of Teaching.

Portland State University. (2006). *Civic engagement.* Retrieved March 16, 2006, from: http://portfolio.pdx.edu/Portfolio/Community_Global_Connections/Civic_Engagement

Putnam, R. D. (2000). *Bowling alone: The collapse and revival of American community.* New York, NY: Simon & Schuster.

Rawls, J. (1971). *A theory of justice.* Cambridge, MA: Harvard University Press.

Saltmarsh, J. (2004). *The civic purpose of higher education: A focus on civic learning.* Unpublished manuscript.

Saltmarsh, J. (2005, Spring). The civic promise of service learning. *Liberal Education, 91*(2), 50–55.

Sullivan, W. M. (2004). *Work and integrity: The crisis and promise of professionalism in America* (2nd ed.). San Francisco, CA: Jossey-Bass.

Torney-Purta, J., & Vermeer, S. (2004). *Developing citizenship competencies from kindergarten through grade 12: A background paper for policymakers and educators.* Denver, CO: Education Commission of the States.

About the Author

Richard Battistoni is professor of political science at Providence College. From 1994–2000, he served as the founding director of the Feinstein Institute for Public Service at Providence College, the first in the nation degree-granting program combining community service with the curriculum. He is author of *Civic Engagement Across the Curriculum: A Resource Book for Service-Learning Faculty in All Disciplines* (Campus Compact, 2002).

3

Characteristics of an Engaged Department: Design and Assessment

John Saltmarsh, Sherril Gelmon

Departments are the units in which the institution's strategy for academic development is formulated in practice.

—Donald Kennedy

The department is arguably the definitive locus of faculty culture, especially departments that gain their definition by being their campus's embodiment of distinguished and hallowed disciplines... we could have expected that reformers would have placed departmental reform at the core of their agenda; yet just the opposite has occurred. There has been a noticeable lack of discussion of—or even new ideas about—departments' role in reform.

—Richard Edwards

Concepts of Engagement: General and Department-Specific

When we talk about an engaged department, what do we mean by "engagement?" *Engagement* is a term that has been overused in recent years within higher education, and it has become necessary to clarify how it is being used. It is perhaps most often used to describe active and collaborative teaching and learning strategies that lead to greater student involvement in the processes and outcomes of their education. In this context, engagement refers to the engaged

27

learning on the part of students. This framework refers to processes rather than outcomes, such that engaged learning can take place in any number of ways—discussions, laboratories, simulations—that do not require students to leave the classroom or the campus and become involved in the local community as part of their learning. Nor does engagement in this context raise the question of the civic purposes of higher education and the design of teaching and learning strategies that lead to civic learning outcomes.

An example of this distinction between engaged learning and civic engagement is reflected in the National Survey of Student Engagement (NSSE). The NSSE measures student self-reports about the characteristics of their learning experiences, processes, and activities such as the amount of discussion in the classroom, the amount of contact students have with faculty (in and out of the classroom), and the degree to which students participate in active and collaborative activities. One result of the NSSE is that the most potent pedagogy for civic engagement—service-learning—is also identified as a potent strategy for engaged learning.

> Complementary learning opportunities inside and outside the classroom augment the academic program... service-learning provides students with opportunities to synthesize, integrate, and apply their knowledge. Such experiences make learning more meaningful, and ultimately more useful because what students know becomes a part of who they are. (NSSE, 2002, p. 11)

The difference here is that service-learning is designed for engaged learning as well as for civic engagement. An essential point made by Russ Edgerton and Lee Shulman in a critique of the 2002 NSSE results is relevant here:

> We know, for instance, that students can be engaged in a range of effective practices and still not be learning with

understanding; we know that students can be learning with understanding and still not be acquiring the knowledge, skills, and dispositions that are related to effective citizenship. (NSSE, 2002, p. 3)

Civic engagement moves engagement beyond effective teaching and learning strategies to education for citizenship.

Engagement as part of engaged department initiatives is undertaken in the context of civic engagement that deliberately connects academic knowledge with community-based knowledge, is grounded in experiential and reflective modes of teaching and learning, and is aimed at developing the knowledge, skills, and values that will be necessary for students to become active participants in American democracy. It is the context of engagement in higher education where "civic engagement means working to make a difference in the civic life of our communities and developing the combination of knowledge, skills, values and motivation to make that difference" (Ehrlich, 2000, p. vi). The focus on the department as the locus for engagement is the kind of effort directed toward institutional renewal that supports civic engagement.

The Department as the Unit of Change

Larger institutional reform efforts, such as the movement catalyzed by Boyer (1990) to redefine faculty roles and rewards, have been undertaken predominantly above and outside the departmental context within which faculty culture resides. Efforts aimed at improving teaching and learning have often occurred at the level of practice by the individual faculty member and have had little impact beyond that individual's classroom and scholarship. It has become increasingly clear, as reflected in the analyses by Kennedy (1995) and Edwards (1999) that open this chapter, that meaningful reform efforts in higher education will have to penetrate the department.

The department is the academic structure that brings together the institution's unique identity and mission with the professional strictures of disciplinary associations along with the standards and expectations of scholarship. It is, as Edwards (1999) writes, "the definitive locus of faculty culture, especially departments that gain their definition by being their campus's embodiment of distinguished and hallowed disciplines" (p. 18). Faculty who are unresponsive to administrative agendas constructed outside the values and disciplinary frameworks of the department are far more likely to engage in reform that is indigenous to the department. There must be a compelling academic interest in civic engagement if it is to be undertaken by a department as a significant initiative.

The Imperative for Engagement

There is now a movement within higher education, in the American context and globally, to reclaim the civic purposes of the college and university mission, affirming and implementing the institution's civic responsibility, whether public or private. At the same time, there have been efforts since the early 1990s to improve teaching and learning on campus. Parallel to these trends has been a strong impetus to value diverse forms of knowledge and to find ways to create new knowledge that addresses the social challenges of the 21st century. These three factors, which one can call the mission imperative, the pedagogical imperative, and the epistemological imperative, all influence the creation of engaged departments. For change to occur along the lines of these imperatives, the department becomes the locus for change, not only in terms of knowledge creation and the transmission of that knowledge, but also in terms of operationalizing the mission of the institution through core academic functions.

The Mission Imperative

Engaged department efforts are driven in part by a movement begun in the early 1980s to refocus American higher education on reclaiming its civic purposes. Newman (1985) asserted that "the most critical demand is to restore to higher education its original purpose of preparing graduates for a life of involved and committed citizenship" (p. xiv); therefore, "the advancement of civic learning...must become higher education's most central goal" (p. 32). Newman's work captured the early stirrings of the "movement" to revitalize the civic mission of higher education as it was increasingly faced with competing and multiple demands. More recently, he forcefully argued the need to stay true to the civic responsibility of higher education: "Higher education must work harder on encouraging the civic education of today's students to ensure the efficacy of tomorrow's democracy" (Newman, Couturier, & Scurry, 2004, p. 129).

In the intervening years between Newman's work, many others embraced the challenge of revitalizing the civic purpose of colleges and universities amidst the insidious pressures of the consumerism and commodification of market-driven education. One example of the countervailing weight of the movement for civic engagement is Campus Compact's *Presidents' Declaration on the Civic Responsibility of Higher Education*, perhaps the most cogent statement on the need for and importance of remaining true to the civic mission of higher education, asserting the role of colleges and universities as "agents and architects of a flourishing democracy" (Ehrlich & Hollander, 2000, p. 3).

The mission imperative for engagement is grounded, fundamentally, in the Deweyian marriage of education and democracy, or as Dewey (1937/1987) wrote,

> Unless education has some frame of reference it is bound to be aimless, lacking a unified objective. The necessity for a frame of reference must be admitted. There exists in this country such a unified frame. It is called democracy. (p. 415)

The mission imperative resists aimlessness and fragmentation and embraces the public purpose of higher education—looking to the academic department as one place, perhaps the most important place, for the academic mission to be implemented.

The Pedagogical Imperative

Much of the success of service-learning over the past quarter century can be attributed to its effectiveness in improving student learning. A growing body of research indicates that all the features of quality service-learning lead to improved learning—its experiential aspect, the continual reflection on experience, the testing of abstract theoretical concepts with practical knowledge, the linking of affective and cognitive development, the application of knowledge (Eyler, Giles, Stenson, & Gray, 2001). These and other factors have led large numbers of faculty from across the disciplines to redesign their courses as service-learning courses. This work has also been embraced by administrators who seek to improve the quality of education on campus and have encouraged service-learning. Higher education is increasingly compelled to improve the quality of teaching and learning in such a way that departments are responsible not only for foundational and professional knowledge, but also for socially responsive knowledge (Altman, 2004). For change that is aimed at improving teaching and learning with a civic dimension, civic engagement must become the work of the departments.

In an interview, John Abbott explained the pedagogical imperative for civic engagement in this way:

> People worldwide need a whole series of new competencies.... But I doubt that such abilities can be taught solely in the classroom, or be developed solely by teachers. Higher order thinking and problem solving skills grow out of direct experience, not simply teaching; they require more than a classroom activity. They develop through active involvement and real life experiences in workplaces and the community. (Marchese, 1996, pp. 3–4)

Departments committed to developing curricula that teach the course content of the discipline and develop the civic dispositions of professional practice in the discipline are more likely to embrace civic engagement as their core work.

The Epistemological Imperative

More than the mission and pedagogical imperatives, perhaps the most compelling interest in civic engagement from a faculty perspective—and hence, in the departmental context—is the question of epistemology. Referring to Boyer's (1990) work, Schön (1995) wrote that "the new scholarship requires a new epistemology" (p. 27). In fact, it may be that a new epistemology requires a new scholarship and a new pedagogy. From a faculty perspective, the creation/production of new knowledge is their foremost interest—from this will flow research agendas and curriculum design. As an example of how this hierarchy of interest can manifest itself on campus, consider this personal experience of working with faculty on advancing civic engagement and service-learning at a highly selective liberal arts college. Few, if any, of the faculty who participated were interested in community-based teaching because it created a richer classroom environment and better teaching and learning. Fewer still were interested in connecting their discipline-based courses to the community to help actualize the civic mission of their institution. Yet when the question of how to best create new knowledge advancing their disciplinary frameworks and presenting opportunities for scholarship was raised, there was deep resonance. The question of interest to faculty—and this is how they framed it as the question they wanted discussed as part of a strategic planning process—was this: "For the sake of creating new knowledge, what is the intellectual space for complementary epistemologies at _____ college?"

Interest in addressing this kind of question is, as Walshok (1995) wrote, "influenced by the ways academics think about knowledge and factor experiences and expertise outside the academy into society's total knowledge development and dissemination process" (p. 13). Universities "will not integrate the experiences and expertise of individuals and institutions outside the academy," she continued, "without a deeper appreciation of the invaluable resources they represent" (p. 13). Within the space created for complementary epistemologies is the opportunity to bring together academic knowledge with community-based knowledge in a way that counters the traditional epistemological boundaries that "treat experience as separate from knowledge rather than as a form of knowledge" (Walshok, p. 14).

In bringing together academic knowledge with community-based knowledge, faculty such as the ones at the college mentioned earlier and others are seeking an epistemology appropriate to engaged teaching and scholarship that makes "room for the practitioner's reflection in and on action. It must account for and legitimize not only the use of knowledge produced in the academy, but the practitioner's generation of actionable knowledge" (Schön, 1995, p. 28). An engaged department will be shaped in large part by the epistemological imperative, the recognition that "knowledge—particularly useful knowledge that can be applied in the economy and society—is something more than highly intellectualized, analytical, and symbolic material. It includes working knowledge, a component of experience, of hands-on practice knowledge" (Walshok, 1995, p. 14).

Building an Engaged Department

Campus Compact's experience since the late 1990s in conducting Engaged Department Institutes suggests that there are certain key characteristics that a department (or comparable academic unit) must demonstrate to successfully undertake and implement an engaged department initiative (Battistoni, Gelmon, Saltmarsh, Wergin, & Zlotkowski, 2003).

First, the department should have a cadre of faculty, preferably including at least some senior individuals, who have experience with community-based education. These may be faculty who have been teaching courses incorporating service-learning or who have been involved in community-based research and have at least some experience with a reflective teaching methodology and with establishing and maintaining community partnerships. Engaged department work is not introductory work; it involves experienced faculty who are prepared to take their individual efforts and contribute to a collective departmental effort. An engaged department agenda includes unit responsibility for engagement-related activities, departmental agreement on the concepts and terminology that allow faculty to explore the dimensions of engaged work most effectively, and a departmental plan of how best to document, evaluate, and communicate the significance of engaged work.

Second, and related to the first characteristic, department faculty should have experience with community partnerships to the extent that relationships with community partners are strong enough to include them in the engaged department initiative. As with the first characteristic, faculty who are in the initial steps of establishing partnerships and who have little experience with exploring reciprocal relationships and developing community voice in the education process are not likely to be sufficiently prepared to play a major role in a departmental initiative. Engaged department work is most effective when community partners help develop the unit's objectives from the beginning and are viewed as co-educators of students engaged in community-based learning.

A third key characteristic of a department that is prepared to undertake civic engagement as a collective strategy is the institutional environment of the campus, including the leadership and support of academic administration. Engaged departments are more likely to develop effectively if there is an infrastructure on campus, such as a service-learning office, intended to support faculty in community-based teaching and scholarship. An institutional environment in which definitions of scholarship have been reconsidered, allowing for community-based scholarship and the scholarship of teaching and learning to be considered legitimate academic work, is more likely to foster engaged department efforts. Moreover, support from the department chair is a key indicator of the success of the engaged department efforts. It is the role of the chair to provide leadership around improving teaching and learning, to encourage and support community-based scholarship, and to advocate for resources and support for the department's engagement initiatives.

Assessing Departmental Engagement

Departments that make a commitment to engagement must be able to demonstrate the impact of the various activities they choose to pursue. How do they ensure the quality of the learning experience for students? What is the evidence of this quality? How do they monitor the impact on community participants? What is the information base that allows the department to make improvements to enhance community benefits and strengthen the community partnership? What data are available to justify resource investments? What is the knowledge base the department uses to inform the improvement and expansion of such programs?

These questions all relate to a fourth imperative—that of having a defined strategy for assessment and evaluation that ensures the department can conceptualize its desired impacts and can design appropriate methods for measuring and/or observing these impacts, has a coherent plan for analysis and synthesis of findings, and strategically reports these results to maintain and/or improve the departmental engagement agenda.

Descriptions about assessment strategies and methods are available in detail elsewhere (see Bringle, Phillips, & Hudson, 2004; Gelmon, 2003; Gelmon, Holland, Driscoll, Spring, & Kerrigan, 2001; Holland, 2001). In the context of this volume, a formulation for assessment is based on the key concepts presented in Chapter 2 and on other fundamental components of departmental engagement.

Civic Learning Outcomes

If a primary strategy for departmental engagement is to develop or enhance civic learning outcomes among students, then from an assessment perspective the department must clearly articulate those outcomes. Outcomes must be stated in clear terms that refer to knowledge, skills, and values. Potential measurable or observable outcomes must also relate to the desired results—demonstration of civic learning, departmental commitment, engaged faculty, and the like. The challenge for many is identifying relevant methods to measure or observe outcomes, some of which may be apparent during or at the end of a specific learning experience (such as a course or a field experience), while others may appear over time with increasing experience and articulation.

Civic knowledge. We often "measure" knowledge through routine assessments, whether a simple pre-test/post-test, or through more rigorous academic methods such as essays, examinations, or oral presentations. In the context of civic knowledge, the assessment must be broad enough to address the many factors defined for civic knowledge—core content areas, knowledge of issues, understanding of root problems, understanding of place. These factors must then be contextualized in terms of relevant disciplinary frameworks or perspectives. Many disciplines have their own styles of teaching, learning, and assessment (such as the portfolio developed by an art student, or the question and answer methods used by a law school professor), and the assessment of civic knowledge should be framed within the relevant context. No single model can be used, rather one should build on what is common in the discipline with adaptation to account for the relevant elements of civic knowledge. Ironically, the core elements of civic knowledge (such as building an understanding of root social or community problems) might be similar across several departments working in a common community, yet each department would likely follow its own assessment strategies that would be relevant to its distinctive style of teaching and learning, assessment, and expectations.

In addition to the elements of knowledge, there are related skills that can be assessed that are linked to the elements of civic knowledge. How do students engage in problem solving? What are their skills in critical analysis, and how are these demonstrated? What opportunities are presented for reflection, and is it feasible to assess the "quality" of these reflections? An excellent resource for a variety of methods to assess student experiences can be found in Bringle et al. (2004).

Civic skills. As illustrated in Figure 2.1 in Chapter 2, a number of civic skills have been identified that link to the various civic engagement frameworks. As with civic knowledge, these skills vary by disciplinary context, with some common elements, but with potentially different expressions by discipline. The level of the learner and the breadth of his or her previous experience are important factors to consider in measuring or observing skills—a novice will have much less expertise than someone who has had multiple engaged experiences and has mastered many of the challenging elements of such work. Undergraduate students may show less skill development than graduate students; however, many students come to higher education today with significant community-based experience through their K–12 education. As a result, they quickly demonstrate skills and abilities related to working with and in communities which may *not* be as evident for the more advanced student who has not had such experiences.

Civic values. Measuring values may be more of a challenge for some departments than measuring knowledge, but the strategy is identical. Departments must begin by clearly articulating the values they hope or expect students to gain from civic engagement experiences. They can then develop an assessment metric that enables students to self-assess before, during, and after the experience (or, if a short experience, through a more simple pre-/post-strategy). Similarly, departments should collectively identify and articulate their values with respect to engagement, then monitor and assess departmental change over time. As described in

Chapter 2, espoused values are influenced by institutional mission and by departmental areas of emphasis and disciplinary values.

Specific Measurement Strategies

To pursue an assessment agenda, the department must carefully consider each strategy it is adopting as part of its work as an engaged department and then determine the appropriate assessment methods for each strategy—whether these are curriculum-based activities or other professional/personal development activities. For course-based activities, one would typically use methods of student learning assessment that include papers, examinations, presentations, and reflections, but could augment these with specific methods to explore the experience—surveys, interviews, focus groups, reflective writing, and observations. In field-based experiences and integrative capstones, it is common to use a reflective portfolio as a method of assessment. Using focused questions can help students to self-assess their personal experiences and provide an opportunity to comment on community interaction, thus augmenting the assessment value of such portfolios.

As suggested in Chapter 2, there are common characteristics among all the various strategies such as placement quality, curricular applications, or practice implications that might lead to relevant assessment methods. These characteristics point to the importance of incorporating questions or discrete assessment items into rubrics that will provide insights into them. Of vital importance is the expression of multiple voices—the student, the community partner, and the faculty overseeing the experience. Thus in thinking about measurement strategies it is also important for departments to clearly identify the multiple potential sources of information to ensure that a variety of perspectives are obtained, giving a full spectrum (or 360-degree view) of opinions and observations.

Departments (or comparable units) also may benefit from conducting an overall self-assessment to gain insights into their level of development with respect to service-learning, civic engagement, and community-engaged scholarship. Useful examples of self-assessment tools designed to measure baseline institutional status and change over time are now available in the public domain (see Furco, 2002; Gelmon, Seifer, Kauper-Brown, & Mikkelsen, 2004). These formats can be easily used by departments as valuable mechanisms for baseline self-assessment and for tracking change over time.

Community-University Partnerships

An essential element of engagement for many departments is establishing, nurturing, and enhancing partnerships with a variety of community organizations. If these partnerships are essential to the department's engagement activities, then the partners' perspectives should be incorporated into assessment by seeking out community perspectives for data collection and by engaging partners in values clarification and the design of measurement strategies (Gelmon, 2003; Holland, 2001). Partners' perspectives should be a substantial portion of the assessment agenda, and should not be limited to assessing only the partnership itself but should include the community perspective on student, faculty, and institutional roles and activities (Gelmon et al., 2001). Of course, engagement may only be successful if a department has partners with whom to engage; the assumption is, therefore, that the department has been committed to developing effective partnerships and has partners to involve in the assessment process (Battistoni et al., 2003).

Faculty Commitment, Development, and Rewards

A final area essential to consider when assessing departmental engagement relates to faculty commitment, development, and rewards. The roles of faculty will evolve as they gain experience and comfort in creating and facilitating various community engagement experiences—in the classroom, through community-based research, and in mentoring students in specific field experiences, internships, or capstones. However, faculty need reassurance that work related to an engagement agenda will be recognized within their department, their institution, and their discipline as a valid focus of their curricular and scholarly efforts. There is increasing evidence that institutions are changing to support faculty engagement as reflected in mandates, rewards, and incentives, but faculty still need encouragement and motivation to become involved in engagement activities that may seem different from traditional disciplinary work (Gelmon & Agre-Kippenhan, 2002). Therefore, another area of emphasis for departments is to carefully assess their definitions of faculty roles, support for faculty (e.g., through faculty development), and methods of reward and recognition.

Implementing Assessment

Regardless of the focus area within the overall assessment of departmental engagement, it is necessary to identify core concepts, measurable or observable indicators, relevant methods for data collection, and appropriate sources of information, and then articulate these into a coherent plan for analysis and reporting. Departments that adopt a comprehensive assessment plan as part of their engagement agenda will be able to demonstrate evidence of accomplishments, as well as challenges and resultant learning, and should be most effective in securing commitments of resources and energy to support ongoing engagement initiatives. The chapters that follow illustrate a variety of departmental approaches to engagement.

References

Altman, I. (2004, Fall). Socially responsive knowledge. *Campus Compact Reader.* Retrieved March 18, 2006, from www.compact.org/reader/fall04/article6-intro.html

Battistoni, R. M., Gelmon, S. B., Saltmarsh, J. A., Wergin, J. F., & Zlotkowski, E. (2003). *The engaged department toolkit.* Providence, RI: Campus Compact.

Boyer, E. L. (1990). *Scholarship reconsidered: Priorities of the professoriate.* Princeton, NJ: Carnegie Foundation for the Advancement of Teaching.

Bringle, R. G., Phillips, M. A., & Hudson, M. (2004). *The measure of service-learning: Research scales to assess student experiences.* Washington, DC: American Psychological Association.

Dewey, J. (1987). Education and social change. In J. A. Boydston (Ed.), *John Dewey: The later works, 1925–1953* (Vol. 11, pp. 408–417). Carbondale, IL: Southern Illinois University Press. (Original work published 1937)

Edwards, R. (1999, September/October). The academic department: How does it fit into the university reform agenda? *Change, 31(5),* 17–27.

Ehrlich, T. (Ed.). (2000). *Civic responsibility and higher education.* Phoenix, AZ: ACE/Oryx Press.

Ehrlich, T., & Hollander, E. (2000). *Presidents' declaration on the civic responsibility of higher education.* Providence, RI: Campus Compact.

Eyler, J., Giles, D. E., Jr., Stenson, C. M., & Gray, C. J. (2001). *At a glance: What we know about the effects of service-learning on college students, faculty, institutions and communities, 1993–2000* (3rd ed.). Nashville, TN: Vanderbilt University.

Furco, A. (2002). *Self-assessment rubric for the institutionalization of service-learning in higher education.* Berkeley, CA: University of California, Berkeley.

Gelmon, S. B. (2003). Assessment as a means of building service-learning partnerships. In B. Jacoby & Associates, *Building partnerships for service-learning* (pp. 42–64). San Francisco, CA: Jossey-Bass.

Gelmon, S. B., & Agre-Kippenhan, S. (2002). A developmental framework for supporting evolving faculty roles for community engagement. *Journal of Public Affairs, 7,* 161–182.

Gelmon, S. B., Holland, B. A., Driscoll, A., Spring, A., & Kerrigan, S. (2001). *Assessing the impact of service-learning and civic engagement: Principles and practices.* Providence, RI: Campus Compact.

Gelmon, S. B., Seifer, S. D., Kauper-Brown, J., & Mikkelsen, M. (2004). *Community-engaged scholarship for health collaborative: Institutional self-assessment.* Seattle, WA: Community-Campus Partnerships for Health.

Holland, B. A. (2001). A comprehensive model for assessing service-learning and community-university partnerships. In M. Canada & B. W. Speck (Eds.), *New directions for higher education: No. 114. Developing and implementing service-learning programs* (pp. 51–60). San Francisco, CA: Jossey-Bass.

Kennedy, D. (1995, May/June). Another century's end, another revolution for higher education. *Change, 27*(3), 8–15.

Marchese, T. (1996, March). The search for next-century learning: An interview with John Abbot. *AAHE Bulletin, 48*(7), 3–6.

National Survey of Student Engagement. (2002). *From promise to progress: How colleges and universities are using student engagement results to improve collegiate quality.* Bloomington, IN: Indiana University.

Newman, F. (1985). *Higher education and the American resurgence.* Princeton, NJ: Carnegie Foundation for the Advancement of Teaching.

Newman, F., Couturier, L., & Scurry, J. (2004). *The future of higher education: Rhetoric, reality, and the risks of the market.* San Francisco, CA: Jossey-Bass.

Schön, D. A. (1995, November/December). The new scholarship requires a new epistemology. *Change, 27*(6), 27–34.

Walshok, M. L. (1995). *Knowledge without boundaries: What America's research universities can do for the economy, the workplace, and the community.* San Francisco, CA: Jossey-Bass.

About the Authors

John Saltmarsh is director of the New England Resource Center for Higher Education at the University of Massachusetts, Boston where he is a faculty member in the Department of Leadership in Education in the Graduate College of Education. From 1998–2005, he directed the Project on Integrating Service with Academic Study at Campus Compact. He holds a Ph.D. in American history from Boston University and taught for more than a decade at Northeastern University and as a Visiting Research Fellow at the Feinstein Institute for Public Service at Providence College. He is the author of numerous book chapters and articles on civic engagement, service-learning, and experiential education. His writings have appeared in *Liberal Education*, the *Michigan Journal for Com-*

munity Service Learning, Academe, the *Journal of Experiential Education,* the *National Society for Experiential Education Quarterly,* and the *Journal of Cooperative Education.*

Sherril Gelmon received her doctorate of public health in health policy from the University of Michigan. She is professor of public health at Portland State University in the Mark O. Hatfield School of Government. She has more than 20 years of experience in applied program evaluation, with two areas of particular expertise: community health program assessment and improvement, and design and implementation of models of assessment of community-based learning. She served as Engaged Scholar on Assessment with National Campus Compact; is an alumna examiner for the Malcolm Baldrige National Quality Award program; a member of the National Review Board for the Scholarship of Engagement; and a member of the Consulting Corps of both Campus Compact and Community-Campus Partnerships for Health. She currently serves as the national evaluator for the Community Engaged Scholarship for Health Collaborative, as well as evaluator for the five-year multimillion dollar Nurse Workforce Initiative of the Northwest Health Foundation.

4

From Rogue Program to Poster Child: A Department's Shaping of a University's Agenda

Paula T. Silver, John E. Poulin, Stephen C. Wilhite

Don't Come if You Don't Plan to Stay!

It was an early evening in November 1995. Seated around the dinner table were five members of the social work faculty and five guests. The guests had been invited as "key informants" for a brainstorming session about ways in which the Center for Social Work Education faculty and students might begin to extend their human resources and professional expertise to the city of Chester, Pennsylvania. The faculty explained that they felt strongly that the center had an obligation to attend to the needs of its local community and wanted advice on the best way to go about it.

The guests, all seasoned professionals and/or public servants who had devoted many years of service to the city, listened politely to the faculty's vision. Without hesitation or the need for consultation, the advice they provided was unanimous:

> Find a partner, already trusted and known by the community, to serve as your sponsor in the community. Without such a sponsor to help, you will be greeted with well-earned cynicism and closed doors. Don't come if you don't plan to stay or you will only engender even greater distrust and resentment of the university. Most importantly, take your time to get to know and understand this city before you do anything. It would be better to do nothing than to raise

expectations and disappoint a community that has been disappointed all too often by self-serving institutions.

After the guests had left, the faculty, while feeling a bit deflated, recognized the wisdom of the advice it had been given. Due to other program demands, it would take four years before the faculty was ready to act on the advice and launch an initiative to become part of Chester's solutions rather than its problems.

Demographics

The University Setting

Widener University is an independent, metropolitan, comprehensive teaching institution whose main campus is located in Chester, a socioeconomically distressed city of approximately 35,000 residents, 14 miles outside of Philadelphia, Pennsylvania. Composed of eight schools and colleges, the university offers educational programs leading to associate, baccalaureate, master's, and professional doctoral degrees. The university's enrollment is approximately 6,200 students, including 3,300 graduate students, 2,400 day undergraduate students, and 500 evening undergraduate students.

Like other metropolitan universities, students at the undergraduate and graduate levels tend to be drawn from the region and remain in the region upon program completion. Widener's undergraduates are predominantly white (approximately 80%), traditionally aged 18- to 21-years-olds. Undergraduates characteristically come from middle-class, blue-collar families, and a significant number represent the first generation in their family to attend college. Most of the university's professional graduate programs are part-time and draw students with busy work/life schedules seeking to enhance their professional credentials or change careers.

The Center for Social Work Education

The Center for Social Work Education was established in 1992 in order to provide a more autonomous governance structure to administer the undergraduate (BSW) program and a newly established graduate (MSW) program. The center has experienced significant growth and development since its formation. As of September 2005, there were 17 full-time and 12 part-time faculty, 52 full-time undergraduate social work majors, and 250 full-time and part-time MSW students.

The School of Human Service Professions was created in 1993 to provide an administrative umbrella for human service–related professional degree programs at the university. In addition to the center, the School of Human Service Professions is the administrative home of the Center for Education, the Institute for Graduate Clinical Psychology, and the Institute for Physical Therapy Education.

Processes

An Idea is Born

The decision to become an engaged department emerged as a faculty consensus early in the Center for Social Work Education's development. While the center's faculty had articulated a mission for its academic programs, they had yet to identify a vision and mission for the center that went beyond providing a sound curriculum. In 1994, the center's faculty held a retreat with the goal of formulating a broader vision and mission for the center. What emerged from that activity was a strong commitment to extend our expertise and human resources to address the needs of our very distressed local community. This commitment was driven by a number of factors.

Needs of the local community. The city of Chester, where Widener University is located, is by any objective measure one of the most socioeconomically disadvantaged in the nation. From the 1950s to the 1980s, the city suffered severe economic decline as its tax base narrowed and much of the middle class moved out following employment opportunities. The city's steep slope of decline continued through the end of the century. By 2000, more than 22% of all families and 27% of all individuals were classified as living in poverty, the unemployment rate stood at just under 10%, 41% of the adults were outside of the labor force, and the city had lost almost 20% of its 1980 population (U.S. Census Bureau, 2001).

The university's fortress mentality. The social work faculty had long been critical of the university's efforts to dissociate itself from the local community. Although the university's former president, who occupied the position from 1982–2002, had worked to establish close ties with Chester's political leaders, his frustration and impatience with a city bureaucracy built on years of one-party domination limited his enthusiasm for any major joint project with Chester. Believing its location in Chester to be a liability to the university's image and enrollment, the administration did its best to present the university, figuratively and literally, as separate from the city. This negative view of the city, coupled with security concerns, contributed to the development of a fortress mentality on campus—a mentality perhaps best symbolized by the daily closing and locking at dusk of a pedestrian walkway over the freeway that separates the Widener campus from most of the rest of the city.

Shared professional values. As social workers, the center's faculty shared the values and ethics of the profession. Social work's professional code of ethics explicitly states that its primary mission "is to enhance human well-being and help meet the basic human needs of all people, with particular attention to the needs and empowerment of people who are vulnerable, oppressed, and living in poverty" (National Association of Social Workers, 1999, p. i). The university's efforts to distance itself from the community were antithetical to the faculty's sense of civic responsibility. In order to integrate social work values into the program's curriculum, the faculty strongly believed that the program should "walk the walk" and "talk the talk" in its own community.

Social work student learning needs. Supervised practicum experiences are a mandated feature of all accredited social work programs. Undergraduate and first-year graduate practicums are required to be generalist in nature, exposing students to a wide variety of social work roles, including direct client service and macro-practice functions such as organizational and community development, program development and evaluation, and policy analysis. Finding truly generalist placements is an ongoing challenge since placement sites in traditional human service agencies rarely provide students with adequate opportunities to engage in macro-practice activities.

Although Chester, with all of its systemic and service issues, would be an ideal setting for students to be exposed to and engage in the micro and macro aspects of social work practice, local, underresourced human service agencies could provide neither the required level of supervised field instruction nor the opportunity for generalist practice. If the center was to use student internships to help address human service needs in Chester, it would have to develop its own internship program that met mandated training standards. The notion that such an effort would be consistent with models of civic engagement and service-learning came later. In effect, the social work faculty "invented" service-learning long before it became aware of its significance in the pedagogical literature.

An Idea Takes Shape

In fall 1999, the director of the Center for Social Work Education appointed a department-level faculty task force led by a senior faculty member to explore the action steps needed to create a community-based field placement site. The task force's charge was to get input from community stakeholders regarding how such a program might best serve the community and, if feasible, develop an action plan or proposal for review by the full social work faculty.

It was already clear to the center that it would need a primary community partner to sponsor its entry into the community. After meeting with several community organizations, an ideal partner, Chester Education Foundation (CEF), was found. The mission of CEF, a private, nonprofit organization, was to support educational excellence and promote community revitalization. Incorporated in 1989, CEF's successful record of program funding, leadership in developing community collaborations, established credibility, and organizational stability met all the criteria the center established for a partner agency. Partnering with CEF had the added benefit of allowing the center to apply for funding earmarked for nonprofits and also for funding earmarked for academic programs.

After establishing a primary collaboration with CEF, six community grassroots organizations were invited to attend a meeting to discuss the emerging concept. Our hope was to enlist some of these organizations as cooperating partners in the project. The concept of having social work interns assigned to work with their organizations to develop social work services for their clients, as well as faculty/student teams to help strengthen their organizational capacities, was met with unanimous enthusiasm.

Once the community partnerships had been established, the concept was presented to and approved by the faculty in spring 2000, and the work to implement the project began. Given that the center could not look to the university administration for support, funding for the project had to be secured from external sources. Despite the full support of the dean of the School of Human Service Professions, the center had to make sure that the project kept a low profile within the university so that it did not aggravate the administration's concern about its identification with the city. In collaboration with CEF, the director of the center and three faculty members set out to secure sufficient grant funding to launch the program in September 2000, an exceedingly ambitious goal.

By midsummer 2000, funding had been secured to operate the program for at least 10 months. Even though the program was not 100% funded, it was decided to proceed with the planned fall semester opening with the hope that additional funding would be secured as the year progressed. Had the faculty been more fiscally cautious and less optimistic, the program would probably never have been inaugurated.

Designing a University-Sponsored
Field Placement Agency

The Social Work Consultation Services, or SWCS as it became known, officially opened in September 2000 with a full-time program director, a part-time field instructor, three one-quarter-time faculty members, 10 MSW student interns, a collaborating community partner, and six cooperating grassroots community partners. Creating an agency from scratch was exciting, but having 10 interns show up for field placement at an agency was overwhelming. Most of the first year was devoted to designing the agency and an array of services, a truly collaborative effort in which students, staff, and faculty worked together to shape a mission, develop policies and procedures, create a culture, and implement the programs.

From its inception SWCS articulated a dual mission—to improve the quality of life for residents of our low-income urban community and to train competent and caring social work leaders committed to serving disadvantaged populations and communities. The SWCS mission was to be accomplished by having undergraduate and graduate interns 1) provide free social work and counseling services to community residents and 2) provide organizational development, research and evaluation, and staff training and development, and other capacity-building services to community-based human service organizations.

SWCS Five Years Later

Five years after the program began, SWCS has developed a wide range of direct services for Chester's children, families, vulnerable adults, and elderly. Services include family therapy and parenting support programs; after school and summer camp programs for middle school children; and case management, counseling, and support group services for vulnerable adults and seniors. In addition to direct services, SWCS interns, under faculty supervision, provide capacity-building services for partner agencies. Through a collaborative process, SWCS and partner agencies identify and design strategies for expanding and strengthening the agency's functioning and service capacity, including program development and evaluation; needs assessments; grant application preparation; community outreach and strategic planning; community education, training, and development; and networking initiatives. These diverse programmatic aspects ensure that all students are exposed to micro and macro social work experiences.

Analysis

SWCS's Influence on the School

The civic engagement initiative launched by SWCS eventually became a central focus of the School of Human Service Professions and Widener University as a whole. The school's executive committee, composed of the dean and the directors of each of the four units of the school, meets regularly to shape the school's agenda. These meetings provided an ongoing forum for the center's director to share her unit's rationale for and experiences with the formation and operation of SWCS and for the dean of the school to use SWCS as an example of how partnerships with community organizations could provide the basis for obtaining grants that would contribute directly to expanded learning opportunities for students and community-based research options for faculty.

In response to this emphasis on SWCS as a resource for civic engagement, the Center for Education was able to launch new grant-funded Chester-based initiatives with Chester organizations. These initiatives are ongoing and involve expanded tutoring by Widener students, staff, and faculty for Chester school children, especially elementary and middle school students lagging furthest behind in academic achievement.

The Institute for Graduate Clinical Psychology, historically the unit of the school with the least formal organizational connection with the Chester community, also partnered with a Chester-based group in a job skills training program funded by a major grant from the U.S. Department of Commerce and Labor. That program became the vehicle for the involvement of several clinical psychology graduate students in community-based intervention. Through federal earmark funding, the program became institutionalized as the Center for Leadership and Organizational Development and is involved in other community partnerships, including one designed to develop the leadership skills of community residents involved in neighborhood associations. With its expanding connections to the community, the leadership center also serves as a catalyst for the transformation of some traditional courses in the Psy.D. curriculum into academic service-learning courses.

Beyond its close association with a major medical center in Chester, the Institute for Physical Therapy Education's primary connection to the Chester community has been through required student projects that focus on health education and promotion. Through funding from a federal appropriation, the institute created graduate assistantships that are designed to help faculty with the identification of community partners for academic service-learning projects.

In all of these instances, the networks of associations with community entities established by SWCS and the firsthand experiences of the academic administrators responsible for SWCS have played a significant role. Without the SWCS model, it is doubtful that any of these initiatives would be developed to the same degree.

SWCS's Influence on the University

In September 2002, Widener welcomed Dr. James T. Harris III as its new president. President Harris was explicit during the interview process about his intention to make civic engagement a cornerstone of his administration. In his inaugural address he called on the university to commit itself to preparing citizens who truly understand collaboration and possess community-building skills.

Immediately after taking office, President Harris launched the first formal strategic planning process in the institution's history; as he did so, he signaled again his commitment to an agenda of engagement by creating a new position of Special Assistant to the President for Community Engagement, reporting directly to him. As he began promoting his vision of an engaged metropolitan university, he seized on SWCS as an example of how academic programs can use community partnerships to promote active learning by students and innovative teaching and research by faculty while simultaneously helping community residents address social, family, cultural, and political issues of immediate concern.

In February 2003, the Strategic Planning Committee created special task forces to investigate a number of key issues. Based on the task force reports and input generated from a campus-wide visioning conference held in October 2003, the Strategic Planning Committee drafted vision and mission statements and strategic planning goals for the university. In the Strategic Planning Committee's discussion of the proposed mission statement, the SWCS model of civic engagement was frequently referenced and clearly helped shape the mission statement's emphasis on "creating a learning environment where curricula were connected to societal issues through civic engagement," inspiring students "to be citizens of character who demonstrate professional and civic leadership," and contributing to the "vitality and well-being of the communities we serve" (Widener University, 2004, p. 2). The SWCS model also contributed to specific language in at least 2 of the 12 strategic goals, placing a clear emphasis on experiential and collaborative learning and linkage between curricula and societal needs (Widener University, 2004).

The Role of Leadership

Leadership at all three levels of the university was critically important in launching the university's current civic engagement initiative. First, within the Center for Social Work Education, the leadership of a senior faculty member and the program director was essential to ensure a collegial process that promoted the faculty's collective ownership of the program and the integration of the program into the center. The senior faculty member assumed the task of building the case for this new model of student placements by systematically assessing the model's efficacy through documenting student learning outcomes and by demonstrating to university administrators that this type of community partnership could be supported in large part by external grants with only modest direct funding from the university.

The center's director was strongly supportive of the SWCS concept from the beginning and worked closely with the senior faculty member to develop strategies for engaging other faculty in the design and implementation of SWCS. She played a central role in establishing the initial SWCS partnership with CEF and was instrumental in securing initial external grant funding. Her success in these areas led to her appointment to serve on the Strategic Planning Committee where she played an active and influential role in shaping the emphasis on civic engagement that emerged from the planning process.

Sensing the compatibility of SWCS's mission with President Harris's agenda for community engagement, the dean of the School of Human Service Professions ensured that President Harris was familiar with SWCS from the moment he arrived on campus. As a member of the Strategic Planning Committee, the dean played a major role in redefining the institution as a metropolitan university committed to promoting civic engagement. When the draft of the plan was presented to the university, the dean's reputation for commitment to collegial governance and academic excellence helped reassure skeptical faculty in other units that faculty will ultimately determine how civic engagement is embodied in their curricula and that field-based experiential learning can promote achievement of student learning outcomes and faculty scholarship of engagement.

Most importantly, President Harris's unwavering commitment to civic engagement has been responsible for SWCS's becoming a widely cited exemplar of how civic engagement in the service of furthering students' acquisition of professional competencies can benefit the university and the community of which it is a part. While SWCS programming would probably have continued to grow even without President Harris's arrival, his leadership in forging the university's new mission and goals has provided a context within which SWCS has served as a catalyst for community engagement across the university.

Impact

Impact on Student Learning

Two types of data assessing student learning outcomes are presented here: quantitative data from three annual student field surveys and qualitative data from four annual SWCS student focus groups.

Field survey findings. This section presents the findings from three annual field surveys (2002–2004) of the SWCS students and a random sample of the program's students placed in traditional field internships. Mean score differences between the interns placed at SWCS and those in traditional placements of the combined three-year surveys are shown in Table 4.1.

As shown in Table 4.1, there were no significant differences between the SWCS and non-SWCS interns' micro practice scores. SWCS interns, however, had significantly higher macro practice scores than did their student counterparts placed in traditional field sites. The mean organization (48.6 vs. 35.3) and community practice (26.7 vs. 15.6) index scores were significantly higher for the SWCS interns. The SWCS interns also had significantly higher overall practice skills scores (276.3 vs. 247.9) than the non-SWCS comparison group.

Focus group findings. Figure 4.1 shows the major positive (strengths) and negative (challenges) themes that emerged from the SWCS student focus groups from the four years studied (2000–2004). The themes were derived from a content analysis of the annual focus group reports prepared by the focus group facilitator.

Table 4.1. Mean SWCS Interns and Non-SWCS Interns Practice Skills Scores

Measure	SWCS (N = 24)	Non-SWCS (N = 38)	T-Statistic	Significance
Helping process	34.3	32.7	1.50	n.s.
Use of self	84.1	86.0	0.61	n.s.
Individual and family client systems	56.2	55.1	0.38	n.s.
Group client systems	26.4	23.3	1.48	n.s.
Organization client systems	48.6	35.3	4.37	p < .000
Community client systems	26.7	15.6	5.07	p < .000
Overall practice skills index	276.3	247.9	2.61	p < .01

Figure 4.1. SWCS Student Focus Group Themes: 2000–2004

Strengths	Challenges
• Excellent generalist experience—broad range of experiences micro and macro • Very supportive staff and safe environment • Felt empowered in terms of running agency and filling service gaps • Good exposure to broad range of clients • Positive connection to community and to working with disadvantaged clients • Unique learning opportunity • Opportunity to develop close bond with staff, faculty, and fellow students	• Expectations higher than at other field placement sites • Heavy workload—students partially responsible for running the agency as well as service provision • Lack of clarity regarding decision-making responsibilities • Lack of clarity regarding roles and responsibilities of administrators

As Figure 4.1 demonstrates, while students identified some challenges, the broad range of learning opportunities and the supportive learning environment were major strengths of their SWCS placement. Overall, the quantitative and qualitative findings indicate that, compared to traditional field placements, SWCS provided an enriched field experience in which students gained micro and macro practice skills and an empowering organizational experience that supported their professional development.

Impact on University Civic Engagement Activities

SWCS's impact on the expansion of civic engagement activities can be seen in the growth of academic service-learning across the campus. The developers of SWCS were not aware of the academic service-learning literature as they launched the service. However, the existence of this formal university-community partnership with its emphasis on combining specific academic learning experiences with service to the community encouraged a multidisciplinary group of faculty to begin exploring academic service-learning as a means of more effectively engaging students in academic life.

The university's new mission and strategic plan have clearly accelerated the growth of interest in academic service-learning. Recognizing the conceptual overlap of academic service-learning and the type of field-based learning experiences provided by SWCS, the dean of the School of Human Service Professions became a leading campus advocate for academic partnerships.

Lessons

In five years, SWCS evolved from a departmental initiative that was forced to keep a low profile to avoid administrative scrutiny to the poster child for a new university administration committed to civic engagement and service-learning. Getting there was not always assured and depended, in part, on two critical factors.

Securing University Buy-In

That the university's new president would support SWCS in spirit was clear from the beginning of his appointment in 2002; however, SWCS needed more than support in spirit. Scrambling for soft funding and service contracts, carving faculty release time out of the center's personnel budget, and gratefully accepting CEF's underwriting of a significant portion of operations costs, SWCS was able to be fiscally viable. Additionally, the university, under its new president, agreed to contribute "cash" to SWCS operations by assuming responsibility for the cost of office space and providing personnel support for preparation of grant proposals. While fiscal security continues to be a challenge, the university's financial and personnel support send the real and symbolic message that SWCS is a valued university asset that merits the investment of fiscal resources. This university investment, in turn, gives SWCS more credibility as it seeks additional external funding.

Maintaining and Solidifying the Community's Trust

After years of feeling neglected and unwelcome by the university, Chester's residents were cynical and distrustful of anything associated with the university. SWCS faced an uphill battle to earn the acceptance and trust of the residents. Partnering with CEF, a highly trusted and visible community organization, was critical to reestablishing community credibility. SWCS, however, had to convince residents and other organizations that it was there to serve and not to study the city and that it intended to become a permanent part of the city's human service infrastructure. Accomplishing this meant engaging in ongoing outreach, diligently following through on all commitments and contacts, developing programs that met the needs perceived *by the residents*, and becoming a good community partner by participating in organizational networks and supporting collaborative projects. After five years of operations, the success of SWCS's programs and its positive reputation have contributed significantly to the university's effort to rehabilitate its relationship with the city.

Vision

Emerging Vision for the University

By 2010, we envision that the SWCS model of civic engagement will be reflected in the creation of a university office for developing and supporting university/community collaborations aimed at addressing regional needs and providing learning opportunities for Widener students. The launching of such an office is a specific action step included in the university's strategic plan. Once established, the office will provide the infrastructure for designing and implementing a comprehensive economic impact plan for the university that includes the development of additional academic courses with a community focus and extensive student involvement in community projects. The office would be further charged with responsibility for coordinating and facilitating the involvement of Widener's academic programs, administrative departments, and community partners in community capacity building and service-learning projects.

External funds will be needed to support this vision,. The university is actively engaged in developing and circulating proposals to a variety of funding sources in an effort to secure sufficient resources to make such an office a reality. The salient fact is that the university has experienced a culture shift and is now committed to a path of community engagement as a way of enriching the learning opportunities for its students and supporting the development of its community. Through demonstrating what can be done by a single department with very limited resources, the Center for Social Work Education has become a significant institutional role model for this new institutional culture.

References

National Association of Social Workers. (1999). *Code of ethics.* Washington, DC: National Association of Social Workers Press.

U.S. Census Bureau. (2001). *United States census 2000.* Washington, DC: Author.

Widener University. (2004). *Strategic plan.* Chester, PA: Author.

About the Authors

Paula T. Silver is director of the Center for Social Work Education, associate dean of the School of Human Service Professions, and associate professor of social work at Widener University. Her research interests include child welfare policy and practice, occupational and environmental health, and the pedagogy of service-learning.

John E. Poulin is professor of social work at Widener University's Center for Social Work Education, where he teaches generalist practice, research, and policy practice courses. He is the former director of Widener's bachelor's and master's social work programs and currently is the executive director of Social Work Consultation Services. His current research focuses on examining the factors that contribute to psychological well-being of socially and economically disadvantaged elderly persons.

Stephen C. Wilhite is dean of the School of Human Service Professions, associate provost for graduate studies, and professor of psychology at Widener University. His research interests include higher education leadership, faculty development, applied cognitive psychology, and educational psychology, especially in relation to the effective design of instructional texts.

5

Samford University's Communication Studies: Seizing an Opportunity

Charlotte Brammer, Rhonda Parker

Tabula Rasa

Our department journey began with an ending. For decades, Samford University had a traditional Department of Speech Communication and Theatre, but in 2000, the theatre faculty, including the department chair (who was the theatre director), left the College of Arts and Sciences and moved to the School of Performing Arts. The "split" was quite friendly; after all, the theatre program obviously belonged in performing arts. The remaining speech communication faculty members, however, were left with little direction and only a vague sense of identity. Many courses were performance based, and without the link to theatre, the curriculum was unfocused. To say that the faculty in our department had diverse interests is an understatement. With backgrounds in debate, writing, and administration, there was no way of knowing that our diversity would become our greatest strength.

We were tabula rasa: We had the rare opportunity to build the kind of department we wanted. While we were somewhat uncertain of exactly what we wanted, we knew we needed a department chair who could help us organize our efforts to rebuild. In fall 2002, we hired a chair with program-building experience. We immediately began to focus on setting goals and creating an identity for the "faculty formerly with the speech and theatre department." Between 2002–2005, we worked hard to build a program that engaged our students, the university, and our community. What follows is an overview of how we engaged each other and our various publics to create a dynamic, growing department.

Demographics

Institution

Samford University, located in Birmingham, Alabama, is a Master's I institution and ranks in the top five in its peer group, according to *U.S. News & World Report*. As a Christian university with 4,416 students, Samford is committed to service. Samford students represent 44 states and 31 foreign countries.

Department

The Department of Communication Studies was formed in 2002 as part of the Howard College of Arts and Sciences. We currently have seven full-time and one part-time faculty members. In spring 2005, the department had 65 majors, with an average GPA of 3.3.

Processes

How Did We Begin?

After hiring a department chair in 2002, our first task was to define who we were as a department and what we wanted to accomplish. An important step in our self-identity was recognizing the central focus of communication and civic engagement that we all shared. Our disciplines ranged from speech communication to rhetoric to composition studies. Every member of the department was actively engaged in service to the university (e.g., the writing center), the community (e.g., the debate program sponsors tournaments for area schools), or both (e.g., incorporating service-learning into appropriate courses), and every member remained committed to such service. We became the Department of Communication Studies, a cooperative synergistic team.

Collective Thinking, Planning, and Action

Rather than work in isolation, laboring on individual projects, we felt that we would be stronger if we took on the major departmental tasks together. For example, rather than appointing one person to manage the assessment of student learning in the major, we would all work on it together. Instead of assigning one faculty member to be in charge of the senior seminar program, each of us would contribute to the course. Rather than working piecemeal on the curriculum with faculty members developing courses independently, we would create a curriculum together, with the intention that it should work as a coherent whole. Importantly, we invited individuals external to our department to contribute to our efforts as well.

While we were busy collaboratively crafting a coherent curriculum built around our faculty's diverse academic strengths, our administration initiated Samford's Transformational Learning Abilities (TLA) project in 2003. This initiative was designed to promote the teaching, learning, and assessment of four key skills that mark a well-educated student: writing, oral communication, information literacy, and quantitative literacy. We were invited to develop the oral communication component of the TLA for the university, and this became our first rallying point for holistic departmental engagement.

After consulting with the associate director of the National Communication Association, we developed the criteria by which the university could assess whether students graduating from Samford demonstrated competency in public speaking and small-group and interpersonal communication. We then developed a series of workshops for faculty who sought to incorporate communication assignments into their courses, such as public speeches and group assignments. We worked with the nursing school to help assess nursing students' interpersonal skills, and we met with individual departments to review their curricula to ascertain what types of communication projects and assessment strategies might work best for them. In short, we developed a university outreach program of sorts for any department or program that was interested in developing student or faculty communication abilities. These efforts soon extended beyond the Samford community. For example, in spring 2005 we helped lead a state teleconference for librarians who were interested in strengthening their public speaking skills.

Because we had worked diligently and quite publicly to support the university's TLA project, we felt that our department should develop a solid approach to assessing our own students' TLA abilities. We began with our curriculum, deciding that our students should have balanced instruction in communication theory and research as well as communication skills development. We created new courses and modified existing ones so that students would gain an understanding of both theory and praxis as they made their way through the major. Students would be required to give a formal speech in every course in the department, and all writing and speech assignments would be evaluated using a common rubric. Working together, we developed a writing rubric. The rubric for speech evaluation was drawn from the National Communication Association's "competent speaker" form (Morreale, Moore, & Taylor, 1993).

To provide opportunities for our students to strengthen their communication skills outside the classroom, we formally incorporated service-learning into some of our courses. Service-learning is valued highly at Samford; in fact, it is a formal component of courses in the core curriculum. For example, in the introductory communication arts course (the equivalent of composition I), first-year students are required to complete a minimum of 10 hours of service-learning in nonprofit organizations ranging from nursing homes to botanical gardens and environmental organizations to rehabilitation centers. With the service-learning foundation already established in the core curriculum, we strive to extend our students' education by integrating service-learning in upper-level courses. Thus far, we have formally incorporated service-learning into our upper-level intercultural communication course, where students work with members of the growing Latino community in our area. The director of service-learning, as part of the Samford in Mission program, has recently awarded us funding for the continued development of this course. Additionally, we have adopted a service-learning model in our 400-level internship program where students work in the surrounding community (often, although not exclusively, in some type of ministerial capacity). Interns are required to complete a series of service-learning-based reflection papers and create a program, product, or service that "gives back" to their placement site—an exchange of sorts for the privilege of gaining valuable learning experiences.

In keeping with our commitments to the TLA project and to civic engagement, we reinvented the senior seminar and designed it for maximum faculty involvement. We regard it as the terminal point for assessment of our students' abilities in writing, oral communication, and information and quantitative literacy. To that end, we require each student in the senior seminar to create an electronic portfolio that demonstrates competency in each of the four TLAs. These portfolios are assessed by all full-time department faculty members and reviewers external to the university.

To incorporate civic education into the senior seminar course, we ask students to create communication workshops for the university and Birmingham communities. The topics for these workshops are based on the students' interests. Some have given leadership workshops to campus freshmen; others have taught area high school students advanced strategies in debate. One workshop invited the community to learn strategies for comforting others in times of loss; yet another focused on developing skill in intercultural communication. Multiple workshop assessment tools have been used to evaluate our students' efforts, and feedback has been obtained from workshop attendees as well as department faculty.

Perhaps our greatest success with civic engagement to date is our debate program. Though we field a highly competitive varsity debate team, we also treat Samford debate as a community resource. Our director of debate created the Birmingham Area Debate League, which has been a major force in keeping debate programs alive in inner-city schools. In years past, only 2 out of 24 schools in our area had debate programs. With cooperation from school district representatives and collaboration with teachers, the Birmingham Area Debate League developed a way to bring debate back to underserved school districts. Together, we developed a format and a plan for tournaments that addressed the schools' resource issues. In the 2004–2005 season, more than 22 schools and 300 students participated in debates on the Samford campus, making this one of the largest urban debate projects in the nation. Importantly, Samford students have been active in every element of this program. Not only do they judge many of the debates, but they also host workshops at the start of the year for new teachers, visit schools that need help starting debate programs, and prepare the results and pairings for the tournaments. The project gives students responsibility for an event that is important in the lives of young students and allows them to use their budding expertise in communication to teach middle and high school students, while empowering them to think critically about the relative strengths of different communication strategies.

Analysis

Moving From "Mine" to "Ours," or the Benefits of "Newness"

For whatever reason, "mine" has never been a significant issue among our department members. For those members who were "formerly with the speech and theatre department," any notion of ownership was surely shaken following the amicable though disruptive split. Additionally, each faculty member seemed less internally focused and more outwardly focused on the new department, the university, and the community at large. Individual faculty did not define themselves by specific courses; they were known more for their civic engagement. Part of their civic engagement became focused on building an interconnected department—a team.

This team emphasis was likely born of our shared goals. After becoming a department in our own right, we recognized that despite our differing areas of communication expertise, we had many things in common. For example, we all wanted to share our love of and knowledge about communication not only with our students, but also with local, national, and even international communities. We opened the floor for discussion and listened to every voice, which led us to become an interactive, open system that was internally and externally engaged. Within the department, every faculty member, regardless of status, took part in planning our curriculum and in creating and using our assessment tools to assess student performance. Meetings were for opening discussions and reaching decisions through consensus. Because we believe that it is not enough *to be engaged*, but that we must also actively *engage others*, we encouraged each other to continue university and community service, whether directing the debate program or the writing center, incorporating service-learning into additional courses, or taking a semester to teach abroad.

We were fortunate to work with an administration that supported our vision; indeed, our move away from individual faculty efforts to cooperative teamwork was partly inspired by Samford's TLA initiative. The invitation to develop the oral communication component of the TLA for the university was significant for several reasons. It was the first university-level project we had undertaken as a department, and it fit squarely in our areas of expertise. More than anything else, our involvement with the TLA initiative launched our team efforts at internal and external engagement with various communities.

Impact

Student Growth

Our collective effort to create an engaged department has had a systemic effect. Exit interviews indicate that our majors tend to be satisfied with their experiences in our department, and they have been effective recruiters for our program: in three years, we grew from 28 majors to 65, largely by student word-of-mouth advertising. Because we focus heavily on the importance of applying knowledge outside the classroom, students have become more civically engaged. Most students are actively involved in various university organizations, particularly the student government association and campus ministry associations; many hold leadership roles, including president of the senior class, chief justice of the values court, and head of student activities as well as presidents of various sororities, fraternities, and the Panhellenic Council. Our students value what they learn beyond the classroom, finding affirmation and application for learning that occurs in class; this was readily apparent in our seniors' inclusion of detailed community involvement narratives in their portfolios.

For us, assessment is the heart of student engagement: An effective assessment plan helped us build a solid curriculum, devise teaching strategies, and create department goals. For example, because we know that we want our students to excel in oral communication by the time they graduate, we assign a formal speech in every course and consistently use National Communication Association guidelines to provide feedback for improvement. At least three department faculty members and one external reviewer assess speeches included in the senior portfolio. This focus has a remarkable impact on our students. Rather than just "another assignment," speeches become part of an educational plan that extends well beyond the classroom. Students take real pride in their speech performances, frequently volunteering to speak at events off campus, which they enthusiastically record and share with the department. In 2004, for example, three of our students were featured motivational speakers at a high school located in one of the poorest areas in Alabama. Another student gave weekly inspirational speeches at a juvenile detention center. Yet another became a youth minister at a nearby church and often led worship services. These students aren't the exception in our department;

the majority of our majors gain impressive speaking experiences outside the classroom.

Community Impact

Our students are not the only ones to respond to the department's synergy. Members of our department also take their expertise into the community. They serve as judges for area speech contests for middle school students and writing contests for Alabama high schools, and as moderators for political debates and community forums. Our Birmingham Area Debate League has revitalized defunct debate programs in 22 schools and provided many under-privileged youth with the opportunity to find their voices in formal debate—an activity all too often reserved for the social elite. Each year, our Summer Debate Institute invites approximately 100 students from around the country to receive intensive instruction in debate. Also invited are prospective debate coaches who come to learn how to begin a debate program. We work hard to make this program affordable to ensure that many people who would not usually have access to debate training can take part in the institute.

Institutional Impact

On campus our department is frequently cited as a model for TLA assessment and curricular coherence, and we have responded by assisting other departments and schools in addressing the oral component of their TLA assessments. Each year we lead assessment workshops in oral communication, and we work with individual departments to tailor assessment plans for their public speaking, group communication, and interpersonal communication assignments.

Lessons Learned

As we have sought to engage our students, our colleagues, and our communities, we are somewhat ironically reminded of how important communication is to what we do. Programs such as the Birmingham Area Debate League and our revised senior seminar require significant resources, and acquiring sufficient resources to implement and grow such programs is challenging. Creating electronic portfolios requires technical knowledge, imparting that knowledge to students, appropriate software and money to purchase it, extensive time commitments from faculty and students, and recruitment of and compensation for external reviewers, among other things. Clearly, such programs require team effort from the department members, administration, and community. While one faculty member may initiate the idea, taking that idea to fruition entails the collective commitment of the department, the students, and the university. Without that team effort, such initiatives, regardless of how innovative or valuable, are unlikely to succeed in the long term.

An important tool for funding our efforts is public relations. When it comes to engagement, we've learned that what happens in the department should not stay in the department—it should be shared with those who have an interest, however peripheral that interest might seem. For example, when we shared our plan for senior electronic portfolios with the head of Samford's Center for Teaching, Learning, and Scholarship, she provided us with digital equipment for recording speeches, equipment that our department could not afford to purchase.

A key factor in our success thus far has been our combined efforts on a comprehensive assessment plan. The TLA initiative made us realize that while university-level plans are good, department-level plans are likely more effective. Working on assessment helped us clarify who we were as a department, where we were heading, and where we wanted to go. It helped us decide what kind of students we want to recruit, what knowledge and skills we want to share, and what strategies we want to use to share information. Our decision that students should be able to apply what they learn outside the classroom had several implications: 1) we had to give them opportunities to apply their knowledge; 2) we had to find meaningful ways to assess their performances; and 3) we needed to develop strong ties to the community—we couldn't simply say "go do service-learning." Clearly, assessment was a catalyst for our engagement, and we suspect the same could be true in other departments. Effective communication, however, was the facilitator.

Engaging the community isn't a linear process: it's a transaction, a conversation in which the community offers critical feedback. Sometimes that feedback is flattering, but other times it can be disappointing. While the senior seminar experience has been fertile ground for learning experiences, we are aware that external reviewers' assessments of senior portfolios can be somewhat uncomfortable. Students who routinely make As in our classes sometimes receive a less enthusiastic evaluation of their portfolios from external reviewers. This can sting a bit: In these situations, students often want further elaboration and justification for the reviewer's grade and may lose sight of the value of the review. Like our students, we may be tempted to resent and resist the external assessment, but we must be willing to look beyond the initial reaction to see reviewer comments for the value they hold precisely because of their external objectivity. Conversely, we found that audiences in the senior workshops were extremely generous when assessing our students' effectiveness. For example, in one semester each senior group (a total of 18 seniors) received almost perfect scores on evaluation forms completed by workshop attendees. Though we agree that our students did exceptional work, we also sense the workshop scores are somewhat inflated. These experiences have taught us that when seeking input from the community, it is important to be clear on assessment criteria. In other words, we must offer evaluators clear rubrics and straightforward grading criteria, and share those rubrics with students prior to the assessment.

The manner in which a department engages has everything to do with the faculty and the organizational climate of the university. Interactions in our department are friendly, open, and usually infused with good-natured humor. We value disagreement and regularly play devil's advocate with each other's ideas. When we hire new faculty members, we seek those who enjoy working collaboratively. For departments with members whose personalities clash or where there is territoriality and direct or indirect conflict, processes of engagement might need careful consideration. Finding at least some common ground between members of a department is an important starting point, and structuring meetings to foster collaborative decision-making is essential. In addition, offering incentives for engagement might also be a tool that can help change the department climate.

Departmental Vision

While we accomplished much between 2002 and 2005, there is much more we want to do. Our vision, as articulated in our five-year plan, includes continued refinement of our curriculum, specifically increasing our current emphasis on intercultural communication and incorporating more service-learning opportunities into our curriculum. This fits well with Samford's Christian mission and commitment to vocational exploration and community outreach. To that end, we hope to expand our current service to the university and larger community.

We have created a Global Communication Initiative (GCI) which links the university's study abroad program to communication courses such as intercultural communication. This is an effort to reinforce Samford's commitment to the theological exploration of vocation while helping the Department of Communication Studies meet our goal of preparing students to communicate effectively in the global village of the 21st century. Whatever path the communication studies' graduates pursue, we want to ensure that they will benefit from the department's emphasis on intercultural communication competence. The GCI will enable our students to share their communication knowledge, interests, and skills in communities outside the U.S.

We also plan to continue working within the university to assist other departments in addressing TLA integration and assessment. Our two writing faculty have already begun working with the university to assist colleges and departments in incorporating and assessing written communication.

Finally, we plan to build a Center for Communication Research, Teaching, and Practice for our department and the extended community. This center will provide communication studies and communication arts students and teachers access to a site ideal for a number of communication-related activities: writing, public speaking, small-group activities, and computer-mediated communication. It will also facilitate research on several communication activities, from individual writers and speakers to small groups involved in collaborative projects to whole classes. We would be able to study, in a world-class environment, communication in a range of contexts, including the teaching of communication and the role of communication in successful service-learning.

Overall, a department that began as "faculty formerly with the speech and theatre department" has actively pursued opportunities to engage and serve our internal and external communities. We plan to garner resources that will enable us not only to continue our current programs but also to expand our sphere of service.

References

Morreale, S. P., Moore, M., & Taylor, P. K. (1993). *The competent speaker speech evaluation form.* Washington, DC: National Communication Association.

About the Authors

Charlotte Brammer is assistant professor of communication studies and director of writing across the curriculum at Samford University. Her research interests include writing pedagogy, technical and professional communication, and electronic portfolios.

Rhonda Parker is professor and chair of the Department of Communication Studies at Samford University. Her research focuses on interpersonal relationships.

6

Geology, Children, and Institutional Change in Southern California

Jay R. Yett

John was perplexed and more than a little skeptical. "What does geology have to do with a soup kitchen?" he asked. He was not alone in questioning the wisdom of presenting a geology-based service-learning project at the Some One Cares Soup Kitchen. But, like most of the Geology 100 students, he needed the points to get the grade he wanted. John had worked hard to design an interesting project based on microscopes and fossils. He set up the microscopes and fossils on one side of the main room in the soup kitchen on a Saturday morning and watched as the men, women, and children came in to eat. Slowly, the children began to come over to see the projects and soon the area was crowded with excited activity. Two young brothers visited all of the projects, but continually returned to John's microscopes and asked question after question. These two boys had been living out of a car for weeks and had been in and out of several local schools. They were starved for knowledge and stimulation. John began to understand the reason for going to the soup kitchen. And he was stunned when both boys came over at the end of the morning and hugged him and asked when he could come back. John went back the next Saturday.

Demographics
Orange Coast College

Orange Coast College is a community college located in Southern California that serves a community that includes one of the wealthiest cities in the country, middle-class neighborhoods, and low-income areas. Approximately 23,000 students enroll each semester in a wide variety of academic, vocational, and technical courses. Many of our students are traditional students who have recently graduated from high school and are taking coursework in order to transfer to the university level. However, the average age of our students is 25, and most of the older, nontraditional students return to college to take courses for professional development, to earn a college degree, or for personal enrichment.

The demographics of our area are rapidly changing. The current composition of our student body is 49% white, 26% Asian American, 17% Hispanic, 2% African American, and 1% Native American. Females comprise about 51% of our student body. Our students represent a wide variety of economic levels and a relatively high percentage work during the school year.

The Geology Department

The faculty of the geology department is composed of two tenured professors and two adjunct instructors. Approximately 950 students are enrolled each semester in a series of freshman- and sophomore-level geology courses including Geology 100, Geology 100 Laboratory (including honors sections), Earth Science for Teachers, Historical Geology, Mineralogy, Environmental Geology, and Natural Science 100. The majority of students take these courses to fulfill general education requirements, and there are usually 8–10 geology majors in the program. The geology program has grown significantly since 2001 as noted by the increased large-group lecture sections for the Geology 100 course.

Our students are representative of the general student body, and we have designed our program to serve all students by offering our courses during the day and the evening. Students vary considerably in their level of college preparation, but at least 30%

of our geology students require remedial courses in mathematics and writing.

Processes
Building a Science-Based Service-Learning Program

Service-learning in our department began in 1998 when the vice president of student services asked our department chair to attend a national service-learning conference held at Vanderbilt University. Upon returning to campus, he designed and implemented a service-learning project working with the local water district. The chair was then asked to become the service-learning coordinator the following semester, and he began working to develop additional service-learning projects across the campus. The turning point in the development of service-learning for our department and the college was an American Association of Community Colleges (AACC) Broadening Horizons through Service-Learning grant that funded the development of science-based service-learning projects tied to our local K–6 schools. These projects were designed so that our students would help K–6 students master basic geologic concepts that are part of the California State Science Standards. The recent addition of science to the state tests dramatically increased the need for help in teaching children about science.

After a series of attempts at designing effective projects, we settled on family science nights held at the local elementary schools and an annual community science night at the college. Rather than have each instructor develop different service-learning projects, the department decided to have all students participate in the family science nights and the community science night. We have standardized the types of projects presented at the family science night by concentrating on certain topics such as Earth materials, energy, or water resources that are included in the California Science Standards and are often areas in which K–6 teachers lack proper training. By presenting these ideas in an enjoyable manner that includes the children and their families, we provide another way for children to master basic concepts related to science.

Family Science Nights: Going Out to the Schools

Our geology students prepare simple hands-on projects for each of the family science nights aimed at the appropriate grade level. Students work in teams to design interactive exhibits and posters that give background information about the topics. All topics are aligned with California State Science Standards, and the projects are designed by the students to actively involve the children in learning about one topic in geology.

Our partner elementary schools are responsible for advertising and promoting the family science nights. The principal sends out flyers two weeks before the event, and the classroom teachers encourage their students to attend. The children must be accompanied by at least one parent, but other family members are also welcome. Usually 40–50 college students meet at the local elementary school, set up the exhibits, and then spend two hours interacting with the children and their families. The family nights are designed as a science fair so that the children and families move from exhibit to exhibit in any manner they find of interest. Approximately 250–300 people attend each of the family science nights.

Our efforts are focused on the west side elementary schools in Costa Mesa, located in an area of lower economic status. These local schools have recorded the lowest scores on the state tests in recent years. Most of the residents are Hispanic, and many of them are new to the area. Since many of the parents do not speak English, we make sure that many of our participating college students are bilingual. We actively encourage family members to join in with their children to learn about geology. We also invite our counselors to attend the events to provide information about our college to the children and the adults. We have presented more than 30 family science nights, and we now offer four or five each semester.

Community Science Nights: Bringing the Families to the College

As part of our AACC grant we designed an annual community science night that offers area K–6 children and their families a chance to visit our campus and tour our science and technology facilities. For many of the attendees, this is their first exposure to a college campus. The first community science night held at the college was a small but successful event attended by about 250 K–6 students and family members; however, the attendance for the subsequent community science nights has grown to more than 3,000 people. About 25–30 science, technology, and allied health faculty open their labs and workshops for the children to explore. More than 200 service-learning students work to put on the event, and many of them design hands-on projects for the children. As a service-learning project, our leadership program students put on a barbecue dinner for all 3,000 attendees. We have presented five community science nights and the attendance has grown each year.

The need for additional help for science education in our K–6 schools is so great that the demand for our service-learning science projects far exceeds the ability of one professor to meet. Students kept telling us that the service-learning experience is extremely valuable and they recommended that we expand service-learning opportunities. For these reasons, the department decided to develop a general service-learning plan for our students. Since we cannot offer service-learning opportunities to all our students, we decided to develop projects for Geology 100 Laboratory students, the Earth Science for Teachers students, and some of the Geology 100 Lecture students. This meant that we needed to include our adjunct faculty in the program, and they have been willing to participate. Over the last several years we have employed a number of different adjunct faculty, and all of them have offered service-learning opportunities.

Our goal is to develop a self-sustaining program of educational outreach, but there is a growing cost to presenting the family and community science nights. Since grant funding was ending, we knew that some limited funding was needed. The professors decided to write a Geology 100 lab manual and use the royalties to help fund future service-learning projects. We believe the sale of the lab manual will provide a steady stream of funding that will allow the department to maintain service-learning projects independent of vagaries of grant or college funding.

Analysis
Why We Developed This Program

All the professors and instructors in the Department of Geology have long observed that some of our entering students are poorly prepared for college science study. This led to the faculty sport of complaining about the teachers at the lower education levels. The past department chair recognized that such complaining was not helping the faculty, our students, or our educational system. Rather, we needed to do something to improve science education at the elementary school level. When this commitment was made, the chair began offering his expertise to the K–12 school districts, where he quickly learned that the fault lay not with the teachers, but with the multitude of other issues that confront our elementary schools. The problem was far too large for him to tackle alone. He then devised ways to involve Geology 100 students in helping the K–6 children through service-learning projects. It was a win-win situation because the college and the K–6 students learned more about the earth sciences.

The geology department was also asked to provide educational opportunities for children outside the formal school setting. In response to a community request, the department developed service-learning projects in earth science education for children in the only soup kitchen in our local area, many of whom live in nearby shelters and may not attend school on a regular basis.

Student and community demand drove the rapid increase in service-learning projects. It became clear that the only possible way to successfully manage this program was at the departmental level. The primary leader in this program is the past department chair and service-learning coordinator who instituted most of the service-learning projects in the department and was able to obtain grant funding for departmental projects. He has worked closely with other faculty to bring them into the program. Fortunately, the dean of mathematics and sciences has long been instrumental in developing science education programs in the county and he provided essential support and advice. The vice president of instruction is a strong advocate for service-learning, and his administrative support was critical to the growth of our program. He continues his support as the current college president.

College and Community Impact

There have been several excellent long-term service-learning projects on campus led by inspiring teachers. The family and community science nights and the geology service-learning projects have given an impetus to service-learning throughout the campus and have especially galvanized the science and technology faculty to work together on a central project. Numerous service-learning projects have been developed by other departments to join with geology service-learning projects at the community science night. Service-learning projects were developed by the biology, microbiology, anatomy and physiology, astronomy, chemistry, marine science, physical anthropology, dental technology, electronics, aviation technology, nutrition science, geography, computer sciences, and leadership studies departments. New service-learning projects are currently being developed in the business, Spanish, English, and physical education departments to support future community science nights.

The community science night has led to institutional funding for the event and for the service-learning program. The college president and vice president of instruction have attended all of the community science nights. The college administration has been so impressed by the science-based service-learning projects and the community science night that funding for the event and the service-learning program has recently been included in the college budget.

The community has benefited greatly by these service-learning projects. Not only have K–6 students learned more about the Earth, but they have been introduced to the college. Many of the elementary school children and their families have never been on a college campus or even considered college as a possibility. When the children and their families interact with college students, faculty, and administrators, they realize that they could succeed at the college level. According to one third-grade teacher, the science nights have made attending college "dinner conversation" topic for many of the elementary school children.

These service-learning projects have also created other important connections between the college and community. They provide an opportunity for K–6 teachers and administrators to visit the campus and see the resources available to them. We have invited additional community partners to join us in these service-learning projects. Project Tomorrow, a privately funded consortium of business and education leaders, has helped us to put on the community science nights. As a result of the success of these community science nights, Project Tomorrow has worked with three other community colleges and one oceanographic museum to develop other community science nights. We have also provided assistance to Fullerton College, Kingwood College, Northwest Indian College and Prince George's Community College to develop their own community science nights.

The Orange County Department of Education has been instrumental in helping us develop service-learning projects. The science education specialists have all worked closely with us to ensure that our projects are designed so that they can be duplicated at other community colleges. They have asked the Department of Geology to partner with them in writing several grant proposals for K–12 science education, and service-learning is now a significant part of these grant proposals.

Most importantly, our students have benefited greatly from the service-learning experience. We ask each service-learning student to write a reflective essay about their project. Almost all have responded that it was a positive experience that has led them to a better understanding of some aspect of geology and a greater appreciation of the responsibilities of citizenship. Many students report that service-learning activities have given more relevance to their studies in geology courses, because they realized that what they learn in class might be of importance to someone else.

These service-learning experiences affect our students in other important ways. The family science nights require students to visit some of the elementary schools in lower income neighborhoods. For some students this is an eye-opening experience. One older student was found crying in the parking lot before one of the family science nights, because she didn't realize that children were being educated in such a "run down" facility. This elementary school was only about a mile from the campus, but she had never been there. Later this same student was amazed by the energy and interest of the children at the family science night and surprised by the parents' involvement. This was a formative event for her. She later became an elementary school teacher.

Not all students are similarly affected by our service-learning activities; however, more than 95% reported that they thought the service-learning project was a good learning experience and they would recommend service-learning to their peers.

Lessons Learned
Be Focused and Build Strong Partnerships

There are two major keys to our success. The decision to concentrate our service-learning efforts on teaching children about geology was significant, because it kept our department focused on a single issue. We selected this issue because it was important to the community and it was one that our department could successfully address. We realized that our general education students were just beginning their studies of geology and that they would feel most confident working with elementary schools. One limitation of service-learning projects in science at the community college level is the limited knowledge that our general education students have obtained in their first year of college. More sophisticated projects could be developed with our majors or with upper-level college students, but we felt that the service-learning option should be available to the greatest number of students.

A second key to the development of our departmental service-learning program has been the partnerships formed between the college and local elementary school children. Early in our work we realized that service-learning could not succeed unless true partnerships were built with local schools and teachers. We built our partnerships by approaching the local school districts at various levels to make sure that administrators, science coordinators, and teachers were all aware of our projects. We also worked closely with the Orange County Department of Education to ensure that our methods and materials were approved for use in local schools.

Partnerships are often difficult to establish and need constant attention to maintain. At first we thought a good partnership with another educational institution would be easy to build and manage. After all, we are all working toward the education of the populace. However, true partnerships between educational partners are rarely attained due to a well-established educational hierarchy and the biases inherent in this system. It is not just the problem of the service provider and the service receiver, but also the problem of a higher-level education institution working with a lower grade-level school. Added to these difficulties is the relationship of the funding partner to the unfunded partners. All of these issues required another approach to partnership building. To bring in true partners for our community science nights, we invited Project Tomorrow, an outside private consortium of business and science leaders, to act as the coordinating agency for the project. They served as central coordinators, bringing all the partners together to design and implement the project. The college representatives and the elementary school partners then could act more as equals. It is still not a perfect partnership, but it allows more input by the elementary school participants.

Our partners have constantly made suggestions for changes in our projects, and we have responded in a flexible manner. It became clear early in our program that although we were experts in our academic discipline, we were not adept at teaching young children. We very quickly learned to rely on the elementary school teachers to show us projects that would work with their students.

Halting Successes and Significant Challenges

The service-learning projects of our department have been developed over several years, and we were surprised by the halting nature of our success. As we began the program, we thought that since every project developed from a firm commitment to a noble goal that every project and activity would be a rousing success. Such was not the case. Mistakes were made, missteps taken, and opportunities missed; however, the commitment to service-learning and helping local K–12 schools kept us on track. Flexibility to our approach was important, and clear communication with our partners was essential. We realized, for example, that classroom presentations were not as successful as we anticipated because our Geology 100 students were not adequately trained to work effectively in a K–6 classroom. The service-learning students, however, really enjoyed presenting their projects in a science fair setting and appreciated having the parents accompany the children. The same geologic concepts could be presented in a more effective manner through the family science night and, importantly, the parents were included in the process.

We also learned that once a successful program is built, many other opportunities arise. After we had shown that we could work with the K–6 schools and districts, the Orange County Department of Education (OCDE) approached us to design and present professional development workshops for elementary school teachers focused on the Earth sciences in the California Science Standards. We responded by giving a number of workshops about rocks and minerals, earthquakes, seismology, plate tectonics, and other topics. Later, OCDE asked if we could lead field trips for teachers, and we did. Now the OCDE contacts us whenever they need help with Earth science projects, teacher workshops, or grant proposals.

Building a service-learning program is beset with significant challenges. The primary barrier to a successful implementation of our departmental service-learning program is the time commitment required from faculty and our partners. Both of our tenured professors teach full academic schedules and the adjunct faculty have other full-time jobs or other teaching jobs. All our partners also have very busy schedules, and many teachers resent any additional assignments. These busy schedules make it difficult to coordinate successful service-learning projects. Unfortunately, time constraints can impose significant limits on the number and types of projects that can be developed. The only solution to this problem is to identify persons who are truly committed to making these service-learning projects succeed and giving them the resources to achieve our goals.

Vision: Where Do We Go From Here?

Our goals for the department are threefold. First, we aim to provide our students with a quality education in geology. This requires that we continue to work at presenting our topics in an organized, engaging, and informative manner. It also means that we must continue to offer meaningful service-learning projects to many of our students.

The second goal is to build a geology program that will fully benefit our community at large. To achieve this goal we are now developing service-learning projects that will include middle and high school students. These projects will be designed to present more technical information to these higher-level students. We encourage middle and high school teachers to access our department for expertise and materials. After-school programs could also be a venue for our service-learning activities—many schools and agencies offer these programs and science education can add to their offerings. We are working with the Orange County Department of Education to design professional development workshops for all Earth science teachers in the county.

The third departmental goal is to serve as a model for science and mathematics departments at other community colleges. More than 160,000 students enroll in science and mathematics courses at Orange County community colleges each year. If we could mobilize even 10% of those students to participate in service-learning projects focused on K–12 education, then we could truly make a significant impact in the community. We have shown that it is possible to enhance science education while serving in the community, and it is our hope that others will follow.

We want anyone in our community to feel that our department is a community resource. Teachers should feel that they could contact us for help with questions about geology. Children and families should know that an educational opportunity exists at our college and that geology is an important aspect of their lives. We aim to help our local children recognize science as an essential element for a successful future. The future is open for all children, even a young child eating at a soup kitchen.

About the Author

Jay R. Yett studied geology at the University of Idaho and the University of Washington. He worked as a micropaleontologist for five years and later was a partner in a paleontological consulting firm. He joined the Orange Coast College faculty in 1984 and has been the college service-learning coordinator since 1999. He currently serves as a national mentor for the American Association of Community Colleges Broadening Horizons through Service-Learning grant.

7

Engagement in the Arts: Commitment to an Urban Experience

Susan Agre-Kippenhan, Elisabeth Charman

An Activist Tradition

In the early 1970s, newly hired Portland State University (PSU) sculpture professor Michihiro (Michi) Kosuge challenged students to address social issues. In one assignment, Kosuge asked his students to design and build a shelter for a homeless person. The shelter had to be durable, lightweight, portable, easy to set up, take down, and pack up, with room to sleep comfortably and the ability to stay warm and dry. The materials had to be inexpensive, the structure functional, and the form artistically interesting. Kosuge introduced the project by asking his students to meet with and interview homeless people.

PSU is an urban campus located in the heart of downtown Portland's business district. The university sits at the south end of tree-lined park blocks and runs almost uninterrupted the length of downtown. A few blocks beyond the campus, small groups of homeless people convened. In the 1970s, the majority of the homeless people Michi and his students encountered were veterans of the Vietnam War, men between the ages of 25 and 35, some of whom were struggling with alcohol and drug-related issues as well as with other social, financial, and psychological problems. The homeless men became engaged in the process, so the students extended invitations to join their critiques. Coffee and hotdogs fueled discussions of the functional and artistic aspects of the shelters. The final requirement for the project was for the students to test their work by spending a night in their shelters on the park blocks where they experienced one aspect of being homeless and gained an appreciation of a life perhaps radically different from their own.

While having students sleep in the park blocks challenged PSU's public safety officers, the idea of tying curriculum to social issues has continued to resonate with faculty and students in the Department of Art. For many years Michi regularly asked his students to address critical social issues through their sculpture; their responses ranged from the practical to installations and highly emotive performance pieces. In the department today, we have built on this activist tradition in ways that respect our history and reflect our present.

Demographics

PSU's urban campus merges seamlessly into the city. The same inviting park-like atmosphere that attracted the homeless men of Michi's day now serves as the outdoor living room of the campus. On any sunny day you can find a mix of neighborhood residents, students from across the campus, children in university daycare, protestors, musicians, and business people on lunch break.

Until the mid 1990s, PSU looked like other institutions in many ways—it was a four-year urban university serving approximately 16,000 students with typical curriculum offerings. Now it is a comprehensive public institution with approximately 25,000 students (two-thirds undergraduate and one-third graduate students) that addresses the needs of its varied community of students by offering more than 100 programs of study. The diverse student population ranges in age, gender, and life experience and, like many similar institutions, PSU serves numerous transfer students, part-time students, and commuters. What precipitated this change? In the mid-1990s, PSU completely reformed its general education program, renaming the integrated thematic approach to learning as University Studies. This reform brought focus to the university's relationship with the community, examining the inter-disciplinarity and application of those disciplines. The institutional results of this reform extend well beyond one program and have moved PSU toward institutionalizing service-learning and civic engagement. New promotion and tenure guidelines approved in 1996 acknowledge civic engagement and support faculty "schol-arship of outreach" that aligns with the institutional mission. A highly visible sky bridge over a main thoroughfare in Portland pro-claims the university motto "Let Knowledge Serve the City." PSU has received significant national recognition, grants, and awards, and in the past four years has earned *U.S. News & World Report's* recognition for service-learning, learning communities, and senior capstone. Currently 7,800 students and 400 faculty are involved in service-learning classes annually. PSU today looks decidedly dif-ferent then the institution of the early 1990s.

At the second annual American Democracy Project National Conference held in Portland in June 2005, George Mehaffy, vice president for academic leadership and change with the Asso-ciation of American Colleges and Universities, lauded PSU for having "created a campus-wide commitment to the community through community-based learning for students, applied scholar-ship addressing community problems for faculty, and a broader definition of service that encouraged linkages between the institu-tion and the community."

It is in this institutional setting that the Department of Art in the School of Fine and Performing Arts has created a mission centered on teaching students to understand and experience ways that artists and their works are involved in a larger social con-text while they gain specific skills, expertise, theory, and historical understandings. The department is one of the largest at PSU, with three undergraduate concentration areas: studio, graphic design, and art history, and a master's of fine arts in studio art. More than 900 majors and well over 300 nonmajors take courses yearly. As described in the department mission, faculty are practicing artists, scholars, and designers "actively engaged in their respective fields and with the extended community" (Portland State University, 2003). Each educator has their own scholarly agenda, range of artistic practice, and community connections.

Processes

Historically, individual faculty in the Department of Art have been engaged in civic work and community partnerships over the past 10 years. Initial efforts in community-based learning and civic engagement in the classroom reflected the scholarship, professional interest, and social orientation of individuals. Artists with an activist approach, like Michi, brought this practice into the classroom. Graphic designers extended their professional orientation of collaborating with businesses and organizations to community-based learning classes. Faculty began to frame their scholarship and work in a range of community venues. For example, art historians gave talks at prisons and an art educator worked on setting statewide educational policy. Faculty began to give assignments that focused on world events, elections, politics, social issues, and social change.

One faculty member whose work carries on the theme of Michi Kosuge's work is Elisabeth (Lis) Charman, associate professor in graphic design and coauthor of this chapter. To contextualize Lis's work, it is critical to understand that Portland's homeless population has changed and now includes many young people. One community group working to address the needs of these often ignored members of society is p:ear (program: education, art, recreation). p:ear describes their work as follows: "p:ear builds positive relationships with homeless and transitional youth, ages 15 to 23. Each year p:ear programs serve more than 350 homeless and transitional young people."

Lis began to work with p:ear through her own professional practice and developed a relationship with the organization. Realizing p:ear needed to communicate with a wider audience, Lis engaged her junior-level communication design students in a community-based learning class on projects to increase awareness and support fundraising. This successful partnership brought p:ear notable public attention and increased volunteer inquiries while demonstrating to students the power of community involvement.

Lis recognized there was still more to be done to address p:ear's significant needs. She organized a group of professionals and submitted a grant proposal to fund additional work. In summer 2005, Sappi paper company's "Ideas that Matter" grant awarded Lis $14,000 to develop a stronger visual promotional tool for p:ear.

Other faculty have made similar links between their own work and their activities in the classroom. An associate professor who joined the department after a 17-year career as an outstanding high school art teacher brought his passion to developing interdisciplinary courses that link K–12 and higher education, developing curriculum, and supporting other faculty in their community work. Another associate professor developed a printmaking course that pairs students with elders in the community to interview them, hear their life stories, and interpret them in prints. The artwork created is exhibited in the senior residencies.

Collective Action

Individual faculty efforts began to converge into a collective effort in 2002 when the department received the first of several key Learn and Serve America grants through the PSU Center for Academic Excellence. This series of grants first moved individual art department faculty and then the entire department through increasingly more sophisticated ways to engage students in communities. These grants have helped to focus our work and to take on a department-wide orientation. We have grown and developed our work by building on departmental expertise and faculty and student interests. We have recognized the unique opportunities and characteristics of the arts and incorporated them into our thinking and planning.

We are developing our own civic capacity, deepening practicum, and helping students identify how their education in the arts fits into a civic society. While focusing on building resources, processes, and support, and on curriculum development, we have become increasingly more comprehensive in our approach. Our work manifests itself in community-based learning courses, a civic emphasis on coursework, research, and cocurricular student activities. These activities are further extended by internships, a gallery operations course, independent student projects, and collaboration with student organizations that focus on community issues.

Increased activities have also widened our scope of community partners and the ways in which we disseminate our work. Our partners are as diverse as public schools, water quality funds, organizations that work with homeless youths, elders, arts organizations, and healthcare professionals. We have disseminated our work through exhibitions, community and public projects, web sites, public presentations, and publications including syllabi and articles on methods and models. Moving beyond our traditional audiences, we have shown work in high schools, community organizations, the mall, the airport, and at community conferences.

Analysis
From "Mine" to "Ours"

This move from an individual to a collective effort is a key evolution for the department and has influenced significant aspects of departmental activities from the faculty we attract to how search committees are formed to the roles students play. In 1995, the department began to recognize the importance of the community voice. What started with the occasional community partners participating in departmental initiatives has led to a more systematic approach of including the community. This new approach was initiated by an influx of new faculty and leadership, bringing faculty to the department with an affinity for collaboration, responsiveness to community needs, and expertise in working with diverse groups. (The normal cycle of retirements has resulted in the hiring of all but one faculty member in the past 10 years.) A natural outcome of hiring personnel with a decidedly collaborative community orientation has been the establishment of a more inclusive approach to incorporating community in departmental activities and decision-making.

Including community partners has now become ingrained in departmental work. Overcoming scheduling issues and logistics, community partners regularly serve on search committees, advisory boards, and critical departmental committees. This practice has myriad benefits: it provides a community perspective in our important decisions, brings in professional expertise, helps support the small number of full-time faculty, and even mitigates against politics in decision-making. We value inviting our community partners into the inner workings of our department as an indication of trust and a measure of our commitment to listening to external voices.

A new addition to the department selected by one such search committee is assistant professor Harrell Fletcher who joined the department in the 2004–2005 academic year. An internationally recognized artist, Harrell's focus is on an artistic social practice. Like many of our newer hires, he was attracted to the institution's and department's commitment to the community. He uses art to create dialogue, providing public spaces for diverse populations to meet and to highlight the unique aspects of neighborhoods. Since 2004, his work has taken him to Bosnia, Vietnam, and France. He is a facilitator who includes artists and nonartists in art making and has extended this distinctive approach to the classroom. In a recent course, Harrell asked students to "focus on a personal fear and to develop a project that engaged the community." A student who fears police officers developed a project where she made rubbings of police officer's badges while the officers were wearing them. She then organized an exhibition of the rubbings in a local café, giving the neighborhood an opportunity to discuss their thoughts about law enforcement.

As we have developed our ability to facilitate and enhance the civic capacity of our students, we have also turned increasingly to them to help guide us. Students have been polled to determine their interests, worked on tandem research projects, identified community partnerships, and been leaders in the classroom. In 2004, two students took a leadership role, compiling a searchable bibliography to serve as a reference for service-learning in the arts. While there are myriad individual sources available, there was not one comprehensive compilation searchable by artists, medium, or type of project. The database offers historic, academic, and contemporary references (see www.art.pdx.edu). We have disseminated it at conferences, and it has assisted several graduate students in the dissertation literature review.

Leadership

Susan Agre-Kippenhan, coauthor of this chapter and chair of the Department of Art, is one of the faculty who began civic work 10 years ago. Long before becoming chair or receiving tenure at PSU, Susan's classes, personal work, and scholarship focused on community engagement. She developed some of the first community-based learning courses in the department and took on the roles of mentor, facilitator, and leader before becoming chair of the department in 2003. The philosophy that has guided her work—community-based learning and civic engagement that can profoundly affect how students define themselves—has become key to the department's work. Students gain a greater sense of how the skills and talents they develop can impact a broader range of concerns from business to the local community to the world. Students see how they fit into and affect the larger context of our society.

Susan's personal work on scholarship in community-based learning and on promotion and tenure has particular relevance for the department. It is critical to faculty that all facets of their work have the potential to be recognized and rewarded. PSU's guidelines allow for such recognition, with the responsibility to create a cogent case placed on the faculty member. Susan has given presentations and written on this topic, and an important aspect of her leadership in this area is her ability to guide faculty through the review process (Gelmon & Agre-Kippenhan, 2002)

Susan's growth in her research and scholarship mirrors PSU's institutional development. Moving from personal projects to institutional ones, she has learned how to replicate successful strategies for the department. Prior administrative experience in the capstone program at PSU (a senior-level required service-learning course in PSU's University Studies) provided her with insight into multiple models for community learning and civic engagement. A key resource she brings to departmental work is writing grants that identify and build on departmental interests and strengths. She has attracted diverse faculty through mini grants that provide funding opportunities, assisted in faculty development, and provided numerous dissemination opportunities. Susan seeks out and supports individual faculty members, helping them connect their passions to civic engagement. Employing an integrated departmental approach that positions experienced faculty as mentors and engages students in all aspects of research and project development has been a successful strategy for the department.

Impact

The department's civic engagement focus is evident in the ways that faculty and students approach their work (i.e., in student and faculty publishing and scholarship) and in the strength of our relationships with the community. It can also be found in the way we regularly integrate scholarship, community service, and teaching.

Student Impact

The impact of departmental civic engagement is reflected in the ways students choose to approach, develop, and create their work. An exemplar of this is work by graduate student damali ayo. Her performance pieces address issues of American slavery reparations and have been seen on the streets of Chicago and New York, among other cities. damali's web site, rent-a-negro.com, and her new book *How to Rent a Negro* (2005), confront race issues using humor and satire. Her pseudo-guidebook is a biting, too-close-for-comfort commentary on black-white racial interactions in America. Seeking to open an honest dialogue, damali's goal is to get people in America thinking and talking about race. Another graduate student addressing sociological issues in a public forum is Micah Perry. With plans for multiple city distribution, Micah's flag project combines the faces of more than 500 Portland citizens with the names, birth, and death dates of recent civilian casualties in Iraq and Afghanistan. Displayed in Portland's outdoor public gathering spaces and outside neighborhood businesses, the waving flags seek to engage people in an open dialogue about a charged social issue.

Individual and class projects and discussions have motivated a group of undergraduate students to form an on-campus organization for investigating ideas of art and community interaction. Intersecting with the community in coffee shops, neighborhood cafés, and on the streets, the students and community members exchange work and develop shared activities.

Faculty Impact

Community engagement has also brought significant changes in our approaches to faculty work, teaching and learning, and our department as a whole. One indication of these changes is the blurring of the boundaries that once existed between professional work, community work (or what is sometimes called community service), and community-based pedagogy. Faculty (and students) have experienced myriad successes where these activities intersect and overlap. Scholarship through articles, exhibitions, and presentations centering on community-based work and teaching more regularly appear on faculty curriculum vitae. One result of this integration is the inclusion of Lis and Susan's syllabi for a community-based learning course in the edited volume, *Teaching Graphic Design* (Heller, 2004). In 2004, faculty presented community-based work at three national conferences, planned and convened regional meetings, and presented their work in lectures as visiting artists nationally and abroad.

Community Impact

The department's connection with the community and community partners has been strengthened through many long-term collaborative relationships. Both established and developing relationships are a direct result of successful community-based projects that have promoted and assisted—and thus created increased visibility and interest in—our partners' organizations. One of the key strengths of these relationships is our belief and understanding that community partners are co-educators, and many have assumed a formal role as co-instructor. One such instructor, a Portland high school art teacher, began at PSU as a community partner in a course that focuses on developing media literacy curricula for high school teachers and students. He subsequently became a co-instructor and most recently developed the capstone course Art and Activism.

The benefits of departmental engagement can be found in the accomplishments and activities of our students, faculty, department, and community partners. As a result of this engagement, students gain opportunities for application and learning-by-doing through addressing civic and social concerns that are critical to our community. And as a department, we are brought closer to the concerns, successes, and life of our community.

Lessons

Successful Strategies

A cardinal strategy of the art department at PSU has been to make intrinsic a philosophy of connecting to and engaging with our community in ways that support our shared agenda. This strategy aligns with PSU's institutional vision and value statement of community engagement which supports "a reciprocal relationship between the community and the university in which knowledge serves the city and the city contributes to knowledge in the university" (Portland State University, 2006). Instead of treating community-based learning as a discrete initiative, we integrate community approaches with multiple priorities and departmental interests and concerns. For example, as we developed a concentration in digital media, we built into the curriculum an interactive team course that contributes senior students' web expertise to nonprofit organizations as a culminating educational experience.

As a department we celebrate student, faculty, and community successes. Acknowledging achievements formally recognizes individual and team accomplishments and it affirms our commitment to being an engaged department. Key to our success has been the sharing of projects and information—we seek out and share scholarship venues and other opportunities. In 2004, four faculty members and four students made presentations at professional conferences centered on community-based learning and civic engagement while another faculty member planned and facilitated two conferences specifically on service-learning and the Arts. In 2005, PSU's annual Civic Engagement Awards, presented by the PSU Center for Academic Excellence, recognized the art department with an award for Excellence in Departmental Civic Engagement and Lis Charman with an award for Excellence in Faculty/Community Partnerships. Such recognition serves to focus institutional and community attention on our work and gives us all a moment to reflect on success. Celebrations also serve as a venue to exchange experiences, ideas, projects, approaches, and methods of dissemination.

Mentorship efforts within the department are effective and indispensable. It only takes one or two key faculty members to model, guide, support, and encourage interested faculty in the development of their own engaged curricula. Mentoring individuals is done through sharing syllabi, discussing and supporting projects, co-teaching, and teaching paralleled sections of the same course. These activities have significantly increased the number of faculty participating in community-based learning and scholarship in the Department of Art.

Finally, we built on our growing achievements by recognizing our faculty's diverse interests and community activities. Faculty approach and apply ideas of community engagement in distinctly different ways. Embracing the diversity of our faculty's pursuits has helped each of us by offering new ways of looking at civic engagement. Locating an individual's interest—where he or she personally connect with community-based learning and scholarship—results in faculty developing and expanding those interests.

Barriers

While we have had many successes, we have also met our share of challenges and barriers, such as addressing the idea that community has a traditional meaning in the arts—it refers to the "arts community." Not mere semantics, it is indicative of a mindset in the arts where faculty often first seek arts organizations for community partners. This narrow focus on arts organizations has inherent limitations. Expanding the definition to mean the community at large not only broadens the pool of community partner organizations but it fundamentally changes the dialogue around the role the arts can play in community work, service, and activism. Broadening the role of the arts in community-based interaction moves us from activities centered on providing arts opportunities and enrichment to a position where the arts can have an expanded function—as a convener, a forum, a galvanizing force for exploring issues critical to our community. An example of this expanded role is found in the work of an assistant professor who has worked with a struggling local high school. Rather than think about the arts as an enrichment activity to supplement a thin curriculum, he has taken on a large, long-term mural project engaging minority students. These students have used mural painting as a way to research, understand, and claim their history and as well as a piece of their school.

Our department composition, 13 full-time, 5 fixed-term, 65 part-time faculty, and a very small, overextended office staff, is another challenge. As these numbers indicate, the majority of art classes are taught by part-time faculty. Successfully mentoring and supporting part-time faculty interested in community engagement proved more difficult and took longer than we anticipated. Most part-time faculty come to campus only to teach a specific course and may not be able to check their mailboxes or email regularly—making distributing information on funding and support less timely and less effective. Part-time faculty interested in civic engagement projects often need additional support and require flexible meeting times. In addition, such a large part-time faculty makes it more difficult for research, scholarship, and community projects (and contacts) to be shared, understood, and integrated into a more centralized and coordinated effort. To directly address these issues we are developing a team of "go-to" or hub people to assist faculty in each area. We have also designated a faculty member from art education to assist all faculty in teaching and learning activities. He is available to meet with any faculty member to help them identify learning objectives, write effective syllabi, and create a more integrated approach to teaching and community work.

The last two barriers we consider are among the more typical challenges faced by service-learning pedagogy. As the research and literature on service-learning demonstrates, we face a ubiquitous challenge in our community-based courses: Some students, accustomed to the insulated nature of the classroom, describe the community-based courses as chaotic. In contrast to traditional courses, which rarely deviate from the term schedule posted on the syllabus and where students come to expect an environment that is fairly predictable, community-based courses challenge this model and these expectations. In community-based courses students are called upon to respond to community partner needs and critical input in addition to faculty direction. Community-based courses often require participants to address changes in priorities, schedules, and goals. Working with a community partner, students confront these realities—outside forces affect deadlines, directions change, and the once theoretical becomes reality. We have found that careful management of student expectations throughout these courses is critical, and periodic check-ins, discussions, and reflection can help students learn to manage competing demands. Discussions with students address their frustrations and point out that sometimes emotionally challenging work can also provide great rewards. Clearly, not all students find community experiences challenging, though many find the experience exhilarating and adapt gracefully to addressing unexpected changes in direction and community partner concerns. Our goal is for all students to realize that these experiences equip them with the skills and experiences they will need to be successful in their personal and professional lives.

Another well-documented and common set of challenges we monitor and address concerns maintaining academic rigor in community-based learning environments. This concern is addressed by assuring that core educational goals and learning outcomes are clearly outlined and addressed for each course. Key course learning objectives are always connected to project goals. The learning objectives, program goals, and course content outlines always guide and direct community-based projects, not the other way around. We understand that meeting educational needs through community-based learning works best when the highest educational benefits for students are maintained while successfully fulfilling community needs.

Key Strategies

Many of our strategies were presented in the lessons sections of this chapter. The strategies we have developed over time have been borrowed, adopted, and adapted from multiple sources, including the successful strategies of other departmental units in our institution and service-learning literature that provides ideas and approaches.

We have developed our approaches organically; our key strategies reflect the structure, diversity, and inner workings of our department. Often, departmental units begin by taking an inventory of courses and program structures and then carefully mapping community-based learning into the curriculum. We have seen this approach work well in other engaged departments at PSU, but it doesn't work for us. The diversity of our curricular offerings make a systematic inventory and mapping approach complex and difficult. The three departmental concentration areas offer variations that translate into seven possible courses of study, each with its own set of requirements and electives. The department employs a decentralized leadership model— while the chair leads the department, each concentration area works collaboratively to make decisions and share responsibilities. A third inhibitor is the imbalance between part-time and full-time faculty that can make connecting people and interests cumbersome.

In contrast to a systematic inventory and mapping, we take a more organic approach. While our strategy may seem counterproductive, it has several benefits. One benefit has been the ability for interested faculty to self-identify—their natural interests lead them to community-based learning and civic engagement—and we have built on those successes. As the faculty grows and collaborates, making greater connections and networks, the entire department becomes more aware and engaged in the process.

We have employed several strategies to accomplish departmental engagement. The first strategy opens all departmental opportunities for grant money, faculty development, and dissemination to all faculty including full-time, fixed-term, and part-time faculty. A cross section of these faculty members from all concentration areas have applied for and received community engagement mini grants. Originating from PSU's Center for Academic Excellence, these grants help support, advise, connect, and celebrate faculty engagement in community-based learning while strengthening connections. The department also offers support and assistance by helping faculty write proposals and apply for grants, and it circulates information regarding development, funding, and dissemination opportunities.

A second strategy addresses our limited resources that most often prohibit the addition of new elective classes. Instead of creating new classes, we locate community activities in existing required courses—essentially redefining courses to include a community component. In 2004, we revised an art education course taken by more than 300 students annually; this course is required prior to applying to PSU's Graduate School of Education for graduate studies. Previously the incorporation of community activity varied from section to section; our revision will integrate the community activities into every section. To support this greater undertaking, we have begun work on partnership identification, project design, and faculty support.

One of the most critical areas of all departmental work is attracting, supporting, and retaining strong faculty. As our departmental agenda has been clearer we can articulate our focus in the interviewing and hiring process. We have prioritized community activity in our new hires, supported their community-based work, and assisted them in navigating the development and support available at the university. We engage new faculty in departmental efforts by either scheduling them to teach courses with a community component or providing them an opportunity to develop courses with community-based learning components that fit their area, expertise, and interests.

Due to our organic development, we capitalized on early, small successes, developing them into larger and larger projects and networks of activity. We modeled effective strategies and adapted them to fit our needs. Above all, when guiding the evolution of an engaged department, it is critical to be flexible, responsive, and willing to try everything and anything that demonstrates possibility and promise.

Vision

From Michi's 1970s idea for an individual assignment that positioned student artists as social change agents, we have moved to a departmental mission that states our commitment to community connection, curriculum, and scholarship—collectively garnering a reputation around the work. What do we seek for our future?

By 2010, the department mission will clearly delineate our commitment to community engagement by involving all majors in a developmental experience with the community. We will deliberately state the vehicles used to integrate community engagement throughout our curriculum and scholarship, and we will create an increasing number of opportunities for students, faculty, and community. As the department moves forward, we will continue to align more consciously with an urban mission, stay open to possibilities, and seek partnerships throughout our region. We hope transformative ideas across the department will continue to lead to shifts and growth in curriculum content, approach, and structure. These developments will directly reflect our civic engagement efforts.

Our future includes a new curriculum strand dedicated to addressing social problems, public art, and visual literacy and which seeks to contextualize social issues through creative processes. This strand will work with traditional mediums like painting as well as more contemporary approaches like performance and installation. The new curriculum will serve as a focal point for community-based work. As part of this strand we envision a new Center for Community Arts that will develop and secure long-term partnerships with community arts organizations, human service providers, environmental groups, and other nonprofit agencies to collectively address our community's needs.

Graduate programs in studio arts and in art history (to be added in 2006) will offer options to focus on the role of the artist and scholar in an urban setting. This focus will both support community-based learning courses and serve as a separate area of engagement.

Finally, each year there will be at least two graduate students admitted specifically as "community artists" with the expectation that their work will include social practice connected to the community. Unlike other graduate students, they will not have a studio space but instead will have a gathering space to convene with key community members, other artists, and policymakers. Supported with scholarship and grant money, they will be known as Kosuge's Scholars, in honor of Michi Kosuge's legacy of commitment to the exploration of social issues.

References

ayo, d. (2005). *How to rent a Negro*. Chicago, IL: Lawrence Hill Books.

Gelmon, S. G., & Agre-Kippenhan, S. (2002, January). Promotion, tenure, and the engaged scholar: Keeping the scholarship of engagement in the review process. *AAHE Bulletin, 54*(5), 7–11.

Heller, S. (Ed.). (2004). *Teaching graphic design: Course offerings and class projects from the leading undergraduate and graduate programs*. New York, NY: Allsworth Press.

Portland State University. (2006). *Our mission, vision and values*. Retrieved March 19, 2006, from www.pdx.edu/mission.html

Portland State University, Department of Art. (2003). *Mission*. Retrieved March 19, 2006, from the Portland State University, Department of Art web site: www.art.pdx.edu/welcome/mission/mission.htm

About the Authors

Susan Agre-Kippenhan is professor of graphic design and chair of the Department of Art at Portland State University. She focuses her teaching and research on connecting educational and community concerns.

Elisabeth Charman is an associate professor at Portland State University where she teaches in the graphic design program. Her work has received recognition from the Art Director's Club, the AIGA, and *How* magazine. Her work has been exhibited and published nationally and internationally in Europe, Japan, and South Korea.

8

Sustaining a Service-Learning Program: An English Department's Commitment to Service

Marybeth Mason, Pam Davenport

> It was my first night of service, and I was skeptical about the importance of my role at ICAN [Improving Chandler Area Neighborhoods], a program to help kids avoid gang participation and drug abuse. Despite my skepticism, one thing was certain: what I was about to experience would change my outlook on my community forever.... As we gathered together, the director asked a young Hispanic boy, Roberto, to lead us in prayer to begin the evening's activities. Roberto prayed aloud that his family would not be shot at any more and that his brother would survive his gunshot wound to the head. Whatever happened to praying to win a basketball game or giving thanks for a good meal? Needless to say, Roberto's prayer came as a shock to me.... Unfortunately, the violence and fear are not limited to other communities, towns, or urban areas any more. Tragically, it is a dilemma rapidly escalating into a nation-wide crisis, leaving few untouched.
>
> —Josh Heller

> March 20—I went in this morning expecting the normal, hectic routine of the activity assistants gathering up residents of the nursing home for the morning's events.

Instead, I was greeted by silent hallways. Three of the four assistants had called in sick on this particular day, so I was asked to cover the Alzheimer's unit by myself. I was a little nervous about the idea of being alone in the unit for the first time, but I thought I could handle it. Unfortunately, all of the prerecorded music often used to entertain the residents was locked away in a cabinet along with all of the musical instruments. I managed to find an oldies station on the radio and a deflated beach ball behind the TV in the corner. I blew up the beach ball and gathered the residents into a circle. After they tossed the ball around for about a half hour, they began to lose interest. One woman, Sophie, who seemed more interested in what was on the ceiling than in tossing the beach ball, even told me I was boring. I tried not to let her discourage me. I picked her up out of her chair and began to dance with her to a folksy rendition of "The Yellow Rose of Texas." This got a smile out of her and everyone else as we waltzed wall to wall around the room.

—Dean Dietzen

These student reflections on their service-learning experiences are typical of the thousands of students at Chandler-Gilbert Community College (CGCC) who have served in their communities over the last 15 years and who have learned a wide variety of lessons connected to their coursework that cannot be taught within the confines of a classroom's four walls. Like most of the students at Chandler-Gilbert Community College who are asked to serve, these students, no matter how reluctant at first, reveal in their written reflections a deeper understanding of the social problems within their own communities, a heightened awareness of their civic responsibility, and creative strategies for problem solving.

Demographics
Chandler-Gilbert Community College

Chandler-Gilbert Community College (CGCC) is 1 of 10 Maricopa Community Colleges in metropolitan Phoenix. CGCC serves approximately 13,000 students each year at three campus locations, offering a variety of associate degrees, university transfer curricula, career and technical training programs, and special interest courses. Among CGCC students, 83% are pursuing academic coursework and 17% are enrolled in career and technical training programs, with 72% attending part-time and 28% full-time. A significant majority of CGCC students commute daily. The student body is 67% Caucasian, 15% Hispanic, 3% African American, 4% Asian, 2% American Indian, and 9% identified as "Other." CGCC students represent a wide spectrum of declared and undeclared undergraduate majors.

The Department of English

Currently, there are 11 full-time residential faculty and 38 part-time adjunct faculty in the CGCC English department. Our English faculty teach developmental English classes, First-Year Composition, as well as lower division literature and humanities courses for university transfer.

Processes
Getting Started: How and When

> I walked into chaos. The coordinator of the unified Bowling League for Mentally Disabled Citizens was trying to organize the teams, hand out nametags and collect money. Despite the confusion, I found my team. I would not only be spending the next eight weeks with these three women, we would become friends and the team known as "The Rat Pack." I had no idea that Lucy, Barbara, and Geri would hook me on serving with the disabled.
>
> —James Lewis

James Lewis was a student in the very first class that required service-learning at Chandler-Gilbert Community College. Service-learning emerged at CGCC in one English 102 First-Year Composition section of 20 students in fall 1991. The theme of the course was career and community. Students were required to research a prospective career as well as a social problem relevant to that career and to serve in a related community-based nonprofit organization. For example, James, who researched a career in engineering, also researched access issues of the disabled and the Americans with Disabilities Act, while serving 20 hours with the Bowling League for Mentally Disabled Citizens and eventually many additional hours as an organizer for the Special Olympics.

An English faculty member teamed with the student life faculty advisor and the director of student life, with support from the vice president of student affairs, to design, implement, and lead this service-learning model. Although placing each of the 20 students individually in an agency relevant to her or his research was challenging, the enthusiasm demonstrated in their journal entries and reflection essays motivated the team to create the Office of Service-Learning in the Office of Student Life to manage the placements. Cultivating relationships with each agency and working with their staff to design meaningful service experiences and orientations for each student took careful attention, deliberation, and time. Eventually the 20 hour service-learning component became a requirement in most English 102 sections.

At first figuring out a way to individually place hundreds of students in agencies and training the faculty in this new method of experiential learning each semester seemed daunting. In response, the service-learning leadership team of faculty, staff, and the vice president of student affairs created a service-learning assistant position, funded by student affairs. Students who had completed service-learning sections served in these roles and received a $100 stipend to go into a classroom each week throughout the semester to help the faculty place each student in an appropriate agency. The service-learning assistants were trained and given a portable box of forms, including service-learning applications, agency timecards, a variety of releases and liability forms, as well as directions for contacting agencies, appropriate dress and demeanor, and journal keeping. The coordinators of the First-Year Composition program conducted faculty development workshops at the beginning of each semester to orient the faculty to the curriculum, the service-learning component, the variety of writing assignments, the database of agencies that had been created, and to introduce each faculty member to his or her service-learning assistant.

With the English 102 model implemented, a service-learning component was also added to the English 101 First-Year Composition curriculum. Centered around the broader theme of creating community in a changing world, the English 101 curriculum required students to participate in Into the Streets, a one-day service event where they served, wrote, and reflected on their learning, choosing from a variety of agencies, such as the Child Crisis Center, Desert Cove Nursing Home, La Mesita Family Emergency Shelter, Save the Family Foundation, the Chandler and Gilbert Boys and Girls Clubs, the Tonto National Forest, the Gilbert Wildlife Refuge, United Blood Services, the Phoenix Zoo, and the Chandler and Gilbert school districts. The coordination of this event was also led by the service-learning leadership team, again with help from student service-learning assistants in coordinating and running this event. Workshops were held to orient faculty to the English 101 curriculum, the theme, the writing assignments, the service-learning component and the Into the Streets event. The college rented buses from a local school district to transport the students to the agencies and provided lunch for the reflection sessions upon their return to campus. Approximately 150 students participated in Into the Streets the first semester. The numbers quickly grew, and in 2005 more than 500 students from a wide variety of disciplines, including 238 from English classes, completed 1,700 hours of service during what is now a two-day event repeated each semester.

For the first few years, the First-Year Composition faculty adopted the Watters and Ford (1995) reader, *Writing for Change: A Community Reader*. Then in 1996, six CGCC English faculty, Kim Chuppa-Cornell, Johnnie Clemens May, Pam Davenport, Sharon Fagan, Chris Schnick, and Caryl Terrell-Bamiro, edited the first edition of their own reader, *Creating Community in a Changing World*. The readings were chosen to connect to the writing topics on social, environmental, and global issues, career exploration, and service in the community.

Collective Thinking, Planning, and Action: A Team Approach

From the beginning, the CGCC service-learning program was led by a collaborative team of innovative English faculty with support from other faculty colleagues, the director and staff of the Office of Student Life, and the vice president of student affairs. Serving as faculty liaisons, the English faculty leaders were given release time from their responsibility of teaching five classes to help lead, implement, and grow the program. Their passion for having students serve in the community motivated them to design a model program that has been sustained and expanded each year since its inception. The English faculty service-learning liaisons continue to work with faculty in all departments on campus to design service-learning assignments that are thoughtfully and meaningfully connected to the curriculum.

The service-learning team now includes two program coordinators, two English faculty liaisons, and a cadre of student service-learning assistants to coordinate agency partnerships and placements. Additional support is provided by the director of student life and his staff, the vice presidents for academic affairs and student affairs, and the president. CGCC's administrative leadership has ensured that service in the community is an integral part of the college's mission and culture.

Analysis

Moving From "Mine" to "Ours": Getting Others Onboard

The faculty service-learning leaders, most of whom were and still are English faculty, had also been the faculty development leaders on campus. In the two years leading up to the emergence of service-learning, they led the campus in a cooperative learning and writing to learn agenda emphasizing the importance of active learning strategies to engage students in deeper learning. Seeing service-learning as a logical next step in their faculty development model, they offered workshops at the beginning of every semester to encourage not only the full- and part-time English faculty, but faculty from all departments on campus, to integrate service-learning into their courses.

In addition, a video titled *A Commitment to Service* was produced to orient faculty in all departments and their students to the CGCC service-learning program. The 10 minute video defines service-learning, illustrates the various models with footage from campus events, and includes enthusiastic testimonials from students, faculty, and staff representing a variety of community agencies. As the program grew and became recognized around the country, this video was, and still is, circulated to other colleges interested in designing and implementing similar service-learning programs.

Since written reflection has always been an integral part of the CGCC service-learning program, in 1994, English faculty Marybeth Mason, with business faculty Maria Hesse and photography faculty Keith Canham, published a book of CGCC service-learning reflections and photographs in *Unspoken*. In 1998, a second publication of service-learning reflections, edited by English faculty Chris Schnick and Kim Chuppa-Cornell, titled *Small Miracles*, was produced. Both of these publications have been widely circulated to colleges around the country. In 2005, Marjorie Ford and Elizabeth Schave Sills included in their reader, *Community Matters*, an essay written by CGCC student Heidi Metzler, "Hats Off to Helpers," which was originally published in *Small Miracles*. The CGCC service-learning web site (www.cgc.maricopa.edu/ learning/service) includes extensive information about the program's rationale, benefits, definitions, models, service-learning assistants, publications, agencies, the leadership team, and forms.

Leadership Provided by Academic and Student Affairs

Over the last 15 years, the leadership for the CGCC service-learning program has been provided by a team of English faculty, the director of student life, the vice presidents of student and academic affairs, and the college president. Although the English department's commitment was the strongest when it was chaired by one of the original service-learning faculty proponents and curriculum designers, as the chair has changed through the years, the faculty commitment to service-learning has remained strong. Over the last decade and a half, as new faculty have been interviewed and hired, their knowledge of and experience with service-learning has been a consideration. The current chair continues to support the department and college commitment to the service-learning program.

Impact: Sustaining a Quality Program

The service-learning program continues to evolve and grow at CGCC. Our students have now served in more than 700 community-based organizations. During the 2004–2005 academic year, approximately 500 English students were placed in service experiences from 45 course sections and served nearly 2,400 hours in the community. Overall in 2004–2005, the CGCC service-learning program placed approximately 2,500 students who contributed nearly 20,000 hours in service to the community. In addition to

English faculty, each semester faculty from sociology, psychology, economics, history, biology, communication, education, humanities, mathematics, business and computer information systems, journalism, counseling, and child and family studies now incorporate service-learning into their courses.

Additional evidence of success comes from various assessments completed by the students, the agencies, and the faculty each semester. The agencies continually report how important our students' service is to the success of their organizations. Helen Sand, the volunteer coordinator at St. Mary's Food Bank, offered this feedback:

> Thank you so much for serving with us. Your group total of 47 hours and 30 minutes is the equivalent of $761.90 or the cost of 508 meals. Your efforts will make a difference in meeting the needs of the less fortunate in our community.

Paz de Cristo's volunteer coordinator, Keith A. Almoney, explained,

> As you know Paz is entirely volunteer driven. Our evening and weekend slots tend to fill quickly; obviously fitting more easily into most school/work schedules. Our weekday Food Box Program, however, has proven to be somewhat problematic; the volunteer shift being Tues./ Thurs., 11 am to 3 pm. Along come your service-learning students to the rescue, in two ways. First, the nature of many of your students' work/class schedules makes our daytime volunteer opportunities very tenable. Second, and most importantly, the enthusiasm and motivation that accompany their efforts becomes a vital part of what Paz de Cristo is about, i.e., serving others in an atmosphere of dignity and respect. Plus from a really pragmatic volunteer coordinator's point-of-view, they actually show up—and on time even.

Faculty report professional and personal satisfaction from an increase in classroom community, a relevance of the service experience to their students' lives and to the curriculum, their own heightened understanding of the needs of the community, and an enjoyment derived from serving and working collaboratively with other faculty, staff, and students on campus and in the community. Furthermore, they have teamed up to collaborate as coauthors and co-editors of the various college service-learning publications.

Most importantly, students continually report that service-learning is one of the most valuable components of the curriculum. They express in their writing having experienced a new sense of civic responsibility and multicultural awareness, as well as a feeling of accomplishment at having actively contributed to the community and to their own learning. Some typical student responses follow.

> It seems I have been living with blinders on, ignorant of the community in which I live. For fifteen years I have been going to work, going to school, and coming home. I have run my usual errands, without realizing that only a few miles from my home, families are living in poverty. Serving at San Marcos Elementary School has helped open my eyes to a broader view of the world in which I live and the needs of others in my own community.
>
> —Donna Thomas

> I have never known what it is like to go to bed hungry. I have always had the luxury of a well stocked pantry and refrigerator at hand. I have followed various diets to try to eat healthy.... I have disposed of food in one day that exceeded my caloric intake that day and dumped food that has spoiled past its expiration date. But working in the United Food Bank opened my eyes to a reality for

many that goes beyond the next fad diet of protein drinks and fat-free frozen yogurt.

—Brent Gibbons

Working with the children at the House of Refuge East [a transitional housing program for formerly homeless families] was by far my favorite part of the semester. Actually hearing from the director about the lives these children had led and what they had experienced at such a young age inspired us as a class to want to do even more.

—Montanna Hughes

Many CGCC students who come to college undecided about a major often discover both a major and a potential career as a result of their service experience. Some have also found employment with our partner agencies. An initially reluctant student from the very first service-learning section began working part-time at Save the Family Foundation after her service experience, and a decade later she was still there in a professional capacity, having completed her bachelor's and master's degrees in social work. Another student, a reentry mother of two, searching for a career, began serving at United Blood Services and eventually became a certified full-time phlebotomist there.

Lessons
Key Successes and Challenges

The service-learning program has endured and grown for 15 years by support from a dedicated leadership team of English faculty, staff, and administrators from both academic and student affairs. We have seen that the enthusiasm in the English department for service-learning is strongest when the chair's commitment and leadership is evident. Furthermore, we have learned that to sustain a college-wide program, a commitment from the administration to support it with budget and personnel is essential. The budget for the service-learning staff salaries and operations now exceeds $100,000.

We have also learned that faculty must participate in service projects themselves in order to make the assignment and experience meaningful and relevant for students before, during, and after the service. When faculty have assigned their students to serve without serving themselves, problems have invariably arisen at the service site as well as back on campus and in the classroom. Both agency volunteer coordinators as well as CGCC service-learning coordinators have reported contending with apathetic, sometimes even hostile, attitudes which carry over into the reflections and evaluations. Consequently, we have come to expect faculty to serve as site leaders at Into the Streets, coordinating orientations with the host agency to which they are assigned and serving with students at that agency. Faculty who have designed other models serve side-by-side with their students. Those faculty unwilling to serve are not encouraged to incorporate service-learning into their courses.

Written reflection is a necessary component to help students begin to analyze the value of the experience and connect it to the classroom curriculum. When faculty simply assign service and hand out extra credit for participation without thoughtful reflection and connection to what is being studied in class, the students miss the relevance of the experience to their lives and to the curriculum, and often feel that their time has been wasted. Therefore, ongoing faculty development has been essential to ensure the design of quality reflections, writing assignments, research projects, and assessment methods. To motivate and reward success, we have developed recognitions and awards for students, faculty, and agencies.

As our college has grown over the last 15 years, it has been a constant challenge to recruit and train new full- and part-time faculty and to meet the ever-growing demand for placements and personnel to support the program. The service-learning team, which continues to include the college president and the vice presidents of academic and student affairs, meets regularly throughout the year to troubleshoot the latest challenges and to adjust, plan, and implement new strategies.

Key Strategies: Written Reflection, Orientation, and Faculty Development

Written reflection. From the beginning, the English faculty understood the importance of writing and critical thinking to the reflection component of service-learning. Therefore, all service-learning assignments in every discipline include a written reflection, an integral component of student learning. The service activities, written reflection, research, and discussions in all classes, culminate in an essay requiring critical thinking, synthesis of ideas, and impressions gained from the service, with research and documentation from credible sources. The service experience has provided powerful primary research and vivid stories that contribute to the overall quality of student writing.

Orientation. Early on we learned that agency orientation was critical to the success of the students' service experience. Having a representative of each agency conduct an orientation for students before they serve supplies essential background information and facts on the realities of the social problems and issues with which each agency must contend, as well as valuable primary research material for the students' writing.

Each year new faculty have been recruited and a wide variety of new models of service has evolved. In some cases, entire classes work at one agency throughout a semester, while other classes are divided into groups and each group is assigned to a different agency. For example, one team-taught learning community class combined First-Year Composition and Sociology 101 around the theme "Weaving the Tapestries of Our Lives." Their students served throughout the semester at the Thomas J. Pappas School for homeless children. The focus of the research and writing was education, poverty, and domestic abuse. The service-learning provided CGCC students firsthand observation and interaction with these very real and complex social issues.

Before the students went to Pappas School, a teacher and social worker came to class and gave students an orientation. The social worker described her day, which begins at dawn as she travels around the Phoenix inner city, collecting the most neglected children from the motels where their mothers ply their trade and do their drugs. She also told of the children of stable parents who were down on their luck. Most CGCC students were surprised to learn how easily families can spiral into poverty and homelessness. Yet, until they went to the school, the students could not have known how profoundly they would be affected by the children. Student Leanna Jones wrote about her service in a class of kindergarteners:

> Angelica was a darling girl, rail thin, with a wide smile. . . . Pearl couldn't sit still or focus on a task. . . . Molly was another shy smart one, but who probably hadn't had a bath and clean clothes in a long time. She too would grow up to be pretty. . . . There were three Stevens, one of whom had rotten, worn-down teeth, and who constantly asked to hold my hand and help him with his alphabet. . . . I wanted to take those kids home with me and tell them that they were worthy, that they were important, loved and valued.

Faculty development. The service-learning team continues to work with faculty to design and provide the support for the model of service and the writing assignment that best fits individual needs and curriculum. The ongoing emphasis on faculty development is key to the success of the CGCC service-learning program. Each semester new faculty are recruited and provided service-learning training in a variety of formats. The English faculty liaisons, working closely with the service-learning program advisors, most often provide small group and one-on-one training for faculty. The newest model for faculty development, the Network for Excellence, also includes a workshop on integrating service-learning into the curriculum. In order to sustain the service-learning program over the years, we have hired and developed new English faculty to take leadership roles, and they have successfully continued the college tradition.

Vision by 2010: A Broader Commitment to Civic Engagement and Global Awareness

Beginning in 2003, we expanded our vision of service-learning to include a broader civic engagement agenda. We now see service-learning as a component of a wider range of political and civic activities. Students are not only serving in community agencies, they are also actively engaged in other primary research activities related to various social, political, economic, and environmental problems in the community.

In spring 2005, a political science faculty member traveled with a team of CGCC students to San Francisco to participate in the Model United Nations program. Our students are taking field trips, attending community lectures, organizing campus discussion panels, letter writing campaigns, and voter registration drives, all in an effort to gain knowledge relevant to issues, multicultural awareness, and practical experience to help them see that their decisions, actions, and ideas can influence change in the world in which they live. For example, after learning community students conducted a cross-cultural study of the campus which included interviews with English as a Second Language (ESL) students, they concluded that there was a need for an ESL tutoring center. They worked closely with the director of the learning assistance center to set up the program, to prepare and distribute publicity materials, and to tutor students in the center. In her reflection, student Ashley Cook noted,

On certain days I have been a teacher, but every day I have been a student. . . . I have seen what it is like to cross into unfamiliar borders, and I have seen what it is like to maintain strength when most of the people watching believe that you will fail. I have seen such hard work and dedication within these students, and it makes me want to work just as hard.

Faculty in many disciplines are writing new curriculum and are in the process of adopting a global theme college-wide with a focus on sustainability. In addition to current options, there are plans to engage students in service activities in Mexico and South America.

In fall 2005, a team of faculty, the director of student life, and the college president visited the Highlander Research and Education Center in Tennessee. Since 1932, Highlander has gathered workers, grassroots leaders, community organizers, educators, and researchers to address pressing social, environmental, and economic problems. Generations of activists have gone to Highlander to learn, teach, and prepare to participate in struggles for justice. We hope to learn from this renowned model and apply it to both local and global issues. We foresee CGCC students, inspired by their service-learning activities, engaged in more civic action in many disciplines across campus.

References

Canham, K., Mason, M., & Hesse, M. (Eds.). (1994). *Unspoken*. Chandler, AZ: Chandler-Gilbert Community College.

Chuppa-Cornell, K., May, J. C., Davenport, P., Fagan, S., Schnick, C., & and Terrell-Bamiro, C. (Eds.). (1996). *Creating community in a changing world*. New York, NY: McGraw-Hill.

Chuppa-Cornell, K., & Schnick, C. (Eds.). (1998). *Small miracles: Service-learning essays, 1997–1998*. Chandler, AZ: Chandler-Gilbert Community College.

Ford, M., & Sills, E. S. (2005). *Community matters: A reader for writers*, (2nd ed.). New York, NY: Longman.

Watters, A., & Ford, M. (1995). *Writing for change: A community reader.* New York, NY: McGraw-Hill.

About the Authors

Marybeth Mason teaches English and humanities at Chandler-Gilbert Community College (CGCC). She has provided leadership for the CGCC service-learning program since its inception in 1991. Most recently, she was a contributor to the monographs *Integrating Learning Communities with Service-Learning* (2003) and *Learning Communities in Community Colleges* (2003), published by the American Association for Higher Education and the National Learning Communities Project. Her work with service-learning and learning communities has been highlighted in John Tagg's book, *The Learning Paradigm College* (Anker, 2003), and in Thomas Ehrlich's book, *Civic Responsibility and Higher Education* (ACE/Oryx, 2000).

Pam Davenport earned degrees at Arizona State University and teaches English at Chandler-Gilbert Community College. In addition to her commitment to service-learning and learning communities, she is involved with encouraging civic engagement among students and mentoring new faculty. Her teaching interests include Native American literature and culture, and she also leads writing retreats for faculty.

9

The Spelman College Total Person Commits to Positive Social Change

Cynthia Neal Spence, Daryl White

An outstanding historically Black college for women, Spelman promotes academic excellence in the liberal arts, and develops the intellectual, ethical, and leadership potential of its students. Spelman seeks to empower the total person, who appreciates the many cultures of the world and commits to positive social change.

—Spelman College Mission Statement

On March 5, 2000, 19 Spelman students, enrolled in a unique course titled Selma—Beyond 2000, crossed the Edmund Pettus Bridge and began a six-day march from Selma to Montgomery, Alabama. The students, along with more than 100 other marchers, were commemorating the 35th anniversary of pivotal civil rights movement events that led to the Voting Rights Act of 1965. The march was just one part of a remarkably multifaceted course offered by Spelman's Department of Sociology and Anthropology. Students also studied and discussed the history and sociology of the civil rights movement. U.S. Congressman John Lewis, who as a student leader had been beaten badly in 1965 by Alabama state troopers on the bridge, visited the class and told his story. Students also participated in voter registration campaigns in Atlanta and Alabama. In addition, to prepare physically for the march itself, the class walked every weekend of the semester, adding more miles to their walk each week in order to make the six-day march possible. The following four students' comments about the course and the march are quoted in Spelman sociology professor emeritus Harry Lefever's (2005, pp. 232–233) recent book about Spelman and the civil rights movement. Comparing the latter march with the former, Taneya Gethers saw disturbing similarities: "There was still an obvious disconnect between high-ranking community leaders and grassroots community members, an inability to train new leaders and pass the leadership torch, and a condescending attitude toward women leaders and grassroots workers and students." Dione Moultrie found special meaning as an Alabama citizen: "My parents had told me about the Montgomery bus boycott, the Birmingham bombings of homes and churches, and the original Selma-to-Montgomery march, but I had never walked a mile in anyone else's shoes. Walking those miles and reflecting upon the original marchers' strenuous journey made me thankful for what their efforts did for our future. Each day gave me a renewed sense of vigor and I began to plan how I could make a lasting impact to honor those who were beaten and bruised for my right to vote." Philathia Bolton wrote: "I returned to Spelman with a challenge to dream and be me, knowing that in the process I would add to the legacy of making life better for others." And Jennifer Grimes described overcoming fears and celebrating a "rebirthing of my spirit."

On September 29, 1934, from a temporary platform constructed on Spelman's campus only a few miles southwest of downtown Atlanta, U.S. Secretary of Interior, Harold L. Ickles, inaugurated the first federal government slum clearance and housing development. Secretary Ickles and Morehouse College President John Hope gave speeches, the assembled crowd sang "Great Day" and "Lift Every Voice," and then (as reported in the *Spelman Messenger* in 1934),

> the Secretary pressed the plunger and across the street below the Spelman campus a small red-painted cottage rose in the air and then fell into a mass of distorted timber,

bricks and broken glass. The audience cheered. The Atlanta University Housing Project was officially begun. (p. 3)

Relations between the colleges of the Atlanta University Center and their surrounding community were not just ceremonial. Students developed social work skills as they worked to reconstruct community. As part of their training some students lived in the project itself. Along with neighboring churches, the colleges also served as social and cultural community centers. Seventy years later, although the communities surrounding Spelman and the Atlanta University Center have changed considerably, University Homes still sits across the street from Spelman College.

Since its founding on April 11, 1881, when 11 hopeful, eager pupils—women not long or far out of slavery—and two New England teachers met to begin lessons in the basement of Friendship Baptist Church near downtown Atlanta, Spelman College has embodied a unique mix of academic education and community service. Every semester large numbers of Spelman students participate in community service and internship activities in schools, clinics, and other nonprofit agencies in nearby communities as well as in social agencies throughout the Atlanta metropolitan region. During the summer some students intern at sites across the country, as well as in Latin America and Africa. Student clubs, religious organizations, and the Bonner Scholars Program, the Shepherd Poverty Alliance summer internships, individual research projects, service-learning courses, and the Bonner Office of Community Service all have been vehicles for involvement in community service activities. Recently, Spelman College President Beverly Daniel Tatum established the Center for Leadership and Civic Engagement to more effectively coordinate existing programs, to develop new initiatives, and to expand and strengthen existing ones (see www.spelman.edu/about_us/distinction/leads/index.shtml). Known by the acronym LEADS, the center emphasizes leadership development, economic empowerment, and advocacy through the arts, dialogue across difference, and service-learning and civic engagement.

Departmental Context

The Department of Sociology and Anthropology is a fortunate heir to a rich and continuing legacy. In the tradition of former Atlanta University faculty member W. E. B. Du Bois, our department uses the Atlanta community as a site for sociological study, analysis, and engagement. Du Bois believed that to study social phenomenon, one must engage the issue "personally not by proxy" (Lewis, 1993, p. 202). This belief has helped to frame service-learning and other opportunities for community engagement directed by the sociology and anthropology department. Whether students walk through Atlanta neighborhoods in preparation for conducting case studies for an Urban Sociology class, or ethnographies for an Urban Anthropology class, or spend six weeks living among women in a homeless shelter, or conduct senior thesis research, the department continues to craft opportunities for students to experience social phenomenon personally rather than by proxy.

The department has a historically sustained commitment to engage students in active learning that is supported by community collaborations. Discourse within the major helps students to recognize their positions of privilege and how they must use this privilege to interrogate status quo ideological frameworks. Students are invited to critique dominant views that do not recognize and appreciate diversity, views that are blind to the reality that individual social ills and problems must be analyzed within larger social-structural matrixes that either help to generate or sustain behavior. Service-learning can provide an excellent—indeed, indispensable—framework for this level of intellectual engagement.

Service-learning as a pedagogical strategy works best when applied across disciplinary areas. However, some selected disciplinary areas more readily adapt to service-learning models than others. Both sociology and anthropology as disciplines invite students and faculty to gain greater understanding of "what is." A common mantra among professors is "Nothing is as it seems or appears." Understanding relationships and reciprocal influences between and among individuals, groups, societal institutions, and cultural systems requires deep analysis and careful contextualization. Effective understanding emerges out of sociological and anthropological knowledge when reciprocities between study, action, learning, and service are brought into intimate contact. Our task as professors is to enable students to experience, benefit from, and take pleasure in discovering these reciprocities and make their own connections between the theoretical, the practical, and the personal.

Demographics

Spelman College is a historically black, private liberal arts college that enrolls 2,000 women from 43 states and 16 countries. The Spelman educational program is classical in its liberal arts focus, while integrating service and fostering leadership. Indeed, in many ways Spelman embodies service. In 2002, when asked on a survey if the chances were very good that they will participate in voluntary community services while at Spelman, 75% of first-year students answered yes. In 2003, 84% of the graduating seniors, reporting on their completed four years at Spelman, revealed they had participated in community service activities while at Spelman.

The Department of Sociology and Anthropology has close to 100 majors, pursuing one of two degrees, and graduates 20 to 25 sociologists and anthropologists each year. The department has nine full-time faculty members, four of whom teach part-time because of research opportunities or significant administrative responsibilities outside the department. In a typical semester, one or two courses are taught by part-time adjunct faculty. The curriculum consists of a core set of three methodology and two theory courses capped by a senior thesis; electives cluster around overlapping concentrations in anthropology, health and medicine, law and criminal justice, gender, and race and ethnicity.

Processes: Aligning Learning In and Out of the Classroom

In the late 1960s—with the addition of new courses, the hiring of new faculty, and the reorganization of administrative offices—sociology along with several other departments gradually emerged out of a general social science curriculum that had principally serviced Spelman's teacher education program. By 1974, the department had instituted the Sociology Internship, a course in which students volunteer in agencies in metropolitan Atlanta. Capping the course is a public forum where students describe their internships and summarize their final scholarly paper on some aspect of their experience. This course has been taught every semester since its inception. Two elective courses with service-learning components have since been added. Other departmental courses that address issues of civic engagement, often through community-based research, include Urban Anthropology, Social Problems, Urban Sociology, Sociology of Health, and Nonviolent Social Change. In their senior thesis, all department majors design and execute a research project, many of which involve action research focused on the study of specific social service agencies such as group homes, clinics, and after-school programs. Grants, often organized across disciplines, occasionally provide opportunities for students to engage in research and civic action. For example, a recent environmental health project allowed sociology and environmental science students to survey surrounding neighborhoods concerning environmental hazards and to share with the community information about symptoms and precautions. Independent of the curriculum, the student club SASSAFRAS (Sociological-Anthropological Sisterhood: Scholar-Activists Reshaping Attitudes at Spelman) promotes civic engagement and activist scholarship. The club was responsible for instituting an annual departmental honor awarded to graduating seniors who demonstrate exemplary scholar-activism.

The Department of Sociology and Anthropology has historically created opportunities for majors to engage their research and disciplinary interests in community-based agencies through the Senior Internship Program, senior thesis, and selected service-learning courses. Most importantly, mastery of selected courses within the department requires an understanding of how methodological approaches and theoretical models must be framed by a personally constructed understanding of how individuals experience and give meaning to their particular social realities. Symbolic interactionism, phenomenology, conflict, structural functionalism, and feminist and critical race theories all provide opportunities for students to engage individuals and their communities in efforts to better understand society. Students are encouraged to deconstruct "what they know" by critically analyzing "what is." Greater understanding of sociological and anthropological concepts, theory, and methodology is often facilitated and enforced through social problem posing and policy analysis strategies.

Analysis

A significant aid in furthering the department's ability to promote civic engagement is its participation since 1999 in the Shepherd Poverty Alliance summer internship program. Organized by Washington and Lee University in 1998, this program places students from Berea College, Morehouse College, Spelman College, and Washington and Lee University in rural and urban social service agencies across the East Coast for funded summer internships. All participants meet and are matched together in a three-day orientation. While performing their internships, they live, work, and reflect together. At summer's end, they reconvene in a conference where students reflect on their experiences while focusing their discussions on issues of public policy. The program continues to expand, with the primary vision of preparing students for service in poor communities and promoting sustained civic engagement.

Collectivity Requires Regular Maintenance

The Shepherd Poverty Alliance program works in large part because individuals from the various institutions actively collaborate to make it work. Similarly, our department's civic engagement is collectively organized because of the synergy between individual faculty members, specific administrators (chairs, deans, presidents), and active students. Yet our departmental environment is not static. The Sociology Internship and senior theses, along with regularly taught service-learning electives, are the constants in an otherwise fluctuating involvement. Despite tendencies for faculty to focus on the courses they develop and teach, at its core the department has a strong sense that the curriculum belongs to the department collectively rather than to individuals. It is this collective sense that requires regular maintenance, at times prodded by students and/or sparked by current events.

It is instructive to examine how this protean collective sense has developed over the last two decades. As administrative emphasis on strategic planning becomes more systematic, departments are required to create their own goals and develop means for assessing progress in meeting them. Tied to the annual budgeting process, strategic planning requires at least yearly discussion among faculty in each department. In addition, every five years departments undergo a thorough department review, including outside reviewers. This planning has been mandated by accreditation processes as well as by general financial conditions that necessitate intentional and effective planning. Yet external mandates do not by themselves create a proactive sense of college ownership by faculty, as the following example illustrates.

Within the department, two courses, Internship and Senior Thesis, have become thoroughly owned by the entire faculty. This was accomplished by rotating the responsibilities for teaching, directing, and advising students taking both courses. Two faculty members each year co-teach both courses for two years on a staggered schedule. Eventually each faculty member co-teaches the course with every member of the department. While the two faculty who teach the thesis course serve as the principal advisors for half of the students enrolled in the course, the rest of the faculty serve as thesis readers, secondary advisors, and graders. At the end of the semester, all the faculty convene in a grading session in which each student's thesis is discussed and collectively evaluated. In addition to these two courses, the core sociology and anthropology courses (which include introductory courses, two theory courses, and three methodology courses) are intentionally structured to help students prepare for their thesis research. At every monthly department faculty meeting, at least one of these courses is discussed. In contrast, elective courses are much more likely to be treated as if they belong to the faculty member who traditionally teaches them; yet even these courses are discussed by the entire department periodically. New courses, whether required core or elective, must be approved by the department faculty before they can be reviewed and approved by the college curriculum committee. Nevertheless, some faculty are more open to collective discussion of "their courses" than others, and it is probably by frequent, informal conversation that our collective sense is most deeply strengthened and our most effective coordination occurs. Nonetheless, periodic department reviews, mandated reaccreditation self-studies, and the occasional opportunity to hire a new faculty member are the times when our most significant structural changes are made possible.

Impact

Continued enrollment in courses and participation in internships reveals steady student interest. Faculty observe that students have been able to connect theory to practice. In our ever-popular Violence Against Women course, students have referenced classroom discussions of theory and course readings to better frame what they actually experience and see at the Atlanta Victim Assistance Program. Community partners request our students specifically when internships become available, and some internships result in job offers. Since almost all students choose internship sites related to their career goals, one of the most important things about our

Sociology Internship course is the way it shapes students' career plans. Most students finish their internships with a deeper enthusiasm to continue their pursuits, while a few learn they need to modify their plans and move in other directions. Either way, interns could not have gained this knowledge without firsthand experience. The popularity of summer internships speaks to the value many students place on civic engagement. In addition to Spelman's involvement in the Shepherd Poverty Alliance program, many students search out independent internship sites. Indeed, many of the agencies where students perform their Sociology Internship were developed by students. Spelman students reciprocally influence our departmental curriculum.

Lessons

It is challenging to find classroom time for students to reflect together on their service experiences and their scholarly development. Completing this circle is perhaps the greatest need. Instigating opportunities for collective reflection seems imperative: more venues outside the classroom, such as public forums and film discussions, are necessary. More effective communication and intentional cooperation between academic departments and the community service office should become the norm now that our Bonner Office of Community Service has been reorganized and a Leadership and Civic Engagement Center has been established. But the bottom line seems to be this: Even with institutional structures in place, how well things work depends on the individuals involved. Our student club will be dormant one year, organizing weeklong activities the next. Effective interdisciplinary cooperation between departments depends on the goodwill of chairs and others involved. Some structural features that isolate departments and link faculty advancement solely to departmental processes can work against interdisciplinary innovation, reduce interdepartmental communication and cooperation, and limit civic engagement and service-learning initiatives. Curriculum development workshops—aided by grants and institutional partnerships (such as the New York University Faculty Resource Network, the Council on International Educational Exchange, the Associated Colleges of the South, and the United Negro College Fund, to name only a few)—have proven to be effective in new and continuing course development.

Vision

By 2010, our department will have a small suite of four or five elective courses identified as civic engagement courses in which service-learning will be identified as a central feature. This will allow the Sociology Internship to become more of a capstone experience and less of an introduction to service-learning. At least one of these courses will be interdisciplinary. Open to majors and nonmajors alike, this suite of courses will better prepare students for lifelong civic engagement. In cooperation with other departments, the college Office of Community Service, various student organizations, and the Department of Sociology and Anthropology will organize activities in and out of the classroom that promote discussion and cooperative action focused on pressing social issues. We anticipate that our departmental efforts will continue to help institutionalize campus-wide engagement.

By 2010, our department will be an integral part of an interdisciplinary minor in poverty and human capacity. Drawing on courses across the curriculum from environmental studies and English literature to economics and sociology, the minor will allow students to pursue their disciplinary major and career goals, whatever their major and career goals may be, and at the same time promote lifelong involvement in issues of poverty and social inequality. Our most far-reaching goal is that throughout their lives our students will demonstrate an ever-deepening commitment to civic activity. The minor will include a required interdisciplinary gateway course for all Bonner Scholars that will be highly recommended for all students interested in any type of community service. This introductory service-learning course will introduce students to contemporary academic discussion and public discourse about poverty and inequality, including historical, economic, political, moral, religious, sociological, and cultural aspects; it will serve as an orientation to the nature of nonprofit agencies, the ethics of community service, the practical, day-to-day challenges of volunteering and working in agencies, and other issues of importance to effective campus-community cooperation. The course will also model service-learning by integrating student service—the knowledge gained by students in service activities—back into the classroom, academic activities, and performances. The interdisciplinary minor in poverty and human capacity will include a capstone course, providing students with opportunities to appreciate the breadth and depth of academic discourses on poverty issues, to reflect on their community service during college, and to understand themselves as student learners, emerging professionals, and public citizens. The capstone course will include events to which the entire college community and our partners in participating social service agencies will be invited. Students will present and perform in the modes of their various disciplinary majors—such as social science research, fine arts performance, and other discipline-specific competencies—how their own civic participation, their interdisciplinary minor work, and the major in which they are graduating have become integrated into their lives.

The Spelman College Department of Sociology and Anthropology, like many departments throughout the country, recognizes and appreciates the call of classical education and social theorists John Dewey (1927) and Alexis de Tocqueville (1945) as they pondered idealized notions of democracy and its relationship to education. Jacoby and Associates (2003) asserted, "Dewey's view of a true democracy could not survive without face-to-face interactions that are governed by cooperative associations to solve the ongoing problems of life" (p. xiii). They further advanced the proposition of de Tocqueville, well known for his commentaries on democracy, that the government is not "them" but "us" and functions best when citizens "guide and assist" in determining and carrying out public policy (p. 292). This perspective provides guidance to those who seek clarity on why educational curricula and principles of civic engagement must work together for the greater good. More recently, Bok (1982) argued that "there is no need for universities to feel uncomfortable in taking account of society's needs; in fact, they have a clear obligation to do so" (p. 301). These ideological perspectives are often referenced as helping to lay the groundwork for the development of civic engagement and service-learning methodologies. Early critiques of the function of higher education in society envisioned education as a tool for the transformation of society. The educated elite were expected to use their knowledge to respond to societal needs and problems.

Civic engagement as a goal and service-learning as a means have been the raison d'etre of Spelman College life and the Department of Sociology and Anthropology throughout our respective histories. Our future holds the distinct promise that Spelman College's intentional involvement in social improvement will continue to expand and deepen.

References

Bok, D. (1982). *Beyond the ivory tower: Social responsibilities of the modern university.* Cambridge, MA: Harvard University Press.

de Tocqueville, A. (1945). *Democracy in America.* New York, NY: Alfred A. Knopf.

Dewey, J. (1927). *Democracy and education.* New York, NY: Macmillan.

Housing project begun. (1934, November). *Spelman Messenger, 51*(1), 3.

Jacoby, B., & Associates. (2003). *Building partnerships for service-learning.* San Francisco, CA: Jossey-Bass.

Lefever, H. G. (2005). *Undaunted by the fight: Spelman College and the civil rights movement, 1957–1967.* Macon, GA: Mercer University Press.

Lewis, D. L. (1993). *W. E. B. Du Bois: Biography of a race: 1868–1919.* New York, NY: Henry Holt.

About the Authors

Cynthia Neal Spence is associate professor of sociology at Spelman College. Her teaching and research interests in the areas of sociology, criminology, law, and violence against women support the law and criminology concentration in the Department of Sociology and Anthropology. She created the service-learning course Violence Against Women. In addition, she serves as the national director of the United Negro College Fund/Mellon Programs. She earned her master's and Ph.D. from Rutgers University.

Daryl White is professor of anthropology and chair of the Department of Sociology and Anthropology at Spelman College. He directs efforts at the college to establish an interdisciplinary minor in poverty and human capacity which will have service-learning at its core.

10

Nursing Excellence: Community Engagement Through Service-Learning

Georgia Narsavage, Evelyn Duffy, Deborah Lindell, Marilyn J. Lotas, Carol Savrin, Yea-Jyh Chen

Successful community-campus partnerships can lead to increased services by community health organizations, enhanced clinical learning experiences for nursing students, and opportunities for faculty practice and scholarship. This chapter describes the development of service-learning in a nursing school at a major research university. A vignette demonstrates transcending the town-gown barrier through a sustained partnership between the Frances Payne Bolton School of Nursing at Case Western Reserve University (CASE) and Mosdos Ohr Hatorah, an orthodox Jewish K–12 day school. The partnership, ongoing since 1996, is a component of the Health to Go! project. Faculty and pre-licensure students in the Community/Public Health Nursing (C/PHN) courses of the Bolton School's bachelor's and doctorate nursing programs partner with community health organizations to provide onsite C/PHN services to clients not currently receiving such services. The partnership is framed on the principles of Community-Campus Partnerships for Health's ([CCPH], 1998) best-practice concepts for service-learning.

Nursing students are oriented to orthodox Judaic beliefs, values, and practices; theoretical concepts of health screening; and the Ohio Department of Health's (ODH) requirements for vision and hearing screening in order to respond to an expressed need for specific health services. Staff and parents of Mosdos are notified about the screenings, and Mosdos students are oriented to the screenings in a developmentally appropriate manner. At Mosdos, nursing students are supervised on site by faculty, with culturally appropriate dress and behavior at all times. Process and outcome evaluations are completed regularly using both quantitative and qualitative methods. The CASE Institutional Review Board (IRB) approval allows dissemination of evaluation findings that reveal compliance with ODH policies and procedures, referral rates in line with ODH findings, culturally and developmentally appropriate care, increased awareness by nursing students of C/PHN roles and functions and the importance of culturally appropriate care, demonstrated value of linking service and learning, opportunities for faculty to practice as a clinical nurse specialist in C/PHN, and successful community-engaged scholarship. This innovative collaboration between Mosdos and the Bolton School of Nursing has resulted in a sustained partnership with positive outcomes for all stakeholders and informed the Orthodox Jewish community of the value of C/PHN practice and community-campus partnerships.

Demographics

Institution

Case Western Reserve University is a private independent research extensive university with broadly balanced strengths in health profession education, including medicine, nursing, and dentistry, as well as in engineering, arts and sciences, and law, management, social work, and graduate studies. The university's mission is to serve society as a leading center for undergraduate, graduate, and professional education and for research that adds to society's store of knowledge and addresses its priorities. Under the president and provost, a focus on community partnership and civic responsibility has been initiated. Approximately 9,000 students are enrolled in the nine schools/colleges, and CASE has almost 2,500 full-time and 200 part-time faculty. An overview of the university and its student body can be found at www.case.edu/president/cir/accreditation/sspdfs/snapshot-fa5.pdf.

Department

The Frances Payne Bolton School of Nursing awards one under-graduate degree, Bachelor of Science in Nursing (B.S.N.), and three graduate degrees, Master's of Science in Nursing (M.S.N.), Doctorate of Nursing Practice (D.N.P.), and Doctorate of Philosophy in Nursing (Ph.D.). The School of Nursing has 82 full-time faculty who teach across programs; part-time clinical faculty are hired per-semester as needed, approximately 10 to 15 per year. There are 248 B.S.N. students (90% complete in four years), 132 M.S.N students, 68 first-year graduate entry M.S.N students, 163 post-masters D.N.P students, and 46 Ph.D. students. First-time pass rates for licensure and certification examinations ranged from 90% to 100% between 2000–2005. The M.S.N program educates advanced practice nurses to deliver comprehensive, high-quality care to assist patients/clients to attain, maintain, and regain optimal health.

Processes
Service-Learning and Civic Engagement Emergence

Service-learning and community-academic partnerships within the Bolton School of Nursing were initiated at the individual faculty level in 1997 in response to student evaluation of the community health nursing course. Student and community response was positive, and faculty efforts were supported within the department. The first course continues to include community engagement through its Health to Go! component.

The vision of departmental community engagement through service-learning programs began by initiating community-based care in the M.S.N. program following award of a grant from the Helene Fuld Health Trust in 2000. The grant began a planned process of commitment to community engagement as the school transitioned from individual faculty support to a sustained program level. Concurrently in the field, the Pew Health Professions Commission identified the importance of healthcare professionals moving from a focus on the health of individuals to awareness of the individual and family within the context of the community and society (O'Neil & Pew Health Professions Commission, 1998). The Fuld grant initiative supported faculty development and initiation of an advisory group of community agency leaders to create a link between community service and academic study so that each enriched the other. The purpose of community-based care is to provide service to the local community based on their needs while providing students with meaningful learning experiences enhanced through academic assignments and reflection. Graduate nursing students complete at least one course that incorporates a community engagement component to produce substantive products with the community agency. Through an integrated service-learning program, students in the B.S.N. program complete 30 hours of service per year for their first three years as a requirement for graduation. The B.S.N. program's primary partner is the Cleveland Municipal School District where many seniors also complete their capstone project on global health.

The community-based care projects included several phases and stakeholders (see Tables 10.1 and 10.2), operationalized through service-learning and community-academic partnerships. Development of a community advisory board to work with faculty teaching in the master's program was a key component of initiating true service-learning versus adding community service. The input and feedback provided by the advisory board—comprised of community agency leaders, university staff, faculty, and students meeting monthly—enriched both the community and academic study and proved to be invaluable to the project's success. For example, student and faculty feedback indicated some discomfort with the phrase *service-learning*. This concern was brought to the advisory group which reached consensus that the project would be called Community Engagement Through Service-Learning (CETSL).

In 2001, CETSL was incorporated into a number of graduate nursing courses such that each M.S.N. student would take at least

Table 10.2. Examples of Roles of CETSL Stakeholders

Stakeholder	Role/Functions
Administrative group	• Timeline, structure, IRB approval, communication coordination, manual, resource to faculty, agencies, students • Promote consistency among courses
Advisory group	• Identify potential community partners • Identify community-wide needs and resources • Consensus building, networking • Input/feedback—formative and summative evaluation
Partnership (faculty, agency, student triad)	• Specific agency (or agency employee) links with specific faculty and students—contributions of each varies • Identify needs/resources of each partner • Orient faculty/students to perspective of each • Collaboration/communication to set goals and objectives, facilitate partnership, evaluate, celebrate, disseminate
Organization (School of Nursing, other departments)	• Demonstrate value and support for CETSL through acknowledgement of faculty service and scholarship, financial resources, public relations, etc.

one course with CETSL. Concurrently, CETSL was integrated into two courses taken by all students in the Graduate Entry M.S.N./D.N.P. program. The B.S.N. program began planning to integrate service-learning and community-based care nursing into all four years, for freshman through senior students.

Faculty teaching a designated CETSL course worked with community partners to determine the manner in which it would be operationalized, course objectives to be met through service-learning, community-partner agency orientation, nature of projects (designed to meet community-identified needs), academic product, and strategies for reflection. Participating in CETSL provided faculty with opportunities to engage in community service,

Table 10.1. Phases of Implementation of CETSL

Phase	Dates	Focus	Activities
I	5/00–12/00	Planning	1) Administrative structure and a timeline 2) Hiring of project personnel 3) One-course pilot project 4) Engage with consultant 5) Education on service-learning and community and academic partnerships for all stakeholders 6) Evaluation plan including instruments and CASE IRB approval 7) Curricular revision as indicated 8) Establishment of a multidisciplinary advisory group 9) Faculty-community agency initial planning for partnerships 10) Initiate linkages with peer organizations at the program level (other CASE departments, Center for Healthy Communities, Campus Compact, CCPH)
II	1/01–12/01	Implementation	1) Implement CETSL in courses such that each student will take at least one course with CETSL 2) Formative evaluation 3) Advisory group: every other month 4) Revise plan based on evaluation 5) Initial dissemination 6) Faculty seek funding for CETSL 7) B.S.N. program integrates service-learning 8) Manual for all stakeholders

Table 10.1. *Continued*

III	1/02–6/02	Summative eval-uation	1) Summative evaluation 2) Report to funder 3) Plan institutionalization 4) Dissemination
IV	Ongoing	Institutionaliza-tion	1) Advisory group meets quarterly 2) Adjust to transitions in leadership, faculty, teaching assignments, staff, partnerships, curriculum 3) Seek School of Nursing financial support for part-time graduate assistant, advisory group meetings, dissemination 4) Graduate Entry D.N.P. program integrates service-learning

professional practice, and community-engaged scholarship such as publication, awards, and funding.

Process and outcome evaluation at the formative and summative levels was initiated during 2001 and is ongoing. Data sources included quantitative and qualitative student assessment, one-minute evaluations at advisory group meetings, one-page faculty and agency evaluations, and a qualitative study of the perspectives of community partners.

The final component of project implementation focused on facilitating faculty scholarship and project dissemination. Focusing on scholarship has produced results: Several faculty obtained funding to support their course-based partnerships, one received an agency award, one received a research award, several articles have been published in nursing peer-reviewed journals, a multi-stakeholder team was invited to participate in a national engaged department workshop, and faculty presented at campus, regional, national, and international conferences.

Collective Thinking, Planning, and Action

When the service-learning (S-L) program was initiated in 2000, most faculty wanted to adopt the concept as an add-on but not make it an integral part of the curriculum. Prior to the Fuld grant initiative, a few faculty had individually utilized community service projects in their courses, but there was no systematic plan or conceptualization of service-learning, nor was there any expectation that it might expand across the entire department or the school. However, nursing faculty took a year to develop meaningful service components that made connections with and were integrated into specific course assignments. By informing students how service-learning was replacing a previously graded assignment such as an exam or paper, the academic link was made to the service experience. The Fuld grant enabled the nursing department to connect needed community service to coursework through doing and reflecting. Subsequently, the M.S.N./D.N.P. faculty incorporated community engagement in the community and gerontology courses, and in 2005 faculty teaching in the B.S.N. program formally integrated service-learning experience and reflection seminars into the curriculum. The School of Nursing with the School of Dental Medicine are now campus leaders as other schools and departments incorporate campus-community partnerships with integrated service-learning into required courses for their professional programs (e.g., social work).

Providing opportunities for scholarship and data-based publications was key to planning the introduction of CETSL into a research university. Faculty became aware of grants that were available to support course revisions provided through Community-Campus Partnerships for Health. Three faculty received course development grants for graduate courses. One site developed through a grant was the orthodox Jewish Day school described in the opening vignette, another was a senior citizen center, and the third was an inner ring suburban school district. The three faculty who received these CCPH grants were those most actively involved in the CETSL activities and have become ambassadors for the remainder of the faculty. Their work has been presented and published regionally and nationally.

The goal of the Fuld grant was that each student in the M.S.N. program would have at least one experience with service-learning. As the concept grew and faculty began to incorporate service-learning into additional courses, one problem arose—some students did not feel they had time to complete service-learning in three or four courses. Nurse practitioner students in the M.S.N. program spend considerable time in clinical experiences, and they became frustrated with the number of hours that were expected in service-learning activities when they were taking multiple clinical courses. Accommodations to apply service in one site to several courses was a practical response, and eventually service-learning activities became distributed among a reasonable number of courses throughout the M.S.N. program. Additionally, the

Community Engagement Through Service-Learning Manual (Narsavage & Lindell, 2001) was a planned improvement for orientation of new faculty, agencies, and students.

During the development of the community sites and service-learning in the MSN department, evaluation of student learning and student attitudes were regularly measured. A one-page survey that received approval from the IRB as submission indicating implied consent was completed by the students at the end of each semester in paper format or electronic and returned to the program director for analysis. The results of the analysis (see Table 10.3) clearly demonstrated that students were learning and growing from their service-learning experiences.

The process of including service-learning in the School of Nursing was an exemplar of a planned change project. There were the early adapter faculty; later, other faculty incorporated service-learning after others had paved the way. It is also acceptable that there are some who will not consider including these pedagogies in their courses.

As CETSL progressed in the M.S.N. program, the B.S.N. program initiated curricular revisions as well. Healthcare education began to move from a heavy focus on hospitals to an increasing focus on the local and global community. The approach to incorporating service-learning into the BSN curriculum, however, was different because there is a clear need to develop skills in beginning college students. Thus BSN faculty decided to concentrate service on one area of need that had multiple facets and extreme limitations in funding—the municipal school district.

Cleveland, Ohio, is identified as the poorest major city in the United States, with more than 50% of its children living under the poverty line (U.S. Census Bureau, 2001). The Cleveland Municipal School District (CMSD) serves a population that is 88% minority, with many families having little or no access to continuous well-child healthcare. Diseases of poverty and lifestyle (diabetes, hypertension, dental issues) are discovered in elementary

Table 10.3. Quantitative Analysis Before and After Service-Learning Projects:
Summer 2001–Spring 2005 (N = 278)

Evaluated Questionnaires (Before/After Scale 1–5)	Mean Before CETSL	Mean After CETSL	t	Post-Test Positive Response
1) Know the types of community resources available for the population with whom I worked.	2.49	3.41	-16.237*	91.5 %
2) Understand how healthcare delivery systems impact my work in the community.	2.79	3.25	-8.536*	80.7 %
3) Know the healthcare needs of the community in which I served.	2.62	3.50	-15.939*	90.4 %
4) Understand the responsibilities of other professionals in a multidisciplinary team.	2.99	3.33	-5.069*	82.3 %
5) Know the barriers to receiving healthcare in the community that I served.	2.63	3.33	-12.128*	86.3 %
6) Understand the impact of socioeconomic status on health and illness.	3.10	3.54	-7.747*	88.3 %
7) Understand how my placement site is perceived in the community.	2.47	3.24	-12.922*	80.6 %
8) Know how to work with clients/patients who have various levels of healthcare knowledge.	3.06	3.54	-8.106*	91.4 %
9) Know what the terms *community resources* and *community service* mean.	2.97	3.71	-13.291*	94.2 %

Note. p < .001.

school-aged children but are left untreated in many cases due to lack of resources. Previously, many of these problems were routinely identified and referred for treatment by the CMSD school nurses. However, the current economic downturn has left the schools with fewer resources to cover growing health needs. In this environment, an ongoing partnership was developed between the CMSD and the School of Nursing at CASE to address the health needs of Cleveland's children. Using a service-learning model, the CMSD and the CASE School of Nursing have developed a collaborative program to provide State of Ohio mandated health screenings and related health education to children and families. B.S.N. students receive an ongoing opportunity to gain clinical practice experience in a culturally and ethnically diverse community setting.

The culmination of the B.S.N. experience is in the senior year when students have a practicum capstone experience and are placed for at least 10 weeks in health projects focused on the needs of underserved populations in diverse settings that may include sites in Arizona, Chile, and Australia. It is during this final experience that students bring together the experiences and insights from CETSL experiences of the previous three years into an increased respect for the views and expectations of those different from themselves, and gain a solid foundation of community-based skills and competencies on which to build their future practice. These service-learning activities enhance students' interaction with the community and assist them in conceptualization of the larger healthcare arena.

The Bolton School of Nursing has also made connections with the School of Dental Medicine and other schools/departments and identified initiatives that had parallel development in the School of Engineering and the College of Arts and Sciences. The hiring of a president and provost from institutions where community engagement was valued provided the impetus for unifying the activities from the separate schools and the opportunity to have an institutional impact.

Analysis
Moving From "Mine" to "Ours"

Key events that helped move civic engagement from the individual faculty level to the collective department level, and then to the university level, were initial and ongoing faculty development; preparation of a manual for service-learning that is available electronically for use by faculty, agency members, and students; formative and summative evaluation of the outcomes for students, faculty, and agencies; and local, national, and international presentations and publications. Nontenure-track faculty were able to obtain grants for course development, leading to recognition on par with research grants. A new university vision that incorporated community partnerships gave credibility to the movement, and curricular changes were made at all nursing education levels except the Ph.D. Tenure-track faculty can develop data-driven outcome programs of applied research, but it is not an easy path to tenure. CASE is one of the sites where a FIPSE (Fund for the Improvement for Postsecondary Education) grant awarded to CCPH is currently attempting to define the scholarship of engagement criteria that can be used to support faculty tenure applications. On the other hand, CETSL has been an ideal way for nontenure-track faculty to meet criteria for scholarship that is especially valuable in light of promotion requirements. This discussion of community-engaged scholarship will remain important for nursing and the university as they strive to recognize and work through these issues both as a department and as an institution.

Faculty Development

During the planning phase, programs were developed to educate faculty, students, and community partners in the principles and implementation of service-learning partnerships. Faculty also attended educational programs on service-learning provided by national organizations such as CCPH and Campus Compact. During the implementation and ongoing phases, faculty in the School of Nursing acted as resources for each other to help identify possible partners, plan the implementation of CETSL into their courses, and seek sources of external funding. Faculty also hosted a national institute to assist other interested universities that sent student-faculty-agency teams to develop plans for implementing service-learning into their community-campus partnership settings.

CETSL Manual

During phases I and II of the project, a CETSL manual (Narsavage & Lindell, 2001) was written with separate sections focused on community partners, faculty, and students. The manual incorporates theoretical content on service-learning and community-academic partnerships, practical tips for success, and copies of all instruments and forms. The manual was provided to all stakeholders and is posted on the CCPH web site (http://depts.washington.edu/ccph/pdf_files/CETSLmanual4.pdf).

Formative and summative evaluation of the project provided data that permitted process and outcome assessment at the course and program levels. Evaluation reports continue to be reviewed regularly by the CETSL Advisory Group and changes are made to the project as needed. Evaluation findings have been shared in presentations at the local, regional, national, and international levels and in peer-reviewed publications (Narsavage, Lindell, Chen, Savrin, & Duffy, 2002; Narsavage, Batchelor, Lindell, & Chen, 2003).

Leadership

The chair of the initiative (the associate dean for academic programs who obtained the initial grant funding) acted as a mentor for faculty development, led the community advisory committee, authored publications with faculty, presented and supported faculty presentations, and was a resource for changing the curriculum. The dean's support combined with the influential role of the president and provost had an immediate impact on providing legitimacy for the initiative. The theme of the president's inauguration had been community-campus partnership, an initiative that continues as "CASE in the Community."

Impact

CETSL in the B.S.N. program integrated experience in providing health teaching and health services to children in public schools using teams of up to 25 students assigned to one of nine CMSD schools in their freshman year. Students continue with that school for the first three years of their nursing program. Nursing students and their faculty supervisor work with the school community in identifying the priority health needs for the community and the services the nursing team can provide to meet those needs. Under faculty, teacher, and school nurse direction, the nursing team provides health teaching, screenings, and health services to address the identified need. Senior students and graduate-level nursing students implement programs for addressing specific healthcare needs that build on the screening and assessment data of the previous three years. Results have been positive as seen in the 2004–2005 school year, when 9,540 hours of nursing services were provided to CMSD; ninth-graders were screened and 31% identified with previously unidentified prehypertensive or hypertensive conditions were referred for ongoing treatment; and health education modules were developed and implemented in the areas of nutrition, asthma, dental care, and general hygiene. Formation of partnership teams of faculty/nursing student/teacher/school/child had another advantage in supporting nursing students' understanding of the cultures represented by the municipal students. Cultural sensitivity helped nursing students recognize and decrease potential ethnocentric bias (Lotas & Aloshen, 2004).

Graduate nursing students contributed 90 to 1,200 hours of service per year to each partner agency, and projects were completed that agencies had needed for years but did not have staff to implement. Process and outcome evaluation continue using both quantitative and qualitative methods. Evaluation findings revealed enhanced leadership skills and social responsibility for students, improved culturally and developmentally appropriate care, increased awareness by nursing students of community-learning and self-learning, and opportunities for faculty practice and scholarship.

The School of Nursing and the university improved their image in the community. The dental school has provided a dental sealant program to every elementary student in the district. The math and science departments have provided summer education to develop teachers' ability to work within a new curriculum. The School of Applied Social Science, through a funded center, has supported implementation of service-learning throughout K–12 schools in Cleveland and the surrounding area. An overview of "Case in the Community" is located at www.case.edu/president/cir/accreditation/sspdfs/ch10-fa21.pdf

Lessons
Key Successes and Barriers

As students develop knowledge of community needs and barriers, they can work more effectively with underserved individuals and groups. Students' activities meet Healthy People 2010 objectives (Department of Health and Human Services, n.d.), allowing community agencies serving vulnerable, urban populations to enhance the quality and quantity of their services, while promoting student commitment to civic engagement. The recognition of nontenure-track faculty through grant writing, presentations, and publication has supported the university and school missions and vision and has begun to dissolve the town-gown barrier.

The main barrier to success of CETSL is the lack of recognition for community-engaged scholarship, which limits faculty who participate to those in nontenure-track positions. Since more than 50% of the faculty are in tenure-track/tenured positions, measurable criteria that would be used for promotion and tenure could double faculty participation.

Several challenges that needed to be addressed were 1) identifying a single dedicated individual at the community site to coordinate student activities; 2) meeting the community agency needs while also meeting the objectives of the students in the class; 3) meeting students' need for a structured plan with a specific timeline for the project; 4) orienting students to the function and culture of the community agency.

Early in the process it became evident that students were having a better experience at certain community agency sites than at others. Additionally, faculty found that certain sites were easier to work with than others. Evaluation of the sites indicated that those where one person in the agency was responsible for service-learning provided the most positive experiences for all involved. Often communication becomes unclear and roles get confused when there is more than one person at the community site who is responsible for communication with students and faculty.

Another problem that developed was that students wanted to be sure that the activity was meeting their learning needs. At the M.S.N. level, many students were working, raising a family, and spending time in clinical. Unless a specific learning goal could be achieved, they were not interested in spending their valuable time in the experience. Likewise, the community agency had multiple demands on its employees' time. Unless a specific agency need could be met, they did not feel the need to spend their time with students. The most successful service-learning sites and courses met both these needs. All graduate courses that incorporate CETSL have very specific objectives included as part of the syllabus. When the faculty could work with the students and the agencies to clearly identify which objective(s) the activities would meet, the students were much more likely to participate wholeheartedly.

We learned that each community agency has its own structure and culture. At first we had some problems when students did or said something that did not fit with the agency's culture. A solution to this problem has been to deliver an orientation to and with the agency to familiarize the students with the agency culture where they will be a guest. When this is done well, the students understand the agency's mission more clearly, and the agency is much happier with the students.

Finally, a challenge to faculty is finding reflection activities that are meaningful and allow the student to develop the connection between theory and practice. There are many examples in the literature of reflection activities: seminars scheduled at strategic times throughout the program, logs, storyboards, PowerPoint presentations, and web sites are all possibilities. Integrating a variety of activities is a good strategy to promote the personal growth of students. Faculty can prepare for their role as facilitator by getting to know the mission and vision of the organization(s) where the students will serve. Successful reflection also requires faculty to consider which of the course objectives are best met by the service.

Key Strategies

Key strategies include the essential need to link service activities to course objectives; to keep regular, open communication among all stakeholders; to provide services based on identified community needs; to have mutual commitment to a sustained relationship; to be flexible; to orient all stakeholders; and to maintain ongoing partnerships. Findings of a grounded theory study of 13 community partners revealed that reflection needs to be an integral part of the entire experience rather than a self-assessment completed at the end of the experience (Lindell, 2003). Reflection provides the opportunity for theory to meld with experience. Additionally, Lindell's study identified critical components of successful relationships including frequent, effective communication; commitment to the partnership; orientation; planning; reciprocity; and evaluation.

By 2010, the Frances Payne Bolton School of Nursing will have criteria for community-engaged scholarship included in the criteria for advancement in rank, promotion, and tenure, thereby increasing the capacity for community engagement in their school and in the university.

References

Community Campus Partnerships for Health. (1998). *Principles of good community campus partnerships.* Retrieved March 18, 2006, from the University of Washington, Community-Campus Partnerships for Health web site: http://depts.washington.edu/ccph/principles .html#principles

Department of Health and Human Services. (n.d.). *Healthy people 2010.* Retrieved March 18, 2006, from www.healthypeople.gov/

Lindell, D. (2003). *Partnership with a graduate nursing program: Voices of the community.* Unpublished doctoral dissertation, Case Western Reserve University, Cleveland, OH.

Lotas, M., & Aloshen, D. (2004). *Service-learning in practice: A partnership between a large urban school district and university school of nursing.* Cleveland, OH: Case Western Reserve University.

Narsavage, G., & Lindell, D. (2001). *Community engagement through service-learning manual.* Retrieved March 18, 2006, from the University of Washington, Community-Campus Partnerships for Health web site: http://depts.washington.edu/ccph/pdf_files/CETSLmanual4.pdf

Narsavage, G. L., Batchelor, H., Lindell, D., & Chen, Y-J. (2003, November/ December). Developing personal and community learning in graduate nursing education through community engagement. *Nursing Education Perspectives, 24*(6), 300–305.

Narsavage, G. L., Lindell, D., Chen, Y-J., Savrin, C., & Duffy, E. (2002, October). A community engagement initiative: Service-learning in graduate nursing education. *Journal of Nursing Education, 41*(10), 457–461.

O'Neil E. H., & Pew Health Professions Commission. (1998). *Recreating health professional practice for a new century.* San Francisco, CA: Center for the Health Professions.

U.S. Census Bureau. (2001). *United States census 2000.* Washington, DC: Author.

About the Authors

Georgia Narsavage is former associate dean for academic programs in the Frances Payne Bolton School of Nursing at Case Western Reserve University. She is currently professor and associate dean for academic affairs at the Medical College of Georgia School of Nursing. She continues to serve as a service-learning consultant for Campus Community Partnerships for Health.

Evelyn Duffy is assistant professor of nursing and coordinator of the Gerontological Nurse Practitioner program in the Frances Payne Bolton School of Nursing at Case Western Reserve University. She is a certified adult and gerontological nurse practitioner and practices at University Hospitals of Cleveland.

Deborah Lindell is assistant professor and director of the Graduate Entry Master's of Science in Nursing/Doctorate of Nursing Practice program in the Frances Payne Bolton School of Nursing at Case Western Reserve University. She has incorporated service-learning and community-academic partnerships into the clinical component of her public health nursing courses since 1997 and was project director for a funded project to implement Community Engagement Through Service-Learning in the Bolton School's Master's of Science in Nursing program.

Marilyn J. Lotas is associate dean for the undergraduate program in the Frances Payne Bolton School of Nursing at Case Western Reserve University. She received her Ph.D. in nursing from the University of Michigan and completed postdoctoral work at the University of Pennsylvania.

Carol Savrin is assistant professor and director of the Master's of Science in Nursing program in the Frances Payne Bolton School of Nursing at Case Western Reserve University. She is certified as both a pediatric nurse practitioner and a family nurse practitioner, providing a comprehensive approach to the care of children.

Yea-Jyh Chen is a former graduate assistant for the Community Engagement Through Service-Learning program. She currently works as project manager on the Intensive Communication for Chronically Critically Ill study in the Frances Payne Bolton School of Nursing at Case Western Reserve University.

11

Community Service-Learning, Research, and the Public Intellectual

Leda Cooks, Erica Scharrer, Michael Morgan

For more than three decades, the Department of Communication at the University of Massachusetts, Amherst has been dedicated to social justice work, but until the early 1990s, little had been done to integrate scholarship and private/personal social justice work with teaching, curriculum, and action in the community. In a land-grant institution that gives public credence to community service-learning (CSL) but privileges and rewards research, CSL can be a hard sell to faculty across all disciplines who need job security and the support of the administration. However, a small movement to recognize faculty who did work in CSL began with a fellowship group (supported by the provost at the time) that met once every month to discuss the "magic" of CSL and, of course, the hard work of planning, organizing, and supervising these projects and partnerships.

From the start of this movement on campus, our department was part of the discussion. As a communication department, we were especially interested in the ways communication creates and structures how we think about community, justice, and democracy. We examined the outreach we were doing as a department and considered how we could build on this work to create collaborative projects among our colleagues and community partners. We needed to build a program that would support junior faculty through the integration of research, teaching, and service. From the outset, our concern was building a strong CSL program that was well integrated with our vision as a department, rather than the sum total of each faculty member's projects or courses. We feel that we have accomplished some of our goals, as this chapter portrays.

In particular, the collaborative Media Literacy and Violence Prevention Program has brought together faculty, graduate students, and undergraduate students in courses on media violence, conflict and mediation, and media and public policy to work with sixth-grade teachers and students in local schools on issues of media violence, media literacy, and interpersonal conflict education. Undergraduate students enrolled in these courses work throughout the semester to create a curriculum that they present in five weekly sessions to the sixth graders. In the last session of the program, the sixth graders, utilizing the information they have gained, prepare, present, and videotape a public service announcement that is shown to third graders. The program has been ongoing since 1999 and has resulted in a rewarding partnership with local schools and a strong teaching and publication record for faculty involved.

Although we have a long way to go before CSL will be rewarded on the level of projects driven by corporate incentives and monies, our department's crucial integration of teaching, research, and service through CSL has resulted in strong collaborations of faculty committed to helping each other and their campus and disciplinary colleagues gain recognition for their work as true "public intellectuals."

Demographic Information
The University

The University of Massachusetts, Amherst is the flagship of the commonwealth's five-campus public university system. Established in 1863 under the Morrill Land Grant Act as Massachusetts Agricultural College, the university sits on nearly 1,450 acres in the scenic Pioneer Valley of Western Massachusetts. The campus provides a rich cultural environment in a rural setting close to major urban centers. The university is part of a five-college collaborative program through which faculty and students may teach or take classes at their own campus or at Mount Holyoke College, Smith College, Amherst College, or Hampshire College.

The campus has 18,000 undergraduate students and 6,000 graduate students from every state and more than 100 countries. Its 10 schools and colleges offer 88 undergraduate majors, 68 master's, and 48 doctoral programs. In 2004, the university awarded 3,919 bachelor degrees, 1,058 master's degrees, and 274 doctoral degrees. Sponsored research activities total more than $100 million a year. The majority (83%) of students are white, about 8% are Asian, 4.2% are African American, and 3.6% are Latino. A small percentage (about 150 students) are Native American or Cape Verdean. Overall, 72% of students are from Massachusetts, and 6% (22% of graduate students) are international.

The Department of Communication

The Department of Communication has 19 tenure-track faculty members and one full-time lecturer. The journalism program (a semi-independent undergraduate degree housed within communication) has an additional six tenure-track faculty. Nine of the 25 faculty are assistant professors working toward tenure. The department has about 1,200 undergraduate majors (800 in communication and 400 in journalism) and about 80 graduate students, most of whom are in the Ph.D. program. Graduate students make a substantial contribution to the department's teaching efforts—on average, about 30 graduate students serve as teaching assistants each semester. Faculty are split evenly between men and women, and six faculty are from minority communities.

Processes

Departmental CSL Programs

Specific examples of CSL work in our department include internships with a variety of local nonprofit agencies, the option of choosing CSL projects in lower level courses or of participating in CSL-focused courses on the graduate and undergraduate levels, and getting honors or CSL credit above and beyond course credit for CSL work and for community-based research in both graduate and undergraduate courses. While these courses are not always specifically sequenced, the courses that are connected to the collaborative project (Media Literacy and Violence Prevention Program) are offered in the same semester, and some students choose to take both in order to make the connections between the topics of interpersonal conflict and media violence that are central to the CSL project.

Collective Thinking, Planning, and Action

Our department is quite diverse in terms of its areas and interests and yet united through a mission that is theoretically driven but activist oriented. In other words, we have a vision of our work that is more about collective action than individually based learning. In a department with diverse fields of concentration and a commitment to civic engagement, our efforts have been concentrated in three main areas that loosely reflect our disciplinary fields: film studies, dialogue, and media literacy initiatives.

Faculty and graduate students in film studies have a long tradition of working in and with the community to sponsor showings and festivals that feature or are produced by marginalized or otherwise "invisible" segments of the community. These festivals were created and/or organized by our students in collaboration with faculty from colleges in our area and community members to highlight marginalized and underrepresented populations. The showings include the multicultural film festival, the Korean film festival, the Irish Film festival, and the Asian film festival, among others.

The dialogue initiatives were created and implemented by faculty in the area of social interaction and have worked to bring together students, faculty, and community members in an attempt to address race, class, and other differences. The projects have helped define and solidify the commitments and concerns of a variety of groups on campus and in the community while serving as the basis for important initiatives in addressing visibility and equity in policy.

The media literacy initiatives have been the strongest and longest lasting in our department. These projects have involved the greatest number of faculty and graduate students and have had the largest evidential impact on the community and on larger national and international audiences.

Analysis: The Development and Integration of CSL in the Department

Key Events

Although civic engagement has long been a part of our departmental mission and vision, the emergence of CSL in the department as a specific pedagogical method began in the early 1990s in courses on conflict, mediation, interpersonal communication, and group decision-making that worked to integrate and apply course concepts with learning in the community. The move to incorporate CSL into existing courses complemented other projects in the department that sought to involve community members in creating their own video projects in teaching media literacy and promoting dialogue among diverse and conflicting groups on campus.

Simultaneously, the university began a CSL fellowship program that invited faculty across disciplines to meet biweekly to share their CSL plans and course experiences. The fellowship program provided a small ($500–$1,000) grant to support faculty who were teaching service-learning courses. As the campus-wide program and focus on CSL grew, so too did faculty interest. Some key events that united faculty interest included the successful partnership between several colleagues on a Media Literacy and Violence Prevention Program in local schools, an on-campus grant program to support departmental CSL initiatives (our department was the first to receive funds from this program), and a variety of individual and team grants for faculty on our campus and in the five-college collaboration.

Another significant boost in our efforts came in 2001 when we were one of nine departments chosen nationwide to participate in a four-day Campus Compact institute on "The Engaged Department." This gave us new ways to think about building service-learning curricula with diverse community partners in interdisciplinary contexts. Other incentives that have helped to increase participation in CSL among faculty are scholarship programs for planning, implementing, and doing research in CSL (a valuable and distinctive aspect of our CSL efforts), recognition from upperlevel administration for department-level work in this area, and recognition of our department by the National Communication Association for our multicourse collaborative project. Over the last 10 years, our department has received more support (in the form of approximately 25 grants and fellowships) and recognition for CSL work than any other on campus. Additionally, two of our faculty have received the highly distinguished University Academic Outreach Award—further recognition of our progress in integrating our research with community needs.

Departmental Leadership

The role of the chair is to manage departmental resources and establish priorities and responsibilities in research, teaching, and outreach. This includes creating a departmental environment in which CSL efforts are encouraged, "normalized," supported, and rewarded. The chair seeks to provide resources needed for faculty to incorporate CSL and to create conditions where faculty not offering CSL components will be motivated to do so.

The chair (and the department) recognize and embrace the fact that CSL will increasingly become a critical criterion by which public higher education is evaluated. Everyone benefits when something of public value results from students' coursework. No amount of support from the chair, however, can substitute for the enthusiasm and commitment of faculty to CSL.

Impact: Assessing Our Programs

Assessment of CSL programs as they relate to community-based research or classroom/community learning outcomes varies in terms of the variety of projects in the department. In the following section, the process and outcome measures we use are discussed. For students and faculty, we focus on integration, application, and retention of course material, satisfaction and enjoyment of the process, commitment to community, and future commitment. With respect to the institution, we evaluate support for faculty by the administration in the form of grants and fellowships, recognition for tenure and promotion, and a centralized office for CSL outreach into the community.

Making a Difference?

Students. Courses offered through our department that emphasize civic engagement are very well received. Students report (via course evaluations and project assessments) that they have better relationships with faculty, have learned and applied course material, will retain course material, and are more committed to doing community work in the future. Undergraduate students who take CSL courses before their senior year look for other course opportunities to build on their experience. The majority of our graduate students who take CSL courses or who choose to do CSL projects or community-based research continue to work with the community groups throughout their academic program. Several have based their master's or dissertation work on community groups and action research.

Faculty/unit. CSL has been the basis around which many partnerships have formed among faculty within our own department and in interdisciplinary groups across the area. Participating faculty have reported renewed energy for teaching and community-based research and advocacy and better relationships with students and with community members. At the department level, we have conducted workshops on planning and implementing a CSL course and on different service-learning opportunities in the community. Several of our newest faculty are interested in working on collaborative projects but are concerned about establishing support for tenure before engaging in what may be perceived as service work. Increasingly, however, CSL is supporting and attracting junior faculty who perceive a shift in support from the administration.

Institutional. The Office of Community Service-Learning (OCSL) provides support services to faculty, students, and community members. The OCSL has a staff of 15, including a director, assistant director, program directors, and other help in the area of independent study coordinators, liaisons, and assessment assistants. Several faculty assist in directing the program and run courses and other initiatives for the office. The office runs two scholarship programs, an alternative spring break and independent study programs for undergraduates, and four grant programs for individuals, teams of faculty, and whole departments. The OCSL has worked closely with communication faculty; four faculty have received multiple grants from the office. The Provost's Committee on Community Service-Learning oversees and administrates the OCSL.

Key indicators. Assessment using traditional methods (i.e., surveys, reflection papers, and journals) and nontraditional methods (i.e., videotaped recordings of interactions between CSL participants) has shown that CSL students demonstrate greater knowledge of course material, improved public speaking skills, and engagement in and commitment to civic leadership. Assessment of the community CSL participants has shown learning about new issues, team and trust building, and appreciation of the partnership.

Lessons Learned

Although we have accumulated a significant amount of "successes" and we feel wiser for having accomplished them, we are continually met with both ongoing and new challenges, some endemic to community-based work and some unique to our particular set of experiences. Despite hurdles along the way, however, we approach all our community-based teaching, learning, and research from the perspective of an unwavering dedication to the principles and promise of CSL.

Key Successes and Barriers

One success of which we are very proud is our ability to cultivate long-term relationships with our community partners. Our Media Literacy and Violence Prevention Program (MLVPP) has been operating through an alliance among members of our department and two particular schools for five and six years, respectively (and shows no signs of stopping!). The long-term nature of these relationships demonstrates our strong commitment to our community partners and ensures that the lines of communication are open between us and them, in addition to eliminating the logistical time and effort involved in having to establish new community partners.

Another key success has been our opportunity to collaborate with each other and a number of members in our department through CSL. The MLVPP has involved 3 faculty members, 3 graduate student instructors, and 12 graduate students in addition to an estimated 100 undergraduates. Through MLVPP, we have also worked with multiple public school administrators, teachers, and more than 500 sixth graders. The multiple perspectives that each of these individuals brings enhances the richness of the experience. We have also enjoyed considerable success in extending CSL across the curriculum, in classes large and small, with undergraduate and graduate students. We have attracted new faculty in our department to CSL and have supported their efforts, resulting in an ever-increasing number of CSL experiences offered each year.

We have also been able to successfully combine teaching, research, and service (the tripartite mandate of academic life) through CSL. At a Research I university such as ours, we quickly learned that this combination was an especially effective use of time and was likely to be favorably received in reviews of our job performance. We also believe that conducting empirical research in association with CSL courses has enhanced the quality of those experiences. We use our research evidence about the effectiveness of the CSL experience for students and community constituents to make ongoing changes in order to improve. We believe that using our CSL efforts as a basis for our research is what makes our efforts especially distinctive; it not only takes the integration of teaching, research, and service to a new level, it also provides a powerful empirical basis from which to improve all three.

Each of these successes has introduces challenges, however. Our long-term relationships with community members have been wonderful, but it is sometimes difficult to meet their ongoing expectations if enrollment in our CSL colloquia is down at the time. We have also had to turn down requests from additional community sites. Our collaborations with each other, graduate students, and undergraduates have undoubtedly brought us closer together and improved our experiences, but they also can come at a cost. Occasionally disagreements will arise and disappointments will be voiced, and juggling so many different schedules and points of view can be a struggle. Although we have brought new colleagues into the CSL fold, we are sometimes disappointed in our failure to convince others in the department to implement CSL into their classes. Finally, attempting to get publishable data from a CSL experience can bring considerable stress to a semester already complicated by including CSL. A related obstacle is the small number of outlets (such as scholarly journals) for CSL research.

Key Strategies

The strategy we have employed in developing long-term relationships with our community partners has been to offer community service-learning experiences to our students without fail every year. This has required the department chair's administrative approval to have our CSL courses offered at the same time every year, but it has been essential in establishing stability and reliability in the eyes of our community partners. Because MLVPP is project-based (involving developing and implementing a set of lessons around media violence and interpersonal conflict mediation for sixth-grade students), the basic parameters do not change dramatically from year to year; therefore, it is easy for the community partners (public school teachers and principals) to agree to participate because the project is a known quantity. Although a project-based CSL course does not allow for the benefits that accrue from longer, more sustained immersion in community settings, its relative feasibility for all parties is a definite strength.

The strategies we have put into place for extending CSL across the curriculum include informing our colleagues about CSL, providing them with resources should they decide to try it, and spreading the word about the successes that CSL can achieve informally and through our scholarship on the topic. For example, we used a small internal CSL grant to hire a graduate student to place sample CSL syllabi and reflection or journal writing assignments and articles and essays on CSL in a publicly accessible area. The student also created a binder for the same central location that contained a list of local agencies and organizations with communication-oriented missions, as well as specific CSL ideas and contact information. We have also invited others in the department to participate in ongoing CSL projects, thereby creating the collaborations previously noted.

Our strategy for incorporating research into our community service-learning is a critical component. When we seek community partners (or contact ongoing partners), we ask for permission to use videotaping, focus groups, interviews, and surveys as an integral element of the community service-learning that will take place. In some cases, as in the MLVPP in which the community constituents are early adolescents, we also secure parental permission before we begin. The mutually beneficial and respectful spirit of CSL ensures that the community partners are not made to feel exploited by the research or that they are providing information without receiving anything in return. We create research questions, form hypotheses, and collect observations to explore them within the context of CSL. For example, we have studied survey responses of college students who chose to participate in a course's CSL option versus students in the same course who chose not to participate. We have also posed questions to community constituents (e.g., "What do young people consider to be 'violent' in the media?") that can be addressed during our community interactions.

Vision: Departmental CSL in 2010

In 2010 our departmental CSL efforts will be strengthened. We envision a CSL capstone course required for majors. Currently, we are developing a fully enriched, team-taught CSL course that will focus on the MLVPP. This course will alleviate some of the time pressure we have felt in administering the MLVPP with a smaller group of students for whom the experience is an added option. In the future, we will work toward expanding the number of CSL course options that can serve as capstones so that eventually there will be a capstone requirement for communication majors in their senior year.

We will continue to bridge teaching, research, and outreach through CSL partnerships and to present and/or publish our experiences and research. The vast stores of data collected over the years will help us to make important observations about changes over time. We also anticipate conducting follow-up research with past CSL participants to determine whether there are enduring effects of participating in our department's community-based experiences. Finally, we predict that we will have long-term commitment to CSL among more departmental colleagues. The forte of our department in activism and community-based teaching and research has helped us to attract new faculty members with a strong interest in CSL. Thus the coming years are sure to see our CSL efforts continue to widen and deepen.

About the Authors

Leda Cooks is an associate professor at the University of Massachusetts, Amherst who teaches interpersonal conflict, mediation, critical pedagogy, and intercultural communication. Based on 15 years of community service-learning (CSL) practice, her research interests in this area center on the intersections of critical pedagogy, critical race theory and CSL, CSL and social justice, and CSL assessment.

Erica Scharrer is an associate professor at the University of Massachuetts, Amherst who has been implementing community service-learning (CSL) into her courses since joining the Department of Communication in 1999. She is particularly interested in media literacy as a CSL topic. Along with coauthor Leda Cooks, she has published her scholarly works in the *Michigan Journal of Community Service Learning, Academic Exchange Quarterly,* and *Communication Teacher.*

Michael Morgan is professor and chair of the Department of Communication at the University of Massachusetts, Amherst. He has authored or coauthored more than 60 national and international studies on the effects of television on images of violence, sex roles, aging, health, science, academic achievement, political orientations, and other issues. He teaches courses on media programming and institutions, media and the family, international media effects, cultivation analysis, and other related topics.

12

Fostering Engagement for Social Justice: The Social Justice Analysis Concentration in Sociology at Georgetown University

Sam Marullo, Kathleen Maas Weigert, Joseph Palacios

Chilean Partnership for Social Justice Learning

Imagine focusing on the worst moment of a country's history as part of your introduction to the country.

For many people, Chile is a guiding light for Latin America. At the beginning of the 21st century, Chile has the most robust economy, the highest literacy rate, and the strongest communications infrastructure of any country in Latin America. Yet, like its neighbor Argentina, Chile has a very recent history of military dictatorship, political repression, and civil strife.

To fully appreciate the social conditions of Chile today, a student of Chile must be familiar with what happened during those years of political repression. On the second day of the Georgetown summer program in Chile, our local university partner—the Jesuit University Alberto Hurtado—organized a critical introductory field trip to visit the sites around Santiago commemorating the era of the fall of democracy and the rise of military dictatorship under General Agosto Pinochet from 1973–1990. The first stop on the students' tour was the Villa Grimaldi on the outskirts of Santiago. For four very troublesome years, 1974–1978, the military regime housed and processed about 5,000 Chilean men and women at the Villa. At least 240 people "disappeared" through torture and subsequent murder.

The students on the tour, which was conducted in Spanish by Pedro Alejandro Matta, slowly realized that the tour guide was telling his own story of detention and torture at Villa Grimaldi. The secret police had constructed different buildings for detention, interrogation, torture, and murder. There, Matta was held for about 10 days and subsequently imprisoned in various detention facilities for more than 13 months before being allowed to go into exile. The secret police tore down the buildings and sold the Villa in 1987. After the fall of Pinochet, Chilean human rights activists were able to galvanize public opinion so the government could acquire the property and preserve the site as the "Park for Peace" and a memorial to those who suffered and died.

After experiencing this socially and politically imbued tour of Santiago, Georgetown social justice analysis practicum students could put into historic context the "new Chile" and why there is a need for long-term truth and reconciliation for Chileans. The coordinator for the 2005 summer experience was a young English woman and graduate of Oxford University who had spent many years studying Chilean politics and justice issues. She brought to the students her experience working with Chilean exiles and those who suffered. Their sociology professor helped establish and staff the Catholic Church's *Solidaridad* ministry during the years of repression. This agency provided financial support and services for the thousands of families who were marginalized by the military dictatorship.

The Alberto Hurtado summer program provides a rich experience for students. They meet the variety of people, neighborhoods, and opportunity structures that Chile actually represents. They live with more well-off families in the better neighborhoods of Santiago because of the nature of housing foreign students in Chile, experiencing how the "new Chileans" live. But they attend Spanish, sociology, and social justice analysis classes at Alberto Hurtado's centrally located campus, where they mix with middle- and working-class students who go to a university named after the great Jesuit advocate for the poor. The university's mission is to offer an excellent and socially aware education for first-generation university students. Indeed, while Chile has a robust economy, it also has the largest gap between the rich and poor in Latin America. Students do their community-based learning projects in the poorest neighborhoods of Santiago where they not only encounter the "losers" in the new Chile but also many of those who suffered the most during the dictatorship. They experience the extreme contrasts in Chilean society and become better young sociologists, especially through the ongoing process of critical reflection that the program provides.

This learning experience for the students in the Social Justice Practicum course brings to life the ideals articulated in the Department of Sociology and Anthropology's vision and mission statements: "We strive to foster a lifelong engagement with questions of social justice. . . . We offer students direct opportunities to develop and apply those skills through research and experiential learning activities in the Washington, D.C. community and beyond" (Georgetown University, 2000).

Georgetown University Background

As a Catholic and Jesuit university, Georgetown describes itself as a student-centered research university. It is a private institution committed to educating "men and women to be reflective lifelong learners, to be responsible and active participants in civic life and to live generously in service to others" (Georgetown University, n.d.). Since 2000, the Department of Sociology and Anthropology has worked intentionally to align its curriculum with this mission and to hold itself accountable to successfully fulfill its mission by assessing students' learning and development throughout the sociology major. Our social justice analysis concentration, the focus of this chapter, is one concrete result of our efforts.

For the academic year 2004–2005, Georgetown had a total undergraduate, graduate, and professional school enrollment of approximately 13,000, with about 52% female and 48% male. Georgetown has roughly 6,000 undergraduates matriculated across four colleges. Students come from all 50 states and more than 130 countries. The university is consistently ranked as one of the most selective in the United States as well as one of the most expensive, with tuition, room, and board topping $40,000. For those who were admitted in fall 2004, about 70% scored above 700 on math and verbal SATs. Ninety-five percent of accepted students were in the top 10% of their class, 59% were valedictorians, and 46% were salutatorians of their high schools. Since 1984, 21 students have received Rhodes Scholarships for study at Oxford University. An additional 39 have been awarded Marshall, Mellon, and Luce Scholarships/Fellowships to study in England, the Far East, and the United States. Fourteen Truman Scholarships have been awarded in the last two decades for study leading to public service.

The university's deep commitment to diversity is reflected in the student population. Minorities represent 24% of the undergraduate student body and 19% of the graduate school. In the undergraduate schools, 7% of students are African American, 10% are Asian American, 6% are Hispanic, and 6% are from overseas. Minority enrollment at the law center is 22%, and at the medical school 27%. For undergraduates, Georgetown is primarily a residential campus, situated in an affluent neighborhood in Washington, DC., with more than 80% of the student body living on campus in university housing.

The social justice analysis concentration is a major and minor in the Department of Sociology and Anthropology, which also offers "traditional" majors and minors. The department consists of seven full-time sociologists and three anthropologists. There are roughly 60–70 declared sociology majors at any time, with roughly 25–30 graduating per year. The social justice analysis concentration completed its second year of operation in 2005, graduating its first cohort of five students with nine in the pipeline for 2006. We anticipate the social justice analysis concentration to grow to

15–20 students graduating per year, with 20 being our maximum target goal due to resource (primarily faculty) capacity.

Processes

Early Development

Since the early 1990s, the Department of Sociology and Anthropology has offered a number of service-learning courses on a routine basis. These include courses that offer an optional service-learning component and those which contain a fully integrated service-learning pedagogy. In addition, Georgetown has long supported a Service-Learning Credit (SLC) program that allows students to add an optional fourth credit to a course pending approval of the student's service-learning contract by the course instructor and a community partner. This option enables the student to integrate at least 40 hours of community service with the course's learning objectives, as demonstrated through the student's writing and reflection. The SLC program—administered by the university's Center for Social Justice Teaching, Research and Service—was recently renamed the Community-Based Learning Credit program to reflect its changing focus, which emphasizes course integration of community-based learning experiences that address community-identified needs.[1]

The number of community-based learning courses offered across the university increased slowly throughout the 1990s, in part due to growing faculty interest and in part due to intentional faculty development efforts. In 1990, a team of Georgetown faculty attended the first "Integrating Service with Academic Study" workshop sponsored by Campus Compact. The team designed and later implemented a faculty development program that each summer worked with a group of about 15 faculty at a weeklong institute, introducing them to the basics of service-learning, supporting their course redesign, and introducing them to potential community partners. During the 1990s, more than 100 university faculty attended these service-learning institutes at Georgetown, becoming the grassroots "critical mass" that would provide a base for further curricular and institutional change. The creation of the Center for Social Justice Research, Teaching, and Service in 2001 greatly advanced the institutional commitment to and work for the integration of social justice and community-based learning throughout the university. The creation of the social justice analysis concentration and other recent curriculum changes in other departments builds on the effectiveness of this strategy.

Departmental Process

It was in this context of slowly growing a grassroots faculty base that the department set out deliberately to integrate community-based learning into its academic program. At the university level, a national Jesuit initiative in 2000 to undertake institutional self-studies of their social justice programs was the catalyst to raise concerns about the lack of institutional commitments—through the curriculum and faculty research—to promoting social justice (Bannan Center, 2005; Reiser, 1995). The Department of Sociology and Anthropology responded to this call for self-study by examining its own curriculum and faculty research interests. We began with a one-day retreat in May 2001 upon the election of a new department chair, ostensibly to draft a department mission and vision statement. In the course of discussions about our collective teaching goals and personal research agendas, we discovered that there were, and are, a number of shared interests around social justice, particularly our commitment to educating students to become effective advocates for social justice, and that many of our own research agendas focused on advancing our visions or commitments to social justice.

To more closely align our curriculum with our mission statement and to build on our faculty members' strengths, we focused our efforts on developing a social justice analysis concentration. The department as a whole first worked with curriculum design experts in our teaching and learning center, the Center for New

Designs in Learning and Scholarship (CNDLS), to rethink our curriculum in light of our learning goals, through a process called backward curriculum design (CNDLS, 2004; Diamond, 1998). We also drew on the support of the university's human resources department to recruit a person with facilitation expertise to help us work through the retreat and curriculum redesign processes. After a year of this collective, intentional rethinking of our curriculum, the authors of this chapter and a community partner were sent to a Campus Compact Workshop in 2003 as a working group to represent Georgetown sociology as an "Engaged Department." The goal was to develop a curriculum reform initiative that would integrate our department's social justice mission with our strengths in community-based learning, thus creating a new concentration. The team started with the department's self-assessment of its strengths, weaknesses, opportunities, and threats (its SWOT analysis) and its enumeration of community-based learning courses, ongoing community partnerships, and faculty members' social justice research interests. We also drew from a study we had undertaken of other similar sociology programs' innovative curriculum initiatives and (the few) interdisciplinary programs we found that focused on social justice issues. Given our department's resources and strengths, and after considering a range of possible options based on other universities' experiences, we designed a concentration that we believed would work for us.

The social justice analysis concentration we designed and implemented is an optional track through the major or minor for interested students to focus on the theories and analyses of structural inequalities. We designated courses to count for the concentration not only because of their substantive focus on inequalities, but also because of the current or potential pedagogical use of community-based learning as a teaching strategy. Our emphasis on community-based learning as a critical pedagogy for the program is important because we believe it provides students with an enriched understanding of the barriers and challenges that undermine social justice, an opportunity to witness the effects of these injustices, and an opportunity to work with others committed to rectifying these injustices. In terms of the students' development as "whole persons," such opportunities enable them to cultivate a sense of empowerment and the civic engagement skills to become more effective agents of positive social change.

Program Structure

The social justice analysis concentration includes the traditional core of the major: Introduction to Sociology, Methods of Sociological Research, Social Statistics, and Sociological Theory. As a replacement to the traditional senior research seminar (a one-semester research colloquium required of all majors), we require a two-semester capstone community-based research seminar, Project D.C., that challenges students to undertake original research in collaboration with our community partners. This seminar provides them with real experiences in applying their sociological skills and understandings to addressing social problems. We also developed a required gateway course for the concentration, Social Justice Analysis Theory and Practice, to introduce students to the theoretical and applied approaches to understanding social justice and social change.

Given Georgetown's location in the nation's capital and our reputation for international education, we intentionally seek out partnerships that have national policy connections and international development initiatives, thereby helping our students to make local-global or local-national policy connections. Further, because a large number of our students participate in study-abroad programs, we did not want to limit our students to DC-based experiences, so we worked with our Office of International Programs and the Center for Social Justice Research, Teaching and Service to create social justice practicum courses that are offered through study-abroad programs (such as the Santiago Chile program described earlier).

Finally, in addition to the four core courses and the three semesters of social justice analysis concentration requirements (the gateway course plus the two-semester capstone course), students are required to take at least one other community-based learning (CBL) course plus one other sociology elective (which may or may not contain a CBL component). The concentration thus requires nine courses rather than the traditional major's requirement of ten courses, but at least four of the social justice analysis concentration courses are four credit-hour courses rather than three credit hours, so the amount of credit hours in the concentration is actually greater than in the traditional major. The model is designed to have a developmental component, with students ideally taking the gateway course in their sophomore year and acquiring their first CBL experience by then (if not sooner). They then have at least one other CBL experience in their junior year and finish with a yearlong commitment to a community-based research project in their senior year that enables them to integrate and apply their sociological learning to their CBL project.

Gateway course. The gateway course for the Social Justice Analysis Theory and Practice concentration introduces students to classical and contemporary theories of justice. With the theoretical groundwork, the course examines current situations of injustice. Students explore how to integrate theory with practical social justice projects that address some issues of injustice. All students are required to work in collaboration with a community partner and, with the partner and the professor, the students design a project that they will work on throughout the semester. The course is a four-credit class that requires the student to devote four to six hours a week to their community project. While the community projects vary according to the needs of the community partner, they are designed so that they incorporate theoretical issues into the sociological issues explored in the course.[2]

Community-based learning and study abroad. We have also designed a way for students to integrate their international study-abroad experiences within the social justice analysis concentration. It is the fruitful collaboration of three Georgetown University offices—the Office of International Programs, the Center for Social Justice Research, Teaching and Service, and the Department of Sociology and Anthropology—that enables us to build on two of Georgetown's traditional strengths: community service and justice work on the one hand, and study abroad on the other (close to 50% of Georgetown's undergraduate students study outside the United States at some point). The newly designed social justice practicum allows students to participate in a community-based project that is rooted in and related to specific sociology course requirements. We drafted a template for the course and shared it with our international partners and, in a collaborative way, adapted it to local circumstances. The practicum is available in five different locations (London, England; Dakar, Senegal; Dominican Republic; Quito, Ecuador; and Santiago, Chile).[3]

Senior capstone. Project D.C. is a yearlong capstone course designed to support students undertaking a community-based research project in collaboration with a community-based organization partner. Students are expected to work at least 80 hours per semester on their projects outside of class time, in addition to undertaking other reading, writing, and class presentation assignments designed to support their projects. By the end of the course, the students have created a portfolio of products related to their research, including a final research report written to academic standards; an executive summary written for community partners' use; an op-ed piece on a policy related to their research; popular education materials used to convey the findings back to the community; an Institutional Review Board proposal to gain approval for their research; a Geographic Information Systems map; reflective journal entries; and a web site to make their findings public.[4] Many of the graduating seniors in this course comment in their final course evaluations or in their final reflective journal entries that this course enables them to understand how academic research is involved in addressing social problems and that the collaborative research project they have just completed has been the most meaningful experience of their college careers.[5]

Analysis
Moving From Personal Pedagogy to Departmental Curriculum

The development of the social justice analysis concentration grew out of a long-term, grassroots institutional change strategy based on the assumption that faculty-driven curriculum changes would lead to permanent institutional changes that would directly impact students' learning. We have also set out intentionally to alter the culture of our department, which we have changed through our interactions and rewards system. We accomplished this by taking advantage of external resources available to us, developing allies and supports found in other units, being intentional about our departmental practices, and utilizing our internal resources to support these changes. The department leadership, and leadership turnover, played a key role as well, as the incoming chair took the opportunity of routine leadership change together with other institutional events to create a catalyst for change. In short, we employed a social movement model of social change, mobilizing and co-opting external resources as well as redirecting internal resources to achieve new ends.

We took advantage of several external resources to help us implement the new concentration. We enlisted the external support of skilled university staff to help us with our strategic planning and curriculum redesign efforts (i.e., the Center for New Designs in Learning and Scholarship, human resources). Small amounts of funding made available through the dean's office and the provost's office were used for curriculum renewal initiatives and new course development. The dean also provided a small pool of money to create a department colloquium series through which faculty could share their research. We focused the first year's presentations on engaged scholarship. We worked with allies in other units, such as the Center for Social Justice Teaching, Research and Service and the Office of International Programs, to help us design and develop quality initiatives that would win widespread faculty and administrative support. The National Campus Compact gave us a safe space, resources, support, and an invitation to undertake serious curriculum reform to promote civic engagement. Finally, the contacts we had developed over time through our community-based teaching enabled us to draw on community partners who could support our efforts by challenging us to do more, by attesting to the value of our students' work in the community, and by helping us to articulate the students' enhanced development that occurs through community-based learning.

We have been careful to address the rewards system needed to sustain such institutional change efforts (Diamond, 1999). The department defines the internal merit review guidelines used for determining annual merit pay raises, and these have been altered to support faculty in undertaking community-based teaching by recognizing the additional challenges and workload involved in employing this pedagogy. We have altered our guidelines to make room for the scholarship of engagement to be counted as "real" scholarship and have articulated these to external reviewers and the university Rank and Tenure Committee when faculty have been reviewed for tenure and/or promotion. The national movement of the American Sociological Association to promote public sociology is another external resource that we have used to legitimize this type of scholarship in the face of faculty colleagues' skepticism (Burowoy, 2005).

Impact: Students and the Community

We have developed several assessment tools to evaluate students' learning in light of our department's teaching and learning goals (Hohm & Johnson, 2001). At the introductory level, we evaluate students' understanding of several core concepts through a pre-test and a post-test administered in all of our Introduction to Sociology sections. At the exit level, our graduating seniors are surveyed each year, which enables us to discover what they perceive to be the strengths and weaknesses in our program with respect to our department's articulated learning goals. Two findings that have emerged from these data are that our students do not feel as strongly competent as we would like in terms of applying research findings to help them understand everyday social problems and in terms of having a solid grasp of the research process (e.g., formulating hypotheses, doing quantitative data analysis, etc.). In response to these findings, we have committed to integrating data analysis and quantitative literacy across the curriculum—in alignment with the American Sociological Association's (1990) recommendation to teach research literacy "early and often" throughout the major—and have created research seminars strongly recommended for our junior majors to help them acquire such competencies.

In comparing students who have completed the traditional senior seminar capstone course with those who enrolled in the social justice analysis program's capstone course, Project D.C., the latter students report higher levels of improvement between the pre-test and the post-test on nearly all indicators, ranging from the more purely theoretical understanding of sociological concepts to the more applied measures of using sociological research to address social issues (see Table 12.1). We expected to see such differences emerge on the applied questions, but were surprised to see such enhanced improvement across nearly all the indicators. Indeed, the least amount of improvement concerns the students' perception of their agency to affect social change (Table 12.1, item 14). Upon closer examination of this finding, we discovered that the pre-test scores on this item are substantially higher for Project D.C. students (due to the self-selection process of enrolling in the concentration and taking this course), so there is much less room for improvement as a result of taking this course. Nevertheless, their average final scores remain higher than the traditional majors' scores.

Table 12.1. Percent Change in Student Learning Between
Pre-Test and Post-Test Responses for Traditional
Senior Seminar Compared to Project D.C. Students

Question/Concept	Senior Seminar: Combined Spring 2002 & 2003 (n = 22)	Project D.C. Combined 2001–2002, 2002–2003, 2004–2005 (n = 18)
1) Integrate theory and research	18.90%	29.53%
2) Apply concepts to real life	4.80%	22.83%
3) Formulate hypothesis	13.80%	18.63%
4) Examine socially important issues	11.50%	17.75%
5) Make reasoned arguments	18.00%	20.32%
6) Apply data to test hypotheses	14.90%	31.26%
7) Analyze quantitative data	16.40%	42.47%
8) Analyze qualitative data	13.60%	39.35%
9) Interpret data	10.50%	17.67%
10) Understand multiculturism	7.10%	17.27%
11) Understand cultural influences	1.00%	18.79%
12) Sense of justice	11.50%	24.28%
13) Critical thinking skills	4.50%	13.31%
14) Sense of agency to affect groups	18.70%	6.55%
Average Change	**11.00%**	**22.02%**

In collaboration with the other Washington, DC–area universities that make up the Community Research and Learning Network, we designed pre- and post-assessment questionnaires for students taking community-based learning courses. The focus of these instruments is on both expectations and outcomes of community-based learning and on civic engagement indicators (self-reported behavioral measures). As a department, we worked on a supplement to these instruments that focuses more on sociological concepts in general and on the links between sociology and civic issues. These instruments and the process are still in a pilot stage.

We have also interviewed several of our community partners to assess the impacts our students have in their organizations. Although both students and community partners acknowledge challenges to undertaking community-based learning projects, our partners are overwhelmingly pleased with the impacts that our students have with respect to the organization's goals. For some of our longer-term partners, they have grown to rely on our students to undertake particular projects that are integrally related to their missions. They report on our students' overall reliability and the quality of the projects they have undertaken which positively benefit their organization. Our partners also report on the growth they see in our students in terms of their civic engagement, cultural awareness, and interpersonal skills in the workplace. We believe that this helps our partners to realize the important role they play as co-teachers of our students. Since a substantial number of our Project D.C. students go on to careers in justice advocacy and non-profit organization management, or undertake post-graduate service positions in the Peace Corps, Teach for America, AmeriCorps, and other similar organizations, our partners see themselves in the role of helping to train the next generation of social justice advocates. In response to our partners' feedback, we have become more intentional about creating work agreements to specify the expected outcomes of a particular semester's work; soliciting partners' feedback as part of students' course evaluation; and improving communications among students, faculty, and community partners.

Lessons
The Importance of Strategically Mobilizing Scarce Resources for Change

There are a number of lessons to distill from our experience. However, before doing so, we state the obvious caveat that such lessons are not automatically transferable to all other departments or programs and that institutional context matters. By way of an obvious example, the fact that Georgetown is a Jesuit and Catholic institution provides us with a mission statement that requires the promotion of social justice as an essential element of all Jesuit institutions. While such an imperative is not the case for non-Jesuit institutions, virtually all higher education institutions have mission statements declaring their institution's commitment to promoting the public good in some form or another or of educating future citizens who will contribute to the larger society. Such mission statements can be used as a motivation and catalyst to provide support for curriculum redesign around civic engagement.

Our experience has taught us these key lessons.

- Utilize internal resources creatively and intentionally to achieve incremental changes that lead toward larger change.
- Take advantage of external resources and mobilize them on behalf of your department's change goals. The sources of such resources may be other units in the university, central administration, national organizations, and even community partners.
- Leadership committed to change is critical. Such leadership need not come from the chair, but the chair does need to be an ally for the change leadership (Ferren & Mussell, 2000).
- Examine the barriers to development and institutionalization (particularly the institutional rewards system) and work intentionally to remove or defuse them.
- Look to develop faculty at the grassroots level and find ways to mobilize them for change. Find or create ways to support the faculty engaged in this institutional change work.
- Locate and collaborate with other on-campus units that have similar vision and goals to advance the institutionalization of social justice opportunities.
- Work with other universities and national organizations to strengthen a wider community involvement in social justice work.

- Look to students as possible allies and find ways to mobilize their energies and desires to be involved with positive social change.
- Draw on the goodwill and support of community partners (without overburdening them) to be advocates and allies in your change efforts. Simultaneously, make sure that your partners are receiving products of value in exchange and/or gaining access to new resources as a result of their collaboration with the university.
- Become the change you seek.

Vision: Small Steps Leading Us to Our Dreams

We have articulated a number of goals and dreams for our program, sometimes publicly and more often within semi-private conversations around the department. These range from narrowly defined hopes for our students' learning successes to our dreams for having national institutional impact. Specifically, we hope to achieve the following:

- Students' enhanced learning—well-measured and documented by our learning assessment instruments—that demonstrates the value added of community-based learning for students' understanding of sociology concepts and the research process; students' enhanced moral and social development, interpersonal skills, and diversity awareness; and practical knowledge of the discipline enabling them to apply theory and research to address social problems.
- Students' increased professionalization and achievement, as indicated by their participation in professional and academic conferences, the quality of their public presentation skills, their receipt of graduate fellowships and other awards, and the nature and status of their employment opportunities after graduation.
- Being a support for other departments, both internal to Georgetown and for other sociology departments around the country, which seek to implement social justice or civic engagement goals

into their teaching and research. Creating the appropriate documentation and publications to codify our promising practices in pedagogy, partnership development, learning assessment practices, faculty roles and rewards, curriculum integration, and development of standards of excellence.

- Create a graduate program that includes formal training and support for students to undertake community-based learning and research.

- Increase institutional support as a center of excellence, thereby attaining additional resources such as endowed chairs in community-based learning and research, additional staff, infrastructure and equipment support.

- Achieve greater community partner involvement with the design, implementation, and evaluation of community-based learning and research.

- Achieve greater public recognition of the work in process and its successful impacts for increasing social justice in the community.

- Build stronger working relationships with like-minded colleagues at neighboring universities to help build a critical mass for positive social change.

We believe that our efforts so far have advanced our work in each of these areas and that we are on the path toward successful fulfillment of this vision. We remain eager to share our experiences with others and to learn from the successes of others as well.

Endnotes

[1] We have also changed our terminology at Georgetown, now using the term *community-based learning* instead of *service-learning*. We have made this change to shed some of the more controversial connotations of the word *service* and to convey to faculty not involved in this pedagogy the rigors and parallels of community-based learning with other venues for students' learning.

[2] For more information on this course or to request a copy of the syllabus, please contact Professor Joseph Palacios at jmp32@georgetown.edu.

³For more information on the practicum, see http://cndls.georgetown
.edu/projects/posters/soc_justice

⁴To view the students' web sites about their projects, see
https://lumen.georgetown.edu/faculty/marullos/public/index.cfm
?fuseaction=poster.fullList
http://lumen.georgetown.edu/projects/posterTool/index.cfm
?fuseaction=poster.fullList&instanceID=33

⁵For additional information about *Project D.C.*, see
http://cndls.georgetown.edu/projects/posters/marullo/index.html

References

American Sociological Association. (1990). *Liberal learning and the sociology major.* Washington, DC: Author.

Bannan Center. (2005). *The commitment to justice in Catholic higher education.* Retrieved March 18, 2006, from the Santa Clara University, Ignatian Center for Jesuit Education web site: www.scu.edu/bannan center/eventsandconferences/justiceconference/commitmentto justice/index.cfm.

Burowoy, M. (2005, February). For public sociology: 2004 presidential address. *American Sociological Review, 70*(1), 4–28.

Center for New Designs in Learning and Scholarship. (n.d.). *Social justice analysis concentration.* Retrieved March 18, 2006, from the Georgetown University web site: http://cndls.georgetown.edu/projects/posters/socialjustice/index.html

Diamond, R. M. (1998). *Designing and assessing courses and curricula: A practical guide* (Rev. ed.). San Francisco, CA: Jossey-Bass.

Diamond, R. M. (1999). *Aligning faculty rewards with institutional mission: Statements, policies, and guidelines.* Bolton, MA: Anker.

Ferren, A. S., & Mussell, K. (2000). Leading curriculum renewal. In A. F. Lucas & Associates, *Leading Academic Change: Essential roles for department chairs* (pp. 246–274). San Francisco, CA: Jossey-Bass.

Georgetown University, Department of Sociology and Anthropology. (2000). *Vision and mission statements.* Retrieved March 18, 2006, from the Georgetown University, Department of Sociology and

Anthropology web site: www.georgetown.edu/departments/sociology/missionstatement.html

Georgetown University, Office of Curriculum and Pedagogy. (n.d.). *Justice report: Understanding the way forward.* Retrieved March 18, 2006, from the Georgetown University, Office of Curriculum and Pedagogy web site: http://socialjustice.georgetown.edu/teaching/justice/understanding.html

Hohm, C. F., & Johnson, W. S. (Eds.). (2001). *Assessing student learning in sociology* (2nd ed.). Washington, DC: American Sociological Association.

Reiser, W. (Ed.). (1995). *Love of learning: Desire for justice.* Scranton, PA: University of Scranton Press.

About the Authors

Sam Marullo is chair and professor of sociology at Georgetown University and director of research at the Center for Social Justice Research, Teaching and Service. He is the founder and board chair of the Community Research and Learning Network of Washington, DC. He has written extensively on community-based learning and research, most recently coauthoring *Community-Based Research and Higher Education* (Jossey-Bass, 2003) and the American Sociological Association's Teaching Resources Guide, *Community-Based Research.*

Kathleen Maas Weigert is executive director of the Center for Social Justice Research, Teaching and Service and research professor in both the Department of Sociology and Anthropology and the Program on Justice and Peace at Georgetown University. She is coeditor of *America's Working Poor* (University of Notre Dame Press, 1996), *Teaching for Justice* (American Association of Higher Education, 1999), and *Living the Catholic Social Tradition* (Sheed & Ward, 2005).

Joseph Palacios is assistant professor of sociology at Georgetown University, where he teaches social theory, social justice analysis, Latino sociology, and religion and society. His research interest is the influence of religion and civil society on political culture. He has recently completed *The Catholic Social Imagination: Cultural Construction of Social Justice Doctrine in Mexico and the United States.*

13

"UCLA in LA": The Engaging Department of Chicana and Chicano Studies

Reynaldo F. Macías, Kathy O'Byrne

What did you learn from the service-learning experience in the community?

I learned the importance of community building, specifically that the needs of the community need to be the priority of the organizing efforts. I learned that it's important to get students involved in the process of assisting communities. This relationship is important because it furthers UCLA students' educational experience by allowing them to apply theoretical concepts to real life issues. It gets students involved in organizing efforts as well as provides the community with valuable outside support and assistance.

How did this course compare to other courses you have taken at UCLA?

This course has challenged me in many aspects that some courses have not. For example, the Barrio Service-Learning course challenged my abilities to synthesize useful information and distribute it to the general population. The class contains a component of civic engagement that all classes at UCLA should promote so that communities can benefit from our efforts.

Would you recommend this course to a friend? Why or why not?

I would recommend this class for those who are interested in taking responsibility in building a better community. In order to take this class one must be passionate about the issues that some of these communities face. I would recommend this course to anyone willing to make that effort to help out those in need.

—UCLA student in Barrio Service-Learning

These reflections represent typical reactions to the service-learning courses across the Department of Chicana and Chicano Studies at the University of California, Los Angeles (UCLA). In this department, there is a commitment to service, social change, and civic activism, almost by definition. It has been a hallmark of the field from its inception in the mid-1960s, partly reflecting its beginning in the social activism of the day. This commitment has been realized in different ways within undergraduate programs in Chicana and Chicano studies throughout the nation—mainly through service requirements of various kinds expected from students who major and sometimes minor in these programs. A few programs are beginning to embrace the notion of an engaged department as a way of addressing the commitment to service and civic engagement reflected in the field. The UCLA Department of Chicana and Chicano Studies and the César E. Chávez Center for Interdisciplinary Instruction did so earnestly beginning in 2001–2002. In concert with the UCLA Center for Experiential Education and Service Learning, now known as the Center for Community Learning, the Department of Chicana and Chicano Studies has continued to develop the notion of an engaged department through its coursework, collaboration with community partners, and involvement in institutional initiatives to promote civic engagement and community-university partnerships.

Demographics

The Institution and Department

UCLA, founded in 1919 as the southern California branch and second campus of the University of California, is part of a 10-campus, public research university system in the state of California. At the beginning of the 21st century, UCLA enrolled about 26,000 undergraduates and 13,000 graduate students in 12 colleges and professional schools. It offered 118 undergraduate and 200 graduate programs, had 3,326 faculty members, a library ranked in the top 10 in the nation with more than 7.6 million volumes, and 174 buildings on 419 acres. The campus sits in the western part of Los Angeles, five miles from the Pacific Ocean, in a diverse metropolitan area of more than 10 million people. The undergraduate enrollment, while not reflecting population parity in its service area, is still very racially and ethnically diverse, with 13% Chicano/Latino, 6% African American, 45% Asian American and Pacific Islander, and 35% white.

Chicano studies began at UCLA in 1969 with an organized research unit, the Chicano Studies Research Center, and created an academic major in 1974, organized as an interdepartmental program (run by a committee of faculty from different departments). It acquired six full-time faculty in a unique academic unit called the César E. Chávez Center for Interdisciplinary Instruction in spring 1993 after a two-week hunger strike by students, a faculty member, and community stakeholders. With a dedicated, full-time faculty, the program grew between 1993 and 2005, achieving departmental status in 2004–2005. Its proposal for graduate programs (master's and doctorate) is currently under review.

The Department of Chicana/Chicano Studies at UCLA has grown to 10 full-time faculty, 6 joint appointments, 15 affiliated faculty (who teach cross-listed courses), and an average of 6 visiting or temporary faculty a year who teach between one and four courses during that year. In June 2005, there were 172 majors, 152 minors, and 59 courses, with a combined student enrollment of

2,600, for the 2004–2005 academic year. Students majoring in Chicana/Chicano studies must meet a service-learning requirement through a single four-unit course (Chicana/Chicano Studies 100SL). It is offered every quarter and enrolled 102 students in 2004–2005.

Whither Service and Engagement?

Service in the communities of Los Angeles has been integrated with the Chicana/Chicano studies major since its inception at UCLA in 1974. This service was called a field studies requirement and was generally satisfied through an independent studies course in which the student undertook the obligation for a community placement and regularly reported to the instructor on a one-to-one basis. In addition to satisfying the field studies requirement through independent studies, individual faculty would teach courses in different communities, focus their content on specific aspects of the community (e.g., a course on planning in minority communities undertook a collaborative survey of community "assets" that was shared with local elected officials and the public at the end of the course), and provide an opportunity for students to do service-learning by allowing a co-enrollment in an independent studies course. This coursework and expectation of service evolved over time. After becoming a Center for Interdisciplinary Instruction in 1993, the full-time faculty engaged in a substantial academic program review and curricular development. This involved a reconsideration of the goals and purposes of this "field studies qua service" requirement.

In 1999, the faculty undertook a series of discussions during faculty meetings, as a curriculum committee of the whole, to clarify this requirement. In anticipation of these discussions, one of our adjunct faculty who had developed a service-learning program for the UCLA Labor Center, assisted us with the literature on service-learning, clarifying different forms of service and how they might be tied to the broader interests and scope of the discipline. In 1999, the UCLA Chancellor's Service-Learning Task Force issued its final report which provided definitions and issued a set of specific recommendations based on the discussions of the 13 faculty members. These recommendations all revolved around the creation of a UCLA Center for Service-Learning to serve as a resource for faculty and students. The idea was to support three key components: community connections, academic courses, and ongoing research. The mission of this new center, now known as the Center for Community Learning, was to focus on campus-wide development of service-learning courses and programs, coordination of faculty and student activities with community partners, and the dissemination of information.

The result of these faculty and student discussions around service-learning was a collectively designed skeleton for a course syllabus as the primary vehicle for meeting the requirement. The faculty also decided that the requirement was to be service-learning, not an internship or community service. This became the basis for establishing a catalog course with its own number (upper division) and course description. Titled Barrio Service-Learning, the course content focused on community organizing and organizations—how the Chicana/Chicano community organized itself for meeting its needs and for social change and justice—and highlighted the service component in its title as well (partly as a marketing strategy).

Our rationale for this service-learning requirement was reinforced as we discovered that the research on service-learning indicated a significant effect on college retention and completion (Bringle & Hatcher, 2002). In addition, we found other benefits had been documented. A national, longitudinal study of more than 22,000 undergraduate students indicated that service participation showed

> …significant positive effects on all 11 outcome measures: academic performance (GPA, writing skills, critical thinking

skills), values (commitment to activism and to promoting racial understanding), self-efficacy, leadership (leadership activities, self-rated leadership ability, interpersonal skills), choice of a service career, and plans to participate in service after college. These findings directly replicate a number of recent studies using different samples and methodologies. Performing service as part of a course (service-learning) adds significantly to the benefits associated with community service for all outcomes except interpersonal skills, self-efficacy, and leadership. Positive results for the latter two outcomes were borderline (i.e., p<.05). (Astin, Vogelgesang, Ikeda, &Yee, 2000, p. ii)

Processes
How We Got Here From There

Establishing an engaged department is a challenge. Our process focused on a number of things over time, including a comprehensive academic program and curriculum review, especially of those requirements that did not work as smoothly as they could. A new chair who was interested in clarifying the field studies requirement and other program requirements for the major and minor promoted a critical discussion and reshaping of the requirement. Critical to this was the sharing among faculty of their individual efforts with off-campus course offerings and research/creative production. The contributions of three individual faculty were especially useful: one an urban planner (who involved high school students and other community members in regular university courses which mapped "assets" of their communities), another in public mural art (developed in collaboration with communities), and a third who taught courses on labor (with strong participation of labor unions and organizations), as well as creatively teaching off-campus courses.

In 2001–2002, the discussions distilled service-learning aspects of the pedagogy within the department, provided a plan for strategic use of resources (e.g., the need and assignment of a teaching assistant if enrollments grew past 20 per class who could assist in the community partner collaborations), and partnership with on-campus partners (the Center for Community Learning) and off-campus partners (identifying and listing them to formalize the connections). In 2002–2003, the department offered a course to satisfy the service-learning requirement, and submitted the forms to establish it as a regular catalog upper-division course. The department also proceeded to change the requirement name from field studies to service-learning in the catalog. Student demand for the course, which was taught by the department chair, necessitated scheduling it every quarter during the academic year. Even students who were not Chicana and Chicano studies majors were attracted to the course based on its title and their desire to have a "structured" service experience.

The support and guidance of the Center for Community Learning was especially helpful. They contributed resources for the teaching assistants, contacts with community partners, forms for the documentation and evaluation of the service-learning, and, perhaps most importantly, introduced us to the national movement in civic engagement. The department was nominated and encouraged to apply to attend a summer institute for engaged departments sponsored by Campus Compact. In June 2002, the department chair, two faculty members, a community partner, and the director of the Center for Community Learning all participated in the institute. It was an opportunity to meet other faculty and administrators involved in the higher education service-learning movement and provided an intensive planning process to set new goals for engagement in the curriculum. The UCLA members who attended the institute established the following goals.

Definition of civic engagement. Civic engagement includes political, economic, and social activities that contribute to the self-determination, betterment, and social justice of Chicana/Chicano, Latina/Latino people.

Goals as an engaged (collaborative) department.
- Expand the institutionalization of service-learning within the department.
- Improve the capacity to implement service-learning.
- Formalize relationships with community partners.
- Increase effectiveness of faculty communication.
- Increase effectiveness of communication with community partners.

Action plan.
- Analyze courses with a community-based component.
- Create the Barrio Service-Learning course for major requirement.
- Develop criteria for service-learning courses.
- Formalize relationships with community partners.
- Formalize procedures for merit review.
- Dedicate instructional staff for service-learning coordination.

Activities addressing community partners' issues.
- Inventory current community partners.
- Conduct site visits (one-on-one meetings) with current and proposed partners.
- Develop written agreements for partnerships, including roles, responsibilities, and expectations.
- Develop a process for ongoing communication and feedback.
- Convene an annual meeting for the Community Partner Council.

Activities addressing faculty issues.
- Mentor junior faculty in service-learning pedagogy.
- Develop formal recognition of service-learning pedagogy within personnel review process.
- Establish new methods for effective communication among faculty members.
- Investigate faculty needs and incentives to engage in service-learning.

Activities addressing department chair's issues.
- Investigate the motivation and commitment of faculty to service-learning pedagogy.
- Host a statewide service-learning conference of Chicana/ Chicano studies departments.
- Work with National Association for Chicana and Chicano Studies to organize sessions on service-learning during national conferences.

Activities addressing student issues.
- Include and involve students in planning service-learning.
- Assess data on service-learning outcomes and satisfaction with current service-learning placements.
- Involve students in identifying and selecting community partners.
- Develop collaborative preparation to orient students to the service-learning, community partners, and neighborhoods.

The institute planning was very useful for the UCLA team because it allowed us to look forward in implementing and broadening service-learning within the departmental curriculum and to consider civic engagement more broadly within the academic program and the campus.

Analysis
How Do We Know We've Arrived?

We monitor our involvement in service-learning and our becoming a stronger engaged department in several different ways.

Impact on students. We see an increase in sustained engagement after service-learning course requirements are met, including enrollment in other service-learning courses, AmeriCorps membership, volunteering outside of class, and the selection of public service careers or graduate programs.

Comments made by students in the evaluation of the Barrio Service-Learning course are typical of those made about service-learning courses throughout the department. Examples include: "Barrio Service-learning is a chance to grow, not a way to fulfill a major and get units." "These last ten weeks have provided a life lesson, enabling me to become a better-rounded individual as I now view the world through a more enlightened lens." "The first day of class we were asked what we planned to give and take from this class and the service-learning. As of now, I have definitely taken more than I have given." "Not only have I had the opportunity to explore the legal realm, which highly interests me, but also I have learned the importance of sharing knowledge because that enables community members to fight for justice."

Impact on faculty. Faculty have more clearly outlined course learning goals and more techniques for implementing service-learning. They have had many opportunities for syllabus development assistance. There is now a department web site that includes service-learning, civic engagement, community-based research, and involvement in initiatives on civic engagement within the University of California System and statewide through California Campus Compact.

Impact on department. There is now much better support of the service-learning requirement and shared responsibility for the placements in identified community agencies. Also, the department has much help setting mutual guidelines for the work and general expectations of all participants.

We monitor the impact on the various constituents by tracking enrollments in designated service-learning courses; we investigate why students are taking these courses; we examine evaluations of the courses and instructors; we host meetings with community partners and employ an inductive Freirean approach to seminar interactions; and we evaluate the "products" associated with the placements. We also monitor a department-wide impact by tracking the number of courses with service-learning components, feedback from faculty and students on the value of these courses, and collaborations with the Center for Community Learning, University Extension, the Labor Center, and others.

Impact on community partners. We look to see if our departmental relations are stabilized. We also regularly query our community partners about their teaching roles and their perceptions about the university. One of our community partners, the Instituto De Educación Popular Del Sur De California (IDEPSCA), recently told us that the "Barrio Service-Learning program has worked closely with IDEPSCA in providing workshops around leadership development, wage claims, work injuries, and labor rights, as well as presidential campaigns. The Barrio Service-Learning program has been vital to IDEPSCA's mission of educating and raising awareness about issues that affect our community."

Impact on institution. The accomplishments of the department would not have been possible without a high degree of institutional support for this work. The Engaged Department Institute coincided with the launch of the UCLA chancellor's "UCLA in LA" initiative and the appointment of a new associate vice chancellor for community partnerships. About the same time, the college renamed the current Center for Community Learning and changed its reporting line to the vice provost for undergraduate education within the College of Letters, Arts, and Sciences, instead of to the Office of Instructional Development within the library. The executive leadership of the campus made it possible for bold moves to take place, enabling the department to integrate the best practices of the field with the curriculum goals of the discipline.

In 2003–2004, the UCLA Academic Senate reviewed and approved new policies on academic standards for service-learning courses and is beginning to expand the commitment to community-based research for undergraduates. This policy also created an "SL" course designation, used as a suffix for courses that meet the service-learning standards. Chicana/Chicano studies was the first department at UCLA to have an SL-designated course. Faculty leadership from all corners of the campus is beginning to work on changing the culture of research and teaching to include engaged scholarship.

The changes at UCLA were echoed on other campuses within the University of California, resulting in a systemwide symposium on civic engagement in June 2005. Cohosted by the provost of the University of California and the California Campus Compact, this event was attended by nearly 90 campus representatives, including the University of California president. The UCLA associate vice chancellor for community partnerships spoke about the national movement to integrate civic engagement into higher education and the need for institutional leadership to build a capacity for such integration. All of the UC campuses sent deans, chairs, and faculty members to this historic event for the express purposes of creating a plan for advancing civic engagement in the University of California System. Chicana/Chicano studies offered expertise and contributed to the vision for deeper and broader engagement as a department.

Vision

By 2010, the department will no doubt have more courses with service-learning components using the standardized criteria approved by the UCLA Academic Senate in their policy on academic standards for internships and service-learning courses. The department faculty will regularly participate as campus leaders to showcase their work as an engaged department to other department chairs and faculty. There will be a series of faculty development events, hosted by the Center for Community Learning, that will provide opportunities for further innovation and creativity for infusing community-based work into teaching and research.

The UCLA Center for Community Learning introduced the department to the California Campus Compact project Graduate Study in Civic Engagement at Research Universities in California. A spring 2006 conference at Stanford University will feature discussions about civic engagement in graduate programs. The Department of Chicana and Chicano Studies will be represented as it seeks to gain approval for graduate programs that include student and faculty engagement in the communities of Los Angeles.

The Center for Community Learning, the Chicana/Chicano studies department, and other academic departments at UCLA will continue to participate in and hopefully lead various University of California system-wide civic engagement activities.

References

Astin, A. W., Vogelgesang, L. J., Ikeda, E. K., & Yee, J. E. (2000). *How service-learning affects students.* Los Angeles, CA: University of California, Los Angeles, Higher Education Research Institute.

Bringle, R. G., & Hatcher, J. A. (2002, Fall). Campus-community partnerships: The terms of engagement. *Journal of Social Issues, 58(3),* 503–516.

Ramakrishnan, S. K., & Baldassare, M. (2004). *The ties that bind: Changing demographics and civic engagement in California.* San Francisco, CA: Public Policy Institute of California.

About the Authors

Reynaldo F. Macías is professor of Chicana and Chicano studies, education, and applied linguistics at the University of California, Los Angeles, and has served as chair of the university's César E. Chávez Center for Interdisciplinary Instruction since January 1999. He is the founding chair of the Department of Chicana and Chicano Studies established in 2004–2005. He served as the national chair of the National Association for Chicana and Chicano Studies, 2004–2006.

Kathy O'Byrne was appointed director of the University of California, Los Angeles Center for Community Learning in 2001–2002. She was the recipient of the 2004 California Campus Compact Richard E. Cone Award for Excellence and Leadership in Cultivating Community Partnerships in Higher Education. Her current research interests include civic engagement and research universities and the development of undergraduate community-based research in service-learning courses.

14

From Engagement to Marriage: A Systems Perspective With Formal and Durable Commitments to Service-Learning

Michael G. Laurent, Judith J. McIntosh,
Rie Rogers Mitchell

Increasing our department's participation in service-learning has been a worthwhile adventure that has had a significant impact on department faculty, students, and community partners. This chapter discusses the steps we have taken, within a systems perspective, to move from an engaged department to a more committed, married one. To introduce our involvement with service-learning, we offer a statement and a vignette from two graduate students.

In reflecting on her service-learning experience, a graduate student in counseling said,

> I now realize I had come from a very sheltered background. I wouldn't have really learned everything I needed to from just reading books. I did my fieldwork in a community where the people were so different from me, ethnically and culturally. It just wasn't for college credit. It changed my life!

We often hear similar comments when students have felt successful in bridging cultural and economic differences in genuine and meaningful ways.

Not long ago, a student was struggling to find a way to relate to the often nonverbal participants in a program for homeless people, where she was placed as a counseling intern. She had been unsuccessful in interesting the participants in having counseling sessions with her. One day, as her mind wandered back to a previous semester, she remembered how deeply she had been touched by an art therapy demonstration that an invited speaker (an agency counselor) had given in her child therapy class. It made her wonder if her homeless clients might feel the same way she did. So, with some trepidation, she brought in a roll of butcher paper the next time she went to the shelter, slowly unfurled it on the floor of the commons room, and began to draw using marking pens. On the first day only one person joined her, but he whispered that he loved to draw bridges. The next time, that man was back and several others joined in, adding their marks and designs to the daily mural. Each time the student came back with her butcher paper and markers (and later paint), the man who loved to draw bridges returned and each time more people appeared, some just watching, others vigorously involved. As time went on, the murals became brighter and less disjointed, and sometimes they even had an integrated theme. However, what most delighted the student was that the participants began to relate to each other! At first, communication was nonverbal—through body movement and sometimes through a color or line drawing. Then participants began to comment about the art activity with a word or short sentence. They also began to talk with her with increasing ease.

The student is still actively involved in using art techniques with homeless individuals. She has moved from viewing homelessness as an abstract concept to personally knowing the toll homelessness exacts on a human being. She doesn't know if she'll continue to work with homeless people throughout her career, but she is now a more knowledgeable individual who will always be interested in the treatment and support of homeless individuals and families.

A Transformative Experience

Throughout the past decade, service-learning experiences for graduate students in the Department of Educational Psychology and

Counseling at California State University, Northridge (CSUN) have advanced from a traditional fieldwork model, where students sit in an office and counsel individual clients, to a wide array of professional development experiences. Students, faculty, and community partners collaborate to serve and transform both the organizations and the children, youth, and families.

For example, at the Mitchell Family Counseling Clinic (a department-based counseling center created to serve the mental health needs of low-income families and individuals living in the diverse San Fernando Valley), faculty members partner with the CSUN Center for Community Service-Learning to recruit and supervise department "marriage and family" students. The students serve as MOSAIC Mentors (Mentoring to Overcome Struggles and Inspire Courage) for at-risk youth in local after-school programs operated by the Los Angeles Police Department or in cooperation with the Los Angeles County Probation Department or other community agencies serving youths in gangs or in danger of gang affiliation. These boys and girls are often victims of divorce, bullying, abuse, family violence, and other traumatic experiences. In another special program, graduate students trained by a community partner lead parent-child groups for children with anger management problems; graduate students are now involved in starting similar programs at local elementary schools.

However, even with the department's strong commitment to service-learning, it was not until a five-member team of department faculty attended a weeklong Engaged Department Institute in July 2003, sponsored by the California State University (CSU) System, that we began to conceptualize how service-learning could become a truly coordinated, department-wide initiative.

At this institute, we drew up preliminary plans for a department-wide, coordinated service-learning model. This model was developmentally oriented; that is, as students moved through their professional training in identified partnership agencies and schools, the model was designed so that students' experiences would become increasingly more complex and challenging, progressively enhancing their skills, knowledge, and contributions to the community. According to this plan, students would culminate this developmental model (and their graduate work) with a significant civic engagement project that would "make a difference" in the lives of clients and students in partnered agencies and/or transform the practices and policies of those who provide services to individuals, families, schools, organizations, or community.

By the conclusion of the five-day Institute, we were aware that we had taken giant steps toward becoming an "engaged" department. To us, and still with most of the general public, the word *engagement* refers to a social and cultural contract to a future marriage and a permanent partnership. However, the term also increasingly refers to a philosophy and call to action for an equal partnership between educators and the community. We felt that we could combine both of these definitions and, if we could implement an egalitarian, collaborative, and comprehensive relationship between the department and community, we would then proceed with a more formal symbol of commitment, one that might be considered a "marriage" between the participants in service-learning rather than just an "engagement."

This chapter describes how we moved from becoming "engaged" to entering a "marriage" (albeit a developing marriage), involving most department faculty members and other faculty in the college. To provide a context for this movement, the next three sections describe the type of environment or system (or family background) in which this engagement and marriage occurred, including the research that influenced our systematic perspective during this process.

Demographics: California State University, Northridge

California State University, Northridge, one of the largest of the 23 campuses in the California State University System, is located approximately 25 miles northwest of central Los Angeles, in the northern San Fernando Valley, a suburb with a multiethnic population of more than 1.8 million people. In fall 2004, the university enrolled more than 31,000 students (23,200 FTEs) of which approximately two-thirds are ethnic minorities, immigrants, and/or international students. More than 1,800 faculty serve in eight colleges that offer baccalaureate degrees in 59 disciplines and master's degrees in 41 fields.

The "Valley" is a hybrid of affluence and extreme poverty. State and county programs for homeless individuals, at-risk children and families, and substance-addicted persons abound; yet gangs, violence, domestic battering, drug and alcohol abuse, and self-injury are of significant proportions in all strata of the population.

The Center for Community Service-learning, established in 1998, is an important part of the university's mission, which emphasizes the value of alliances with community partners. Currently, students in approximately 60 classes per semester now perform a wide variety of education, outreach activities, direct aid, or public policy analysis and research in community settings.

Department of Educational Psychology and Counseling

The Department of Educational Psychology and Counseling is one of six departments in the Michael D. Eisner College of Education. Primarily a graduate department, it offers three master's degrees and seven options. The 30-unit Master of Arts degree in education/educational psychology has two options: early childhood education and development or learning, and instruction. The 60-unit Master of Science degree in counseling has five options: career counseling, college counseling and student services, marriage and family therapy, school counseling, and school psychology. The third degree is a Master of Science in genetic counseling offered in conjunction with the biology and special education departments. With completion of state requirements, graduates are eligible for various professional licenses and credentials. Many graduates continue their education into doctoral programs and also develop post-master's specializations. They are often leaders in their fields. As the university's second largest graduate department, approximately 200 master's candidates are admitted each fall. Over one-half of the graduate students are ethnic minorities, immigrants, and/or international students.

The faculty and staff are committed to a student-centered teaching and learning approach. Our programs strive to prepare students for highly effective, ethical, and satisfying professional careers as educators, counselors, psychotherapists, and psychologists, while instilling in our graduates a sense of civic engagement—a commitment to serve all people regardless of economic status or ethnicity and to influence the way in which these services are delivered to ensure access and equity. Therefore, we seek to provide students with a wide range of service-learning opportunities so they can learn to effectively work with diverse individuals, groups, and/or families with a range of issues at varying locations. Department programs and a faculty of 20 full-time and 50 part-time members have achieved national recognition for program design, scholarship, professional leadership, and teaching excellence.

Processes
Systems Thinking: Promises and Persistent Challenges

The research on systems theory was important in helping us conceptualize how to implement a coordinated, department-wide developmental service-learning model within an already existing system—the department structure.

Most family therapists receive training that includes a systems approach, a perspective evolving since the 1940s, originally focused on trying to organize and explain the structure and functioning of mechanical and biological units. Such an approach can also relate to communication systems that exist for an engaged department. A systems perspective or systems thinking views situations in broader contexts of interrelationships and tries to probe into longer-range implications as well as more immediate effects of actions and relationships. It requires viewing a person, situation, or organization in relation to a full range of its internal components and the external factors, stakeholders, and trends with which it interacts. As Senge (1990) put it:

> Systems thinking is a discipline for seeing wholes. It is a framework for seeing interrelationships rather than things, for seeing a pattern of change rather than static "snapshots." It is a set of general principles distilled over the course of the twentieth century, spanning fields as diverse as the physical and social sciences, engineering, and management. And systems thinking is a sensibility for the subtle interconnectedness that gives living systems their unique character. (pp. 68–69)

Walsch and McGraw (2002) state that systems approaches to personality and counseling are qualitatively different from individual and psychological approaches. Compton and Galaway (1999) used the term *ecomap* to diagram a family's connection to larger social systems. However, Corey (2005) expressed that while the seeds of this movement were planted more than 60 years ago, it has been very difficult for Western counselors and therapists to make effective use of the systems perspective. Nevertheless, Goldenberg and Goldenberg (2004) found that early pioneers did provide valuable ways to look at how a system communicates, offering new concepts that involved feedback loops, a focus shift from content to process, a free sharing of information, and attempts to look at the community at large.

Historical Participation in Service-Learning

The Department of Educational Psychology and Counseling sponsors various programs that serve the community and are also service-learning sites for CSUN students. As part of their closely supervised service-learning experience, many graduate students provide counseling, consulting, assessment, mentoring, training, and teaching services through various department-run community programs.

Valley Trauma Center. This nonprofit, multicultural organization is dedicated to the elimination of sexual and interpersonal violence through healing, empowerment, and increased public awareness of prevention strategies. Staff and service-learning students work with individuals and communities to provide quality crisis intervention and counseling services, training, and prevention education to promote social change.

Family System Service. This large program, instituted by the Valley Trauma Center, provides intensive in-home services to families with the goal of coordinating multidisciplinary services in the community to alleviate and/or prevent abuse and neglect.

Mitchell Family Counseling Clinic. This on-campus agency is dedicated to serving the mental health and development needs of adults, children, couples, and families in the community. It builds satellite programs in the community, such as the Samaritan Center for homeless individuals, Gault Street Elementary School, and Magnolia Science Academy, and serves as a training, research, and support facility for graduate students in counseling programs.

Early Childhood Education Consulting Program. Through this program, graduate students and faculty work together as consultants in partnership with early childhood programs in the community to build curriculum, develop staff, enhance programs, improve management, and support the development of early childhood programs.

Analysis: Moving From "Mine" to "Ours"

After returning from the transformative experience of the CSU Engaged Department Institute, the five participants were enthusiastic about implementing a developmental service-learning model that would culminate in a civic engagement project. However, we still had to convince other department faculty members to join with our idea. We decided to present our ideas at the department faculty retreat in fall 2003.

To most faculty members at the retreat, service-learning was not a new idea (although some viewed service-learning as only fieldwork and this had to be clarified). However, two proposals were new: 1) that service-learning needed to be integrated into the graduate curriculum across the options, and 2) that service-learning needed to be viewed within a developmental frame—students would start service-learning in one of the prerequisite courses (child and adolescent development), followed by increasing participation in service-learning each semester (i.e., for either two or four semesters, depending on the number of units required for the master's degree), and culminating for most students in a civic engagement project.

Although the proposals received relatively little resistance, we were aware that the faculty's enthusiasm did not match ours. This did not surprise us because they had not been involved in the same process we had experienced at the CSU Engaged Department Institute. On the other hand, curriculum for most of the options was already designed for cohorts that moved developmentally through their program (i.e., courses were built on foundations laid out in previous courses and became more complex as students progressed through the semesters). Therefore, a developmental service-learning model could be instituted easily, and it seemed that the coordinators of each of the options were supportive of doing that. In addition, initiating service-learning into the prerequisite course had already been accomplished before the institute. One of the team members at the CSU Engaged Department Institute had previously received a grant to add a service-learning component to the prerequisite course in child and adolescent development. However, it was not until we attended the institute that we conceptualized this course as leading to service-learning experiences in the master's programs. Although our presentation was well accepted by faculty, it was clear that there were diverse levels of understanding of and commitment to full service-learning integration into the curriculum.

Impact: Transforming Partnerships

During 2002–2003, faculty members, especially those in the marriage and family therapy (MFT) option, began to discuss how to increase effectiveness in organizing and identifying partnerships. The MFT option is a two- and one-half year full-time program, the largest within the department, with an average of 200 students enrolled at any given time. Before graduation, students are required to complete a minimum of 600 hours at nonprofit service-learning sites under the supervision of a licensed marriage and family therapist, clinical social worker, psychologist, or psychiatrist. Students continue earning hours after graduation for a total of 3,000 hours before they can qualify for state board examinations and eventual licensure.

In response to the need for a more fully integrated service-learning program, the department hired a part-time service-learning coordinator in 2003. The department coordinator's role is to 1) build partnerships with community organizations to ensure the professional quality and appropriateness of fieldwork placement sites; 2) engage community organizations to join with faculty in a more expanded role as co-educators in the learning of graduate students; 3) act as a liaison among MFT students, faculty, and community organizations, and 4) develop an approved service-learning site list as a resource for MFT students.

Almost immediately, the coordinator conducted a student survey to identify and gather information about community organizations that were currently providing placements for MFT students. She found that students were placed at nearly 60 sites drawn from an area of approximately 30 by 70 miles around the university. Most students reported satisfaction with their placement, with only a few reporting unresolved issues with the site. From this survey, she compiled a list of active community organizations as a starting point in the development of an approved partnership list.

Later that year, the coordinator and an MFT faculty member contacted community organizations and began discussing the formation of a formal partnership arrangement. These organizations were brought together at a Partners in Supervision luncheon hosted by the department. The purpose of the meeting was to initiate a dialogue between faculty and community organizations, as well as among the community organizations themselves; introduce the concept of service-learning and how it relates to the traditional MFT fieldwork model; and invite the organizations to work with the faculty as field-based members of the teaching faculty. Representatives from 19 organizations participated. Overall, attendees were enthusiastic about engaging in more intimate partnering with the department and were especially interested in finding ways to aggregate resources.

Fortunately, the department's newly hired service-learning coordinator had joined the team that attended the Engaged Department Institute. There, she learned about various CSU initiatives, including one to support risk management personnel on each campus. Campus-based risk management personnel utilized this information to review and revise documents, and a new service-learning agreement was developed.

An outcome of the coordinator's work was the creation of the "Community Partner Guide: MFT Fieldwork and Service-learning," which introduces CSU service-learning as it relates to MFT fieldwork, gives information about MFT student coursework and fieldwork requirements, introduces new and revised forms, and provides requirements and instructions for inclusion in the department-approved service-learning site list. The guide also serves as a vehicle for making contact with community organizations that did not attend the Partners in Supervision meeting. In addition, all mutually approved partnership sites were placed on the department web site.

We are excited about working with our formally identified partners. It feels as though we have increased the number of our faculty dedicated to service-learning and that we have even more people and resources on our team to help educate our students. These are people we know and trust, and who share new ideas and energy concerning how to meet real community needs.

Connecting to Other Departmental Initiatives

In addition to the MFT program, other curricular options within the department have developed strong models of collaboration with community partners. For example, school counseling students are involved from the beginning of their program to the end in developmental, school-based service-learning and civic engagement activities. School psychology students become active participants in service-learning activities in their second year of training. By the third year, they are nearly full-time participants at school sites. Graduate students in the first year of the college counseling and student services master's option mentor CSUN first-year students in freshman experience courses to improve retention and graduation. Later in their program, these students participate in service-learning experiences at community colleges and universities throughout the Los Angeles area. Career counseling students are placed in diverse education, business, government, and industry sites. Students in early childhood education are involved in developing curricula, managing programs, and creating new methods of teaching and learning for public school sites.

Vision: Engagement or Marriage?

In writing this chapter, we kept two questions before us: 1) Are we a very engaged department or can we now consider ourselves married? 2) Do we have permanent, committed relationships—ones in which we are still actively pursing ways to interact more effectively and enrich the relationships—or are these impermanent relationships with inadequate energy or commitment to proceed further?

By early 2006, we believed that the department had progressed to a new marriage relationship, with more yet to be accomplished. We have an official and contractual relationship with many of our partners through our service-learning agreements, and we have established stable, egalitarian relationships with a wide range of community organizations. Further, CSUN faculty and many of our partners are excited and committed to discovering new ways to communicate and develop our relationships. We believe our marriage has a promising future.

References

Compton, B. R., & Galaway, B. (1999). *Social work processes* (6th ed.). Pacific Grove, CA: Brooks/Cole.

Corey, G. (2005). *Theory and practice of counseling and psychotherapy* (7th ed.). Pacific Grove, CA: Brooks/Cole.

Goldenberg, I., & Goldenberg, H. (2004). *Family therapy: An overview* (6th ed.). Pacific Grove: Brooks/Cole.

Senge, P. M. (1990). *The fifth discipline: The art and practice of the learning organization*. New York, NY: Doubleday.

Walsch, W. M., & McGraw, J. A. (2002). *Essentials of family therapy: A structured summary of nine approaches*. Denver, CO: Love.

About the Authors

Michael G. Laurent is an assistant professor at California State University, Northridge. He is both a licensed psychologist and a licensed marriage and family therapist with extensive experience providing mental health assistance to African-American and Latino community members in greater Los Angeles.

Judith J. McIntosh is a licensed marriage and family therapist and clinic administrator for the Mitchell Family Counseling Clinic, a community-based counseling clinic at California State University, Northridge. She also serves as the service-learning coordinator in the Department of Educational Psychology and Counseling.

Rie Rogers Mitchell is professor and chair of the Department of Educational Psychology and Counseling at California State University, Northridge, where she received the Distinguished Teaching Award. As a licensed psychologist, she specializes in therapeutic work with children. She is coauthor of *Sandplay: Past, Present and Future* (Routledge, 1994).

15

Continuums of Engagement at Portland State University: An Institution-Wide Initiative to Support Departmental Collaboration for the Common Good

Kevin Kecskes, Amy Spring

We all need food. Where does that food come from? How do we access it? Who might not be getting enough to eat, and what are children being served in our public school lunch programs? These are some of the questions educators, urban planners, linguists, natural scientists, and community health faculty, among others, have been jointly considering and acting on at Portland State University (PSU) since 2004.

Today, there are many visible outcomes on campus that have been inspired and supported by this faculty, staff, student, and community partner work group, such as a community garden and a sustainable café that specializes in serving locally grown organic foods. Also, new science and civics courses have been developed and select curricula relating to food systems have been translated into several different languages. Moreover, strong partnerships have been formed with more than a dozen Portland Public Schools to create school-based edible gardens involving hundreds of undergraduate and graduate students and thousands of school children. Grants have been written and received, with more planned, and a community-wide vision for sustainable community food systems is beginning to emerge. Indeed, synergy within and among departments focusing on the common public issue of food is continuing to transform teaching, research, and service on campus and in the community.

These accomplishments would not have happened were it not for PSU's intentional choice in 2001 to make a strategic institutional commitment to support entire departments (versus individual faculty) in community-based work. This chapter highlights key parts of the story, shares results from ongoing research, and offers some lessons we have learned along the way to help create and support engaged departments.

At Portland State University, a university known internationally for its deep commitment to promoting civic engagement through active teaching, learning, and research partnerships, this level of intra- and interdepartmental collaboration suggests that there is a healthy return on more than a decade of investment in faculty, organizational, and institutional development. But it has not always been like this. In this chapter we will 1) briefly explore PSU's history and context for supporting and sustaining service-learning (known on campus as community-based learning, or CBL), as well as other civic engagement strategies; 2) highlight the rationale and program design for PSU's institution-wide effort to support departmental engagement; 3) share emerging research findings from our continuing efforts to ascertain what is happening and what works within departments; and 4) discuss recommendations and provide short examples and conclusions useful to chairs, faculty, and administrators who are interested in increasing unit coherence focused on the public purposes of disciplines.

Civic Engagement at Portland State University: A Brief History

In the early 1990s, PSU was in a morale and fiscal crisis. The Oregon University System was in the middle of long-term funding reductions for higher education, freshman retention rates were low, with approximately 75% leaving college or transferring to another institution, and frustration with the existing undergraduate general education curriculum was high (Davidson, 1997; Davidson, Holland, Kaiser, & Reardon, 1996).

Campus faculty and leaders responded to this crisis with a scholarly approach. A faculty working group was selected to investigate current research on effective teaching, learning, student retention, and the changing nature of postsecondary education. Their findings recommended to the faculty senate that 1) the traditional distribution model for undergraduate education was not as effective as an integrated model that aligned university-wide curricular strategies with emerging research findings pertaining to effective adult education (Barr & Tagg, 1995), 2) higher education must respond to Portland's critical needs in a time of economic crisis (Holland, 2001), and 3) pedagogy must become more student-centered, focusing on active learning methodologies. Initial efforts led to the development of small learning communities, an approach that blurred the boundaries between the university and the community (Davison, Kerrigan, & Agre-Kippenhan, 1999).

In the span of just a few years, community-based learning became one of the central pedagogies of PSU's new general education curriculum, known as University Studies. As early-adopter faculty returned to their home departments after a few terms of teaching in University Studies, many active teaching and learning methodologies—especially community-based learning—began to spread to courses in the majors across the institution (Kecskes, Kerrigan, & Patton, in press). This was a natural progression for PSU given its clear and consistent history of community connection and access since its founding soon after World War II. Thus PSU's propensity toward community engagement garnered additional legitimacy and became more intentional with the general education reform process and resultant development of the University Studies program.

At PSU, the development of service-learning and other civic engagement strategies continue to be a "'process of accretion'; that is, it builds upon what has gone before" (Driscoll, 1998, p. 150).

Figure 15.1. Pathways for Civic Engagement at PSU

From the outset, the university adopted a wide understanding of its role in society. In the 1990s, when PSU focused attention on its urban role and mission, campus leaders adopted the broad language of *community-university partnerships,* recognizing service-learning as an important curricular integration strategy, but not as the entire partnership building enterprise. Today, leaders commonly use *civic engagement* language to capture the attention and continue to quantify the diverse community-focused activities of faculty and staff. Figure 15.1 illustrates the multiple pathways to engagement commonly understood at PSU today. Maintaining this broad focus invites faculty to connect with their department's engagement agenda via one of several possible pathways. Helping members of academic units realize and remember that they *can* be part of an engaged department agenda and do so without necessarily using service-learning methodologies is a key strategy for success. Many faculty, for example, have used community-based research as an engagement strategy for years and are often enthusiastic to connect their work with departmental colleagues.

Portland State University's collective understanding of the diverse forms of community engagement continues to expand. Concomitantly, the locus of activity has widened to accommodate partnership building activities worldwide. Many partnerships, unfortunately, remain invisible to those not directly involved. Therefore, in an institutional effort to more fully understand and make PSU community partnerships more transparent on a global scale, the Center for Academic Excellence (CAE) is beginning to track partnerships on a new PSU community partnership map. This database-driven web site utilizes emerging geographical information systems (GIS) technology to spatially display PSU's community-university partnerships worldwide. Making partnerships more transparent via this new web interface has begun to help various constituents recognize, utilize, and leverage the multiple relationships that exist. Given that PSU is engaged in more than 1,000 partnerships worldwide, this has been a daunting and exciting project (see www.partner.pdx.edu). Clearly, the process of accretion continues at Portland State University.

Before we discuss PSU's specific engaged department work, it may be helpful to know how we approach professional development work through our Center for Academic Excellence. The CAE is centrally located and reports both to the Office of Academic Affairs and to the Office of the President. When first established in the early 1990s, the CAE approached faculty development in the same way most teaching and learning centers on campuses nationwide did: We worked with individual faculty in traditional areas, such as syllabus and portfolio development. However, unlike other development centers, the CAE's charge is not only to support faculty in these more traditional ways, but also to integrate assessment and community engagement strategies into teaching and research activities and ultimately into the core of university life. The faculty development efforts of the CAE, therefore, support the ongoing transformation of PSU into a more deeply engaged campus. Thus the CAE employs an integrated

Figure 15.2. Portland State University's Development Model

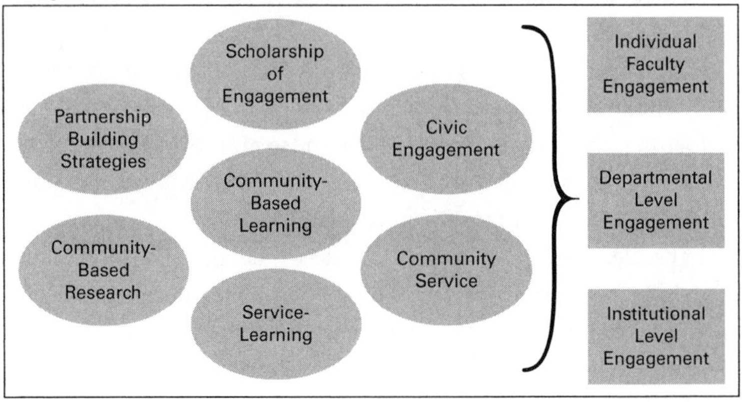

approach to pedagogy, assessment, and community engagement that supports faculty, students, and community partners on multiple levels simultaneously. These levels are conceptually organized in the following manner: Level I programming initiatives focus on supporting faculty at the micro or individual level. Level II activities are typically more collective in scope and focus on working at the small-group cohort or meso level. The Engaged Department Initiative, according to this schema, is a level II activity. Level III activities focus on institutional support and transformation largely directed at the macro level. Figure 15.2 diagrams how these three levels are integrated. For a longer discussion on how professional development centers can support and sustain university engagement efforts, including numerous programmatic examples from each level, see Kecskes, Spring, and Lieberman (2004).

From "Mine" to "Ours:" Rationale for a Department-Level Focus

For several years, one way that PSU has encouraged faculty participation in service-learning is by providing faculty with individual incentives that support and reward their efforts. One of the incentives administered by the CAE has been a competitive, peer-reviewed, small service-learning grant program. More than 250 faculty have received these grants for service-learning course development or enhancement over the past decade. This strategy has significantly facilitated the expansion of service-learning at PSU, and for this reason we continue to employ this strategy today. However, some PSU faculty have expressed concern that an individual grant focus sometimes requires them to be in direct competition with their departmental colleagues for these limited resources. They have also reported frustration with the lack of departmental resources to support their civic engagement work. Therefore, shifting to a departmental incentive strategy encourages individual faculty within units to work together and provides funds to help support the development of a sustainable departmental infrastructure for ongoing engagement.

The CAE has worked with 20 departments (see Table 15.1) since 2000. Not all units have participated each year for various reasons including changes in leadership, perception of lacking sufficient progress, perception of insufficient funding compared to the effort required, and insufficient unit cohesiveness to reach consensus on a collective agenda. We do *not* conclude that any unit demonstrating less than five years of participation is not committed to the work of engagement in its department. Some departments did not begin this work until the third year of the program, for example. Indeed, every unit that has participated in this program has reported utility regarding this collective approach. Most units have developed mechanisms to sustain this departmental approach.

Program Structure and Methods for Study

To extend the opportunity for participating in community engagement to all departments on campus, the Center for Academic Excellence determined that a competitive request for funding proposals was appropriate in support of the Engaged Department Initiative. To increase participation in obtaining this funding, center staff identified departments that had previously demonstrated

Table 15.1 Participating Departments in the Portland State
University Service-Learning Grant Program

Department	Number of Participating Years
Applied Linguistics	5
Art	5
Community Health	5
University Studies (General Education)	5
Urban Studies and Planning	5
Women's Studies	5
Geology	3
Political Science	3
Portland International Initiative for Leadership in Ecology, Culture and Learning (PIIECL)	3
Public Administration and Policy	3
Architecture	2
Center for Science Education	2
Education, Policy and Foundations	2
English	2
Foreign Languages and Literature	2
History	2
Mathematics	2
Physics	2
Psychology	2
School of Business	2

an interest in community-based learning and encouraged them to participate. The proposal guidelines prioritized project proposals that purposefully integrate community-based work into teaching and scholarship, develop community-based learning as a regular part of the academic content and expectations of a sequenced curriculum, and/or develop and implement plans for departmental coherence for engagement in scholarly and service activities. CAE's ongoing assessment of this project is based on five primary sources of evidence: annual reports from each participating department, poster displays created by each participating unit annually, collective meetings that bring all departmental grant recipients together, meetings between individual departmental teams and CAE program staff, and individual interviews. The findings and recommendations outlined in this chapter build on an initial study of PSU's engaged department program conducted after one year of implementation (see Kecskes, Gelmon, & Spring, 2006).

Findings: What Have We Learned?

The CAE Community-University Partnership division at PSU is in its fifth year of implementation of the Engaged Department Initiative. The lessons learned fall into three broad categories: general insights, central development office programmatic strategies, and successful unit-level strategies.

General Insights

- *Keep definitions and expectations broad.* Reminding faculty that service-learning is just one of many civic engagement strategies is helpful. It is important for a departmental cohort to remember that many in the unit can be engaged in attempting to address a specific social issue and perhaps working with a small set of well-defined community partners over time, yet only some of the faculty may be using service-learning pedagogy. It can be a relief for some department members to know that they can still support unit-wide engagement but do not have to use service-learning methodologies. As noted in Figure 15.2, one alternative that faculty commonly employ is community-based research.
- *Ask foundational questions.* Generally, faculty, staff, students, and community partners gravitate toward technical interventions and quickly focus on questions concerning the mechanisms

of engagement (e.g., assignments, teaching strategies, etc.). For these interventions to have long-term, transformative impact, we have found that asking the largest-picture questions early on can help "place" unit-level engagement work in the broadest context and pique the imagination. Questions to consider asking might include: "What does (community or civic) engagement mean in discipline X?" From there, suggesting a departmental scan or mapping of engagement activities would be a logical next step. Or, "What are some current social issues that members of your department X are working on? What are some recent scholarly treatments from your field that address some of these issues?" Undergirding these inquiries is one of the most fundamental questions: "What is the public purpose of your discipline, and how might that manifest for you in your teaching and other scholarly activities?"

- *Systematic and/or organic program growth.* When initiating engagement efforts at the unit level, many departments attempt to take a systematic approach (e.g., taking a scan of all community-based activities associated within the department, aggregating results, etc.). However, other departments have taken an organic approach, building on faculty interests in unexpected and creative ways. See PSU's art department approach (Chapter 7) for a salient example. Several departments have used a simple planning matrix to define and track strategies and tasks (see Appendix A).

- *Internal politics and credibility.* Having a tenured, respected member of the department leading the engagement initiative will enhance credibility and traction within the department.

- *Chair leadership.* In units where the department chair wrote and submitted the engagement proposal, we see increased commitment to incorporating the effort throughout the curriculum. In many cases where the chair leads the effort, there are higher percentages of engaged faculty, increased numbers of opportunities to disseminate the work (especially publicly), and a higher number of courses in the curriculum that were revised and/or made permanent in the core curriculum.

- *Disciplines vary.* Civic engagement is defined differently across units, and the disciplinary influence of how it is defined, taught, and assessed should not be underestimated. Each discipline has a unique approach to defining its public purposes, and each has a distinct set of civic skills it values and specific scholarly reward systems in place.
- *Professional development needs change and grow.* As engagement work grows within a department, it increases the need for professional development activities that help participants understand how to effectively use engagement strategies.
- *Connect unit work to larger community agendas.* Intentionally recognizing the connections to and leveraging community-based learning and research agendas with broader community priorities can attract resources and quickly extend the reach of unitwide initiatives.

Centralized Programmatic Strategies

- *Common beginnings, endings celebration.* The following four strategies appear to be an efficient use of professional development staff and faculty time.

1) Hosting an initial meeting at the beginning of the year to help people become familiar with each of the projects.
2) Providing written material on each of the projects, including pertinent contact information, to the entire group.
3) Sponsoring and promoting an end-of-year poster session.
4) Conducting individual meetings with each of the teams.

- *False starts.* Convening multiple departmental engagement teams for a regular series of meetings seems to have less utility than we anticipated. There are wide differences between the departments and their associated initiatives, thus the meeting time is often spent on nonspecific, nontransferable discussion items.

We have found that limiting the number of cross-departmental meetings to two—one at the beginning of the year and one at the end—is the most effective use of staff and faculty time.

- *Maintain contact, assess.* Regular (two annual) meetings with chair and department leaders provides opportunities for participants to share ideas, define and summarize successes and challenges, troubleshoot, and help maintain focus.
- *Gather chairs.* Gathering the participating department chairs can help in developing cross-unit conversations about engagement activities, challenges and opportunities, and ways to collectively support deepening and expanding engagement work within departments.

Successful Departmental Strategies

- *Someone assumes responsibility.* There should be a point person in the department so those faculty who want to incorporate community projects into their work know who to contact for assistance. This point person should be an advocate for increasing the depth and number of the partnerships, not someone focused on his or her own individual scholarly agenda.
- *One (key) course at a time.* Some departments begin their engagement efforts by simply revising one critical course that is then set strategically in the disciplinary core curriculum to ensure that nearly all majors take it. This is a good start, but if the effort is not led by department leaders (i.e., the chair or a well-respected faculty member), then the single course is less likely to expand to include additional community-based course offerings in the departmental curriculum.
- *Specific theme or partner focus.* Several departments realized substantial success with unit-wide engagement by defining a (set of) partner(s) or a particular theme to focus their engagement work. This makes it easier for colleagues within the unit to understand how they might be able to connect to the work (e.g., PSU's women's studies department continues

to deepen relationships with three long-term partners, and the linguistics department works with a single elementary school). In both cases, additional faculty within the unit have been able to work with either the same partner or focus on the same common community issue. Having a defined set of community partners or a single theme for the partnership work allows students to work with the same partner or topic beyond a single course, over extended periods of time. This is a particularly useful strategy to address the persistent "problem of time" when deepening community-university partnerships (Wallace, 2000).

- *Take stock, innovate, communicate.* A series of meetings within the department can help those involved in engagement activities to connect, discuss innovations, share resources, and increase communication effectiveness across the unit (see Appendix B). Where this has occurred, we have seen increased numbers of faculty within the department participating, development of unit promotional materials to share with students about engagement activities, emergence of sequenced partnership activities throughout the department, development of engagement assessment rubrics to be used across courses, and increased collaboration between faculty and students in their courses.

What Difference Has This Made? PSU Departmental Success Stories

Department-wide engagement efforts, implemented well and sustained over time, can have powerful effects on faculty, students, community partners, and unit culture. PSU's art department has expanded and strengthened several community partnerships and now involves community partners in all faculty hiring processes (see Chapter 7). The following brief examples illustrate the positive effects of this initiative on several additional PSU departments.

Department of Applied Linguistics

The Department of Applied Linguistics is deeply engaged in several rich and long-established partnerships. For example, for many years the faculty has been working closely with Portland Community College as a community partner to run a large English as a Second Language (ESL) Lab School. The department also supports after-school and evening programs for parents and families in need of ESL services at several Portland public school sites. Coinciding with the advent of PSU's Engaged Department Initiative, in 2001 the Department of Applied Linguistics began substantially increasing its engagement activities with Atkinson Elementary School, a Title I school where 55% of its diverse student body qualifies for free or reduced lunch and where more than 40% of the students are English-language learners. The multifaceted engagement efforts of the applied linguistics department with Atkinson Elementary are supported by a faculty leader and involve eight faculty and more than 120 students per year.

Focusing their efforts on this one elementary school has intensified the contributions made to the organization and has allowed students and faculty to build on the experiences from previous classes because of the continuity of the partnership. One faculty member said,

> Having students in my Language Policy class work on a policy for a school that they had spent time in previously—where they knew some of the teachers, parents, and children—allowed them to develop agreements that reflected the culture of the school. Without this deeper understanding of the school that is a direct result of multiple experiences over time, we would not have been able to produce a policy that would have utility for the school.

One student reported that she worked with Atkinson Elementary initially in her Language and Society class where she completed a research project on the relationship of language, culture, and environment. For another class, she investigated the sustainability of cultures in relation to eating habitats and food sources. This research was used by Atkinson to develop a multicultural garden. The student ultimately completed her thesis project for her degree program in collaboration with Atkinson teachers and students.

A faculty member who is closely involved with the Atkinson community was selected to shepherd the partnership between the applied linguistics department and the elementary school. As faculty lead, the individual convened a meeting between unit faculty and the teachers at Atkinson. A joint visioning process inspired many ideas which later turned into classroom projects, research efforts, and practicum experiences for applied linguistics students and faculty. Without this unit-level point person to assume responsibility for brokering the partnership with the school, the number and scope of ideas that came to fruition would have been significantly limited.

Department of Women's Studies

The Department of Women's Studies has a long tradition of engaging its students in local activist initiatives. Individual scholars and community members have typically been involved as activists working on social justice issues. Given the existing commitment to community work in the unit, one might ask, How can this department possibly advance its engagement efforts? This department chose two foci: 1) improving communication within the unit about extant community connections, and 2) helping students develop civic competencies that enhance their ability to act as change agents in communities. Improving communication and becoming clear about student learning outcomes was the department's strategy to streamline the multiple engagement activities into a cohesive package, one that allowed students to have a sequential educational experience.

In the early 1990s, the department viewed its work in communities as unorganized, and the faculty felt uninformed about their colleagues' community-based work. What students were expected to learn and how their community-based experiences were to facilitate that learning was not clear within the unit. Students were involved in several community-based experiences without the means to connect these important but isolated projects across their various courses. Additionally, community partners were typically working with several different faculty on separated projects. The unit utilized the Department Engagement Initiative to discover, outline, and address as many of these issues as possible.

The department began by scheduling two retreats annually for two sequential years. These retreats focused on helping the faculty within the unit learn about others' activities and about how their teaching connected with various community organizations in the region to facilitate student learning. These unit retreats served to create a forum for faculty to share expertise and to deeply explore curriculum and pedagogical issues concerning civic education. The department also created a set of assessment benchmarks for students as they moved through the required women's studies courses. The benchmark identifies specific civic education learning goals appropriate to courses at each level from first year to senior year. Department faculty also explored how students move through the set of courses required of women's studies majors and developed a conceptual map of how students will build specific skills as they move through the curriculum. Faculty identified strategies for in-class activities, materials (e.g., readings, films), and community-based learning projects that build students' confidence in their ability to organize and educate others and to have an impact on public policy decisions. The women's studies department also decided to focus its engagement efforts on two community organizations. These two partners served as the primary partners for the entry-level courses offered to first-year students as well as to the senior-year students. Having these developmentally diverse students work with the same set of limited partners has simplified the partnership management required of these community agencies and augmented agency personnel understanding of the capacities, needs, and sensibilities of these undergraduates.

Portland International Initiative for Leadership in Ecology, Culture, and Learning (PIIECL)

PIIECL is an interdisciplinary graduate program in PSU's Graduate School of Education and the Mark O. Hatfield School of Government in the College of Urban and Public Affairs. PIIECL was established in 2002 to enhance sustainability education through a graduate degree in leadership in ecology, culture, and learning (LECL). By 2005, the program served 75 graduate students, offering a master's specialization in LECL, and a sustainability education specialization theme for doctoral students. Each year, hundreds of PSU undergraduate students are also involved in LECL course offerings. From its inception, this program has intentionally created a teaching and learning environment where students and faculty bridge theory and practice. Each PIIECL course requires that students engage with the community a minimum of 30 hours per 10-week term. PIIECL's research on edible learning gardens and sustainability education, as well as its outreach and publications, have earned wide recognition and grants from the U.S. Environmental Protection Agency and the city of Portland, among other sources. Due to its focus on multisensory and multicultural education, PIIECL engages the hands and hearts of students and faculty—through engagement in the community—as well as the mind—through academic research which is applied to local, bioregional, and global issues. PIIECL students, faculty, and partners keep an active scholarship and publication agenda and have published working papers, books, teacher guides, modules, and interviews in collaboration with scholars and practitioners. Since 2004, collaborative work has existed with Portland Public

Schools around learning gardens and food and garden-based ecological education. PIIECL also manages web sites (see: www. piiecl.pdx.edu and www.web.pdx.edu/~feed) used in local settings and employs resources from national and international arenas. Engagement in these departments touches the teaching, learning, and scholarship of faculty, students, and community partners.

School of Community Health and School of Urban Studies and Planning

This departmental engagement effort is a tripartite partnership among PSU's School of Community Health and the Nohad A. Toulan School of Urban Studies and Planning and the regional nonprofit organization Community Food Matters (CFM). These two academic units developed specific partnerships with CFM in order to engage faculty and students from their departments in community activities that address food systems throughout the region and state. The faculty associated with this initiative work with many different partners and are involved in projects and research related to local food systems. CFM plays an important role in helping faculty to develop partnerships with local farmers, food policymakers, and environmental and social service organizations. This engagement effort focuses on two complementary goals: 1) to introduce students to the theory and practice of community food systems, and 2) to teach many of the civic skills necessary to address two of Oregon's most pressing social issues—hunger and the urban-rural divide. Efforts to address both goals have been successful. For example, several courses have been revised to engage students in community-based learning. These revisions range from including a child and family studies (CFS) unit and associated readings into extant courses to fully redesigning community-based learning courses around the theme of CFS. Students from the two units collaborated to develop several community forums on supporting local food systems. Additionally, more than 40 faculty, adjunct faculty, and students involved in CFS teaching, research, and service have organized the food and community work group. This work group has developed a CFS-oriented web site and has reviewed food and community certificate and degree programs, institutes, centers, and policies at comparable institutions. First formally convened in 2005, this group has crafted a vision statement to guide programmatic efforts and has committed to working together to build PSU's effectiveness as a leader in service-learning and scholarship on food and community issues.

Recommendations

Based on four and a half years of programming to support departmental engagement as an institutional priority, the following insights emerge as recommendations to three distinct campus cohorts: senior academic officers, department chairs/faculty leaders, and community service directors/staff of service-learning or civic engagement offices.

Senior-Level Administrators

- *Institutionalize.* Central office support is critical. Budgetary allocation should be commensurate with the institutional impact that is desired.
- *Make it count.* Acknowledging and supporting the academic legitimacy and importance of this work can accelerate efforts. For example, PSU's (2004) promotion and tenure review guidelines state, "PSU highly values quality community outreach as part of faculty roles and responsibilities."
- *Shine the light.* Spotlight successes via formal and informal mechanisms (e.g., annual awards ceremonies, departmental meetings, incorporate messages into campus-wide communications such as newsletters, campus publications, etc.). Talk about these efforts in public meetings and speeches. Invite committed faculty to speak publicly about their work.
- *Incentives can work.* Provide resources especially to support release time for a faculty point person or other unit-wide staff

who have responsibility for supporting and tracking processes and outcomes.

- *Be a connector.* Assist faculty to see broad overlaps in understandings regarding community engagement so an increasing number of individuals recognize that they can be part of something larger while remaining faithful to their specific disciplinary understandings
- *Ask the right questions.* Continually remind everyone of the highest purposes of higher education. Ask how units are creating knowledge that builds healthy and safe local and worldwide communities. Support the best efforts with words, actions, and resources.

Department Chairs

- *Take stock, synergize.* Develop an inventory of extant engagement efforts among department faculty, staff, and students in the major (Kecskes, 2004).
- *Make time.* Provide regular time in departmental meetings to discuss and clarify terms, highlight successes, problem solve, and collaboratively plan for future unit-community partnership initiatives.
- *Notice, appreciate.* Notice and take advantage of success by spotlighting excellence in unit publications, and incorporate accomplishments into public relations materials.
- *Students as assets.* Identify and work with the most articulate students in the major so they can tell their stories to potential funders, other departments, and to future students in the major.
- *Find money.* (Re)allocate resources in support of a departmental point person.
- *Envision expanded community partner roles.* Provide regular opportunities for key community partners to collaborate on curriculum and program development. Invite them to partner on grants and to teach in your unit. Find ways to make at least a few of their recommendations come to fruition.

- *Evaluate.* Encourage and support documentation and assessment, both for continual improvement and as a future resource generation strategy.
- *Ask the right questions.* Unit leaders can encourage conversations about commitment to the explicit public purposes of the discipline.

Community Service Directors/Service-Learning Support Staff

- *Define.* Define *departmental engagement* broadly.
- *Stay open.* Remain open to significant definition variation among departments (there is no one right way or one right answer).
- *Listen for discipline-specific needs.* Provide resources and support as deans, chairs, and department faculty define their needs.
- *Understand first.* Seek first to understand disciplinary propensities and then help faculty recognize how community engagement can assist them to reach individual and collective outcomes.
- *Encourage communication.* Provide departmental case studies (such as those in this book, among others), and offer to facilitate unit-wide discussions concerning salient topics.
- *Not for everyone.* Expect fallout. No two departments will proceed along exactly the same pathways, and some may not proceed much at all.
- *Remember the service-learning triad.* Help the three main service-learning constituents—faculty, students, and community partners—to understand their various roles and the interdependence of their activities. Involve students and community partners in activities as often as possible.
- *Support scholarship.* Assist faculty to identify publication outlets regarding their unit development. Encourage collaborative publications, possibly including students and community partners.
- *Shine the light.* Highlight successes whenever possible. Annual campus-wide civic engagement (or other) awards celebrations

can elevate the profile of this work. Invite donors, elected officials, and senior-level administrators to these events.

- *Continue raising the stakes.* Recognize and appreciate all civic engagement efforts and publicly applaud the best initiatives. Regularly challenge everyone to create greater impacts, seek greater inter- and intraconnectivity, and explore deeper teaching, learning, and applied research methodologies.

Conclusion

We all live in an individual context, connected to larger professional and other social environments. Each of these contexts is unique. Individually and collectively, we must find our own unique ways to thrive. With this first principle in mind, we offer these modest, initial insights based on our efforts to support engaged department work institution-wide. As we discussed earlier, at PSU's Center for Academic Excellence, we simultaneously support civic engagement initiatives at three levels: with individuals, with cohort groups, and institution-wide. Focusing our work most recently on assisting departments to increase unit-level coherence around appropriate themes of civic engagement has led to both increased activity and depth of community-based teaching, learning, and research. This work, supported in concert with more traditional individual-level efforts and institution-wide programming, has helped PSU become even more connected to communities in Portland and in the state of Oregon. Additionally, PSU's civic engagement work has begun to intentionally connect to universities and other institutions worldwide. This emerging global focus for higher education—also known generally as internationalizing the curriculum—is critically important (Cornwell & Stoddard, 1999). Community-based learning and other civic engagement strategies will help build the reciprocal partnerships necessary to increase global understanding. Connecting engaged departments across colleges and universities and across continents can hasten and deepen this work and has great transformative potential for the common good.

References

Barr, R. B., & Tagg, J. (1995, November/December). From teaching to learning—A new paradigm for undergraduate education. *Change, 27*(6), 13–25.

Cornwell, G. H., & Stoddard, E. W. (1999). *Globalizing knowledge: Connecting international and intercultural studies.* Washington, DC: Association of American Colleges and Universities.

Davidson, S. (1997, Spring). Divide and flourish: nurturing the nucleus of faculty change. *Journal of Public Service and Outreach, 2*(1), 26.

Davidson, S., Holland, B., Kaiser, M., & Reardon, M. (1996). *Practical changes at a large urban public university: Portland State University.* Paper presented at the Capstone Symposium of the W. K. Kellogg Foundation. Retrieved March 19, 2006, from www.msu.edu/unit/outreach/pubs/capstone/ch3_2.html

Davidson, S.L., Kerrigan, S. & Agre-Kippenhan, S. (1999, Winter). Assessing university-community outreach. *Metropolitan Universities: An International Forum, 10*(3), 63–72.

Driscoll, A. (1998). Comprehensive design of community service: New understanding, options, and vitality in student learning at Portland State University. In E. Zlotkowski (Ed.), *Successful service-learning programs: New models of excellence in higher education* (pp. 150–168). Bolton, MA: Anker.

Holland, B. A. (2001). Toward a definition and characterization of the engaged campus: Six cases. *Metropolitan Universities: An International Forum, 12*(3), 20–29.

Kecskes, K. (2004, Summer). Engaging the department: Community-based approaches to support academic unit coherence. *The Department Chair, 15*(1), 7–9.

Kecskes, K., Kerrigan, S., & Patton, J. (in press). The heart of the matter: Aligning curriculum, pedagogy, and engagement in higher education. *Metropolitan Universities: An International Forum.*

Kecskes, K., Spring, A., & Lieberman, D. (2004). The Hesburgh certificate and Portland State University's faculty development approach to service learning and community-university partnerships. In C. M. Wehlburg & S. Chadwick-Blossey (Eds.), *To Improve the Academy: Vol. 22. Resources for faculty, instructional, and organizational development* (pp. 287–301). Bolton, MA: Anker.

Kecskes, K. J., Gelmon, S. B., & Spring A. (2006). Creating engaged departments: A program for organizational and faculty development. In S. Chadwick-Blossey & D. R. Robertson (Eds.), *To improve the academy: Vol. 24. Resources for faculty, instructional, and organizational development* (pp. 147–165). Bolton, MA: Anker.

Portland State University, Office of Academic Affairs. (2004). *Promotion and tenure scholarship.* Retrieved March 28, 2006, from the Portland State University, Office of Academic Affairs web site: www.oaa.pdx .edu/PromotionAndTenureScolarship5

Wallace, J. (2000, Fall). The problem of time: enabling students to make long-term commitments to community-based learning. *Michigan Journal of Community Service Learning, 7,* 133–141.

About the Authors

Kevin Kecskes is director of Community-University Partnerships at Portland State University. He oversees faculty and departmental development for community engagement as well as institutional civic engagement initiatives and events. His research and scholarship interests include community-university partnership development, faculty development for service-learning and civic engagement, social sustainability, and institutional transformation in higher education.

Amy Spring is assistant director of Community-University Partnerships at Portland State University. She facilitates campus-community partnership development and delivers training and technical assistance to faculty, departments, students, and community-based organizations on service-learning pedagogy and other civic engagement strategies. Her research and scholarly interests include student leadership development, assessing service-learning impact, and the scholarship of engagement. She is currently editing a monograph on integrating civic learning strategies into university courses.

16

A Journey of System-Wide Engagement

Season Eckardt, Erika F. Randall, Lori J. Vogelgesang

The collaborative work of an engaged department is inspiring, thought-provoking, challenging, and far-reaching. As illustrated by the various exemplars in earlier chapters, the curricular coherence, faculty dialogue, and cooperative work that result from the efforts to be an engaged department have positive impacts on student learning, faculty research, faculty satisfaction, and communities surrounding the university.

Given the enormous contributions of an engaged department, what then would be the impact of an *institution* that makes a commitment to transform not only one academic department, but the entire institution? Those impacts are clearly demonstrated by Portland State University as discussed in Chapter 15. Based on these findings and experiences, one might then ask, what happens when a *statewide system* of higher education makes a commitment to become an engaged system? How is it done?

The California State University (CSU) made such a commitment beginning in 1997. The journey, while not yet complete, has been a remarkable one in which many lessons have been learned. One of those lessons has been the effectiveness of the Engaged Department Initiative. We hope our experience with this approach—across multiple campuses and varied disciplines— can be useful to other systems of higher education, consortia, and individual campuses and departments. Before discussing the lessons learned in our journey to engagement, however, we must start at the beginning.

Aren't We There Already?

In the beginning, the general sentiment in the CSU system was "We've succeeded. We now offer service-learning opportunities to 40,000 students each year across our 23 campuses, and our board of trustees passed a resolution in support of community service-learning. We have reached the summit of our journey."

Or so we thought. That was in 2000. After three years of committed, intensive system-wide work across all 23 campuses, the CSU Board of Trustees passed a resolution calling for the chancellor and each CSU president to "ensure that all students have opportunities to participate in community service, service-learning, or both" (CSU Board of Trustees, 2000). While this at first seemed like a happy ending to our system-wide efforts to institutionalize community service-learning, we quickly realized that in fact our work had only just reached the midpoint of the mountain, not the summit, and still had much further to go.

The California State University is the nation's largest university system, with 23 campuses and 7 off-campus centers, more than 400,000 students and 44,000 faculty and staff. Each CSU campus has its own unique identity. Some CSU campuses are in large urban settings with student populations of more than 25,000, while other campuses are located rurally and have much smaller student populations. All CSU campuses have distinct features and programs but share the same mission—to provide high-quality, affordable higher education to meet the ever-changing needs of California.

To support its mission, faculty, administrators, staff, students, and alumni across CSU have dedicated themselves to developing partnerships and building bridges, particularly through community service-learning. In 1997, representatives from all CSU campuses came together to develop the CSU Strategic Plan for Community Service-Learning. This plan stated a primary goal of offering service-learning and community service opportunities for each CSU student prior to graduation and outlined specific objectives and action steps to help reach this goal. In 1998, the Office of Community Service-Learning in the Office of the Chancellor was created to provide leadership and coordination for CSU campuses as they developed and implemented community service-learning initiatives. A service-learning coordinator was appointed on each campus. At the system-wide level, workshops were offered, grants were written, meetings were held, and campus subgrants were awarded. By the 1999–2000 academic year, more than 1,000 service-learning courses were offered in the CSU. Then, in March 2000, the CSU Board of Trustees passed a landmark resolution to ensure that all CSU students had opportunities to participate in community service and service-learning. The university was on a whirlwind journey of engagement, and now its governing board was giving this effort its strongest endorsement.

By 2000, hundreds of faculty members in the CSU had incorporated service-learning into their classes with great enthusiasm. According to one CSU faculty member,

> When I discovered service-learning, I can say without exaggeration that it fundamentally changed me as an educator. It allowed me to move to that next phase of teaching that I had read about and aspired to but didn't quite know how to reach. It *revolutionized* how I viewed teaching, learning and the purpose of education.

Yet by 2000, what we really had was not a system-wide *revolution* but rather hundreds of mini innovations—committed, individual faculty members who were using service-learning. However, those individual works were not necessarily connected to or congruent with the overall teaching and research expectations and priorities of their departments, colleges, or the university. In order to create a revolution, something more was needed.

From Individuals to Departments:
The Engaged Department Initiative

In fall 2000, Campus Compact approached the CSU system-wide Office of Community Service-Learning in the Office of the Chancellor with that something—the Engaged Department Initiative. Campus Compact, with support from the Pew Charitable Trusts, was focusing attention on the department "as a unit and to effect institutional change by developing strategies aimed at curricular coherence and faculty collaboration shaped by service-learning and civic engagement" (Battistoni, Gelmon, Saltmarsh, Wergin, & Zlotkowski, 2003, p. 4). The CSU's efforts to become an engaged system would depend on working with academic departments because it is within the academic department that expectations and norms for faculty and students are articulated and carried out. The foundation for this departmental work had been built. CSU had hundreds of individual service-learning champions spread over many academic departments in the system. Now we would call on those champions to engage their colleagues in departmental conversations and participate in Engaged Department Institutes.

The Engaged Department Institute was designed to include several faculty members from a department, the department chair, the institution's service-learning coordinator, and a community partner. The purpose of the institute was to help departments develop strategies to include community-based work in teaching and scholarship, include community-based experiences as a standard expectation for majors, and develop a level coherence that will allow departments to model successfully civic engagement and progressive change (Battistoni et al., 2003).

The call for participants went out from the Office of the Chancellor through campus service-learning directors, the service-learning faculty champions, and the directors of teaching and learning centers. Delightfully, there was ample response. Through a competitive application process, 12 departmental teams were selected to participate in the first Campus Compact Engaged Department Institute for CSU campuses. The disciplines represented included communications, sociology, linguistics, art, urban and regional planning, educational psychology and counseling, health science, and political science. Teams started their work for the institute in the months prior by completing a pre-institute planning document that enabled team members to discuss their department's readiness for this effort, their views of civic engagement, their aspirations for becoming an engaged department, and their general strategies for getting there. Prior to the institute, the facilitators reviewed the pre-institute planning documents.

Teams arrived with varying levels of knowledge of service-learning and civic engagement. However, an introductory service-learning workshop brought everyone to a common understanding of the various terms and concepts that were used throughout the institute. The teams then participated in two- and one-half days of large- and small-group activities and working sessions facilitated by national experts. Topics included the academic and civic effectiveness of community-based work, discipline-specific models of service-learning integration, supporting and assessing community-based work at the faculty and student levels, community-based work as a vehicle of curricular integration, the community partner as departmental resource, and the department as community resource. During the final session of the institute, each team created and presented an action plan which would serve as a guide for team members to continue their work at their institutions. Energized, educated, and prepared, team members then returned to their campuses ready to transform their departments into units of engagement.

Nine CSU departmental teams participated in the 2002 CSU Engaged Department Institute and 11 teams participated in 2003. Over a three-year period, a total of 32 departments representing 16 of the 23 campuses in the CSU participated in the institute in order to become engaged departments.

There are some unique aspects to offering the Engaged Department Institute within a statewide system of higher education (or a consortia)—momentum, shared resources, and the potential for future collaboration. Issuing the call for participation from the Office of the Chancellor and sending participating teams back to their campuses as change agents created a momentum felt by all—participants were pioneers in an exciting system-wide effort that would lead to systemic change. The momentum that had been built from the CSU Strategic Plan and the Board of Trustees' resolution carried the impact of the institute even further. Additionally, institute teams benefited from the shared resources within the system to support their work, particularly from the Community Service-Learning Office. Institute participants became members of a listserv that provided weekly updates on innovations in service-learning and civic engagement, funding opportunities, and the availability of materials and publications to assist departments with their engagement work. Teams also had access to an interactive online database of service-learning practitioners from across the CSU and received additional support from their campus service-learning directors. Many departmental teams connected with related discipline teams from other CSU campuses, and several teams left the institute with plans to collaborate with departments on other CSU campuses in the future.

Evaluating the Impact of the Engaged Department Institute

An important aspect of any new initiative is evaluation. This effort—to transform academic culture through academic departments—is no exception. In addition to the evaluation that all participants completed at the end of each institute, the CSU Office of the Chancellor collaborated with the Higher Education Research Institute (HERI) at the University of California, Los Angeles to examine the impact of the 2001 institute on the departmental teams

(Vogelgesang & Misa, 2002). The evaluation study examined the following questions: How, if at all, did participation in the institute facilitate the process of becoming an engaged department? What barriers and facilitators to becoming an engaged department exist? What changes, if any, have occurred in the department as well as in the community partner organization since the institute?

The study relied on data collected through a survey of faculty and staff participants, structured telephone interviews with community partners, and in-depth case studies of two departmental teams. Thirty-one of the 42 participants (74%) responded to the anonymous paper-and-pencil survey conducted about six months after the institute, and eight of the nine community partners attending the institute participated in interviews. The site visits for the case studies at Humboldt State University and California State University–Fullerton took place nearly one year after the institute. The findings offer insights into the impact of the institute and general efforts to create change within academic culture.

Faculty Views: Supports and Barriers to Becoming Engaged

In the faculty survey, participants indicated the degree to which different sources and resources supported their work toward becoming engaged. There was no single source of support (such as the faculty, the dean, the department head, the disciplinary association) that emerged as particularly powerful. Rather, participants identified multiple sources of support for each of their goals. The exceptions were in the areas that pertained to evaluation and integration of this work into the faculty reward structure; for these areas, no sources of support were identified.

The survey also queried the degree to which resources, such as leave time and printed materials that supported becoming a more engaged department, were available at each institution. The most common source of support among those listed was on-campus professional development opportunities, with nearly all respondents saying it was at least a minor support. Frequently, these on-campus opportunities (such as a campus-wide service-learning fellows program) are coordinated by the service-learning office. Printed materials and administrative support appeared to be available and of at least some support to most respondents, and off-campus training was seen as a support by two-thirds of the respondents. Leave time was not a typical form of support, with about 60% of respondents saying it was not available/not a support.

Community Partner Views: Strengthening Partnerships

The community partner phone interview addressed how the community-based organization representative viewed the academic department and the partnership. The types of organizations as well as the strength of the relationship with the university partners varied greatly among teams. In several cases, the partnership did not exist before the institute and/or no longer exists. In other cases, the partnership was seen as quite strong and mutually beneficial. The department teams partnered with small social service agencies, county organizations, public schools, and other nonprofits. In some cases, a faculty member initiated the contact; in others, the community agency approached the university.

Despite the wide range of partnerships, several common issues emerged. Almost all of the community partners felt that the institute was valuable because it allowed team members to become further acquainted with one another and it facilitated a planning process by structuring time together. Several partners commented that the institute provided an opportunity for them to form a relationship with the department, or at least with individual faculty members beyond the one person they had known prior to participating in the institute. Challenges to a strong partnership, according to community partners, include finding time to meet faculty partners in person and following up on the work of the institute in general.

Case Studies

Two case studies that were conducted a year after the institute resulted in many interesting findings contextualized by the individual campus and community cultures of Humboldt State University (a midsize, rural campus in northern California) and California State University–Fullerton (a large urban campus in the Los Angeles region). However, there are overall themes that emerged from both campuses.

- One person can play a very influential role in galvanizing a critical mass.
- The Engaged Department Institute provided leverage—both teams have moved from having *the* service-learning person to having a critical amount of buy-in from the department.
- The institute helped to strengthen the support of the department chairs; they have better understandings of reflection and connecting course material to experience.
- Dialogue among faculty about what it means to be an engaged department has deepened conversations about what they want students to learn.
- Both teams have connected the work of the institute to larger department goals.
- Teams want to take advantage of personnel transitions in departments to recruit and hire faculty interested in community-based work.
- The broader academic culture is seen as a barrier to junior faculty involvement in both departments.
- This work continues to be underfunded.
- Departments are not (yet) implementing evaluation.

This relatively short-term study revealed some of the barriers and facilitators to departmental change and engagement that parallel some of the lessons learned in the months and years following.

Several years later, the work of 32 pioneering CSU departments to become engaged still continues.

The Various Paths: Lessons Learned

After nearly a decade, our journey toward engagement continues to evolve. The work of these departments, and other departments that have joined the expedition, has yielded new knowledge and practices for departmental change and engagement. The CSU Office of Community Service-Learning supported these efforts and also has a unique system-wide vantage point from which to view and understand these changes. The lessons learned fall into four stages, which we refer to as "paths" on our journey toward engagement. While most departmental teams seem to be progressing through them somewhat sequentially, other teams move from path to path, depending on local influences. Descriptions of each of these four paths follow.

The First Path: Developing Departmental Coherence Around the Meaning of Engagement

Many departments came to the institute thinking that the primary focus of an engaged department was service-learning. Broadening notions of an engaged department was a critical part of the institute. Although service-learning is an important component, there are other elements to becoming engaged. Revising a department's mission to reflect an authentic commitment to addressing community needs, incorporating community-based research projects into faculty research agendas, and mapping out when community-based learning experiences take place within the curricular sequence are some of the other possible avenues. Figure 16.1 illustrates the many components—both at the policy level and the activity level—of departmental work that can be directly connected to engagement.

One component of an engaged department's work is teaching civic responsibility (sometimes referred to as civic learning). Since

Figure 16.1. A Map of Key Components for Creating the Engaged Department

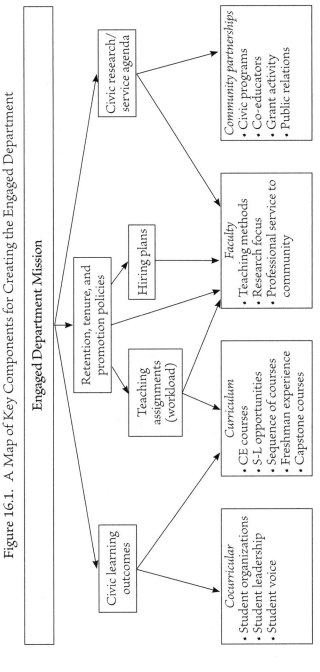

Note: Adapted from Eisman, G. S. (2005), unpublished source. Used with permission of the author.

the first CSU system-wide institute in 2001, strengthening civic responsibility has increasingly become a part of national conversations through high-profile books, meetings, and research initiatives. This national discourse has furthered the understanding of various curricular and cocurricular models for civic learning that can occur within the department. As a result, department conversations across the CSU have led to examples of building civic responsibility, including a service-learning course that explicitly incorporates civic learning objectives, such as increasing awareness of political processes in our state; a course that focuses on changing policy to address an issue identified by the local community, such as students researching the need for a stop sign at a busy intersection and presenting that information to the city council; a capstone course with a community-based research component; student representation in the decision-making process for the department; and student clubs that are connected to the department and provide social and educational opportunities for students.

The HERI study found that six months after the institute, teams reported the most progress in areas related to strengthening awareness of and support for service-learning and engagement at the department level. This was true whether the department was perceived as unfamiliar with service-learning prior to the institute or already had some awareness. Clearly, this is a major strength of the institute. Some of the practical outcomes of conceptualizing a broad meaning of engagement include more opportunities to connect engagement with faculty interests. Because there are so many ways to think about engagement beyond service-learning, there are more opportunities for a particular engaged practice to resonate with each individual faculty member in the department. Additionally, student learning opportunities are increased, thus reaching a broader range of learning styles.

In addition to exploring broader notions of engagement, an important result of the team work at the institute was fostering departmental coherence and consensus. Faculty autonomy is part of our university culture, and this traditional characteristic can impede departmental collaboration. However, through the efforts of the Engaged Department Institute, we witnessed departments working more collaboratively and more coherently than ever before. The format and content of the institute provided a vehicle for faculty to conceive of their individual endeavors as part of a team effort. One faculty team discovered that before it could effectively work on developing its action plan during the institute, it needed to address some dysfunctional working experiences in the department. The department chair remarked that the institute process positively transformed the way department faculty work with one another.

With the departmental teams unified and more broadly informed about engagement, institute participants were ready to lead conversations with their colleagues and increase faculty involvement in the department back on campus.

The Second Path: Finding the Right Fit

On the second path, institute team members work to foster an ongoing dialogue about engagement and to engage other faculty members in departmental discussions. The goal of the second path is to explore and prioritize with the department the various expressions of engagement, whether it be in the curriculum, retention, tenure, and promotion policies, or cocurricular activities supported by faculty advisors. The second path is not a place for decision-making; it is simply a medium for gauging the possibilities and constraints of how far the department can move forward with this effort. For instance, at CSU Chico, there are currently six engaged departments working with the two service-learning directors. Most of these departments decided to use grant funds for department-wide retreats as they started their journey (D. Berg, personal communication, June 17, 2005). This concept of holding retreats is important for two reasons. First, it allowed faculty members who did not participate in the institute the opportunity to hear from their colleagues about the conversations that occurred, thus broadening the base of understanding on engagement issues. Second, the retreats gave the faculty time and space away from daily distractions for dialogue on the bigger questions that emerged from the institute. Many of the teams from other campuses also planned faculty retreats to discuss their work at the institute and plan for future action.

This second stage is an ideal time to begin the conversation about faculty attitudes and perceptions about whether departmental reward structures appropriately recognize various forms of engagement. According to HERI's evaluation, teams reported that integrating service-learning into faculty review processes was one of the two areas that was the most challenging to address. This is not surprising given that only about six months elapsed between the institute and when the evaluation took place. It is important to facilitate conversations about departmental retention, tenure, and promotion (RTP) policies with a new perspective in order to make progress in this area. A service-learning faculty scholar from the Office of the Chancellor and a professor in computer science, describes one exercise that he uses frequently with departments (G. Eisman, personal communication, June 15, 2005):

> Small groups within the department are presented with a list of scenarios describing faculty work that exemplifies community scholarship which goes beyond the traditional definition of teaching, research, and service. The scenarios are selected from actual experiences of colleagues throughout the CSU. For example, one scenario involves a faculty member in history who combines his own knowledge of historical events with an architectural assessment of a neighborhood conducted by his students to present a proposal to city government to designate a certain building as an historical landmark. The application of knowledge is apparent and the consequence is

significant but the presentation is aimed at an audience that does not consist of faculty peers, but rather those in local communities. The group is then charged with determining on the basis of their view of scholarship whether or not these activities would count within a RTP review, and where in the review policy they would be recognized. These conversations are invariably animated and informative as participants struggle to defend or challenge existing policy as being inclusive of a non-traditional activity.

These conversations can reveal whether a department is ready to reexamine its reward structure. After there has been adequate time to explore issues and come to consensus, departments can move to the third stage of implementing the action steps that have been agreed upon.

The Third Path: Implementing Action Steps

Implementation can be viewed in multiple ways. A department may choose to focus on one component, accomplish it, and then move on to another area; or it may decide to address many components of its action plan all at once. The specifics of implementation truly depend on the culture of the department, the faculty and staff members involved, available resources, and goals for engagement.

The sociology department at CSU Fullerton is an exemplary model of the significant changes that can be implemented in this third stage. In 2001, the five-member team that attended the institute consisted of an outgoing department chair, the incoming chair, a faculty member who up until the institute had taught all of the service-learning courses, a fourth faculty member who would later become the department chair, and a community partner (L. Prinsky, personal communication, June 23, 2005). The team was energized and united during the institute, and they returned to campus and planned a department retreat to share the team's recent experiences and insights.

During the retreat, the department explored and prioritized various expressions of engagement. The faculty committed to creating a service-learning requirement within the major. For the next several months, the faculty and staff discussed the most effective way to implement the requirement. During that time, mini grants were given to faculty members interested in teaching service-learning courses, and a faculty partnership luncheon was held to increase faculty awareness of local community partners. As a result of the conversations, the faculty collectively identified several strategies for implementing the service-learning requirement. One suggested approach was to pinpoint a major course that would fulfill the service-learning requirement; however, some faculty felt that this intruded on their autonomy. The final approved plan gives students the option of taking a major-based service-learning course at any point during their coursework. The department has examined the curricular sequence and offerings to ensure this is possible for all students. Once the requirement was implemented, students provided 12,000 hours of service to community agencies in just one semester (Prinsky & Bedell, 2003). Now, the department has started to examine whether its RTP policy encourages faculty to utilize service-learning, and new faculty hires are being informed about the requirement and asked about any prior experience with service-learning.

According to the HERI evaluation findings, departments cited various successes in implementing their action plans: offering more service-learning courses than planned, establishing a resource center, and securing outside funding. On the other hand, those that were not on track in implementing their action plans stated that lack of time, the need for a project coordinator, and limited time available for community partnerships were reasons for the delay in making progress on their action plans.

The fourth path on the journey to engagement speaks to the challenging task of overcoming barriers and ensuring successes into the future.

The Fourth Path: Sustaining and Expanding Engagement

Identifying ongoing strategies to move a department forward with its vision for engagement characterizes the fourth path of sustaining engagement. Given serious budget cuts to the CSU and a significant number of faculty retirements, this process has become increasingly complicated. One department chair commented on wanting to encourage commitment, but she felt tremendous pressure to maintain higher than normal faculty-to-student ratios in the classroom. Larger class size and heavier teaching loads can affect the quality of a service-learning experience and dissuade faculty from wanting to use service-learning. Faculty members within the seven engaged departments at San Jose State University have suggested that a student assistant to oversee community partnership logistics, cofacilitate reflection sessions, and organize paperwork would be immensely helpful to their efforts. The coordination provided by the service-learning offices also plays an essential role at this stage in areas such as preserving quality partnerships with community agencies, providing faculty training, and in some cases offering financial resources.

There are other strategies that help engagement to stay at the core of departmental work, including validation from disciplinary associations, funding evaluation efforts, and enlisting the support of academic leadership. Receiving recognition from disciplinary associations has a mutual benefit for the department and the association—it reinforces the commitment by the department and gives the association an opportunity to learn about and disseminate innovations in the field.

Another strategy includes allocating time and resources to assess and evaluate the impact of the engaged work. The HERI evaluation identified evaluation as one of the two greatest challenges faced by departmental teams. Several years after this initial finding, we conclude that institutions are not yet engaging in systemic evaluation of their engagement efforts and suspect that they would cite lack of resources—time and funding—as the reasons. Still, where evaluation is happening, it can inform the ongoing work of the department and sometimes can provide evidence of positive results.

College deans can play a significant role in sustaining engagement if they are familiar with and conscious of the impact an engaged department approach can have. If college deans are educated about this effort and embrace it, they can have a powerful role in ensuring a long-term commitment to engaged departments. At CSU Chico, the dean of the College of Communication and Education is an enthusiastic supporter of the engaged department concept. She encouraged department chairs to apply when she heard about the opportunity, attended some of the engaged department trainings to learn more, and communicates with her fellow deans about the value of civic engagement. As the work advances, we need to see progress in these three areas in order to fully institutionalize the concept of engaged departments.

New Journeys and Future Directions

Our ongoing journey toward engagement is leading the CSU system in new directions. Since 2003, CSU Chico and CSU Fresno have offered their own spin-offs from the traditional two- and one-half day Engaged Department Institute. Both campuses have monthly meetings with their engaged departments on the standard topics throughout the semester. CSU Chico works with multiple departments at the same time, whereas CSU Fresno works with one department at a time. The service-learning codirector at CSU Chico is thinking about future adaptations. In spring 2006, the campus service-learning office hosted a summit for six engaged departments where interdisciplinary working groups were launched. The working groups provide another way for faculty to come together to exchange ideas and design an action plan around a specific topic, such as RTP policies. At CSU Fresno, the director of civic engagement and service-learning would like to see grant funds be given to a department for two years (C. Fiorentino, personal communication, June 17, 2005). Work during the first year would focus on the first two paths described in this chapter—defining engagement and finding the right fit. The second year would address the third and fourth paths—implementing action steps and examining ways to sustain engagement. A recent success at CSU Fresno is a graduate program that has become engaged. Looking toward the future, the potential to intentionally work with graduate programs is quite promising because of the practical application of the work in professional programs.

At the CSU Office of the Chancellor, we are also pursuing other ideas that dovetail the goals of the engaged department. In the 2005–2006 academic year, a Civic Learning Institute for First Year Experiences was offered for campus teams. Participants examined ways to instill civic skills, knowledge, and values into the first-year experience and developed a plan for strengthening civic experiences for freshman or transfer students. Instead of working within the discipline like the engaged department format, the institute translated to a campus-wide program. A second effort involved hosting a Teaching and Research Conference for CSU faculty that enhanced research skills and transformed current views to ensure that community-based work can be infused into all three aspects of a faculty member's dossier: teaching, research, and service.

Reaching the Summit?

The work of a system of higher education to become engaged is complex, dynamic, and evolving. The California State University has discovered that the engaged department approach has been effective in creating change within departments, colleges, and universities. While the CSU has still not reached the summit of its journey, the paths created by the engaged department approach have been well traveled—albeit winding and rocky at times—and have enabled the CSU to get much closer to the summit of engagement. Despite the changes that we expect will continue on our journey, we know the direction of our journey will lead us to fruitful shifts in our thinking and actions that will result in greater engagement with our communities, our institutions, our colleagues, and our students.

References

Battistoni, R. M., Gelmon, S. B., Saltmarsh, J. A., Wergin, J. F., & Zlotkowski, E. (2003). *The engaged department toolkit.* Providence, RI: Campus Compact.

California State University, Board of Trustees. (2000). *Community service: Responding to the Governor's call* (Rep. 03–02–00). Retrieved March 28, 2006, from the California State University, Office of the Chancellor web site: www.calstate.edu/csl/initiatives/resolution.shtml

California State University, Office of the Chancellor. (1997). *Strategic plan for community service-learning at the California State University.* Retrieved March 28, 2006, from the California State University, Office of the Chancellor web site: www.calstate.edu/csl/initiatives/resolution.shtml

Prinsky, L., & Bedell, J. W. (2003, November). *12,000 hours in 15 weeks.* Paper presented at the International Conference on Civic Education Research, New Orleans, LA.

Vogelgesang, L. J., & Misa, K. (2002). *The Engaged Department Institute and the California State University: Progress, process, and challenges.* Long Beach, CA: California State University, Community Service-Learning Office.

About the Authors

Season Eckardt has been working in the Office of the Chancellor at the California State University since 2000 and currently serves as the administrative director for the Office of Community Service-Learning. She collaboratively works with the service-learning practitioners at each of the California State University's 23 campuses to promote greater institutionalization of service-learning and civic engagement efforts on each campus.

Erika F. Randall is a consultant in higher education and a member of the executive board of Youth Service California. From 1998–2003, she was the director of Community Service-Learning in the Office of the Chancellor at the California State University. She holds a master's in education from Harvard University's School of Education, where her studies focused on administration, planning, and social policy.

Lori J. Vogelgesang is director of the Center for Service-Learning Research and Dissemination at the Higher Education Research Institute at the University of California, Los Angeles (UCLA). She currently directs the multiyear grant "Understanding the Effects of Service-learning: A Study of Students and Faculty" and works with the Chancellor's Center for Community Partnerships at UCLA to implement and evaluate a partnership program for faculty, staff, students, and community agencies.

17

Engaged Disciplines: How National Disciplinary Societies Support the Scholarship of Engagement

Sherwyn P. Morreale, James L. Applegate

The philosopher Marcel Proust observed that the real act of discovery lies not in discovering new lands but in seeing with new eyes. With the reconfiguration of the demographic, economic, and social character of America in the 21st century, new demands are being placed on higher education. We are called upon to see ourselves with Proust's new eyes, to rediscover our responsibilities to society. Society appropriately is asking that we justify the huge investment made in research and teaching institutions in higher education. Campuses configured as ivory towers and disciplines huddled in silos where members communicate only with one another are no longer acceptable. The academy is responding to this public mandate. The term *engagement* captures much of the spirit of this new work

Following Boyer's (1990) discussion of multiple forms of scholarship, higher education associations and disciplinary societies are now helping to advance the idea of a scholarship of engagement. A glance at the themes and titles of just a few recent national conventions confirms this. The Association of American Colleges and Universities convened a November 2005 conference titled The Civic Engagement Imperative: Student Learning and the Public Good. The January 2005 annual meeting of the Association of American Law Schools focused on Engaged Scholarship. In May–June 2006, the Community-Campus Partnerships for Health's ninth annual conference was titled Walking the Talk: Achieving the Promise of Authentic Partnerships.

This scholarship of engagement redefines research and teaching in ways that demand change from faculty, their disciplinary associations, and their academic institutions. Attempts to relegate this form of scholarship to purely a service function, in fact, marginalize it. Rather, the scholarship of engagement redefines our basic research and teaching missions to include, at their core, a concern for using scholarship to address real-world problems. A new approach therefore is necessary that reconceptualizes the relationship of all forms of scholarship in a way that acknowledges the complex connections among them. Continued funding for higher education's research efforts will in large part depend on reconceptualizing research, both basic and applied, as engaged. And there is strong public support for new concepts for teaching and curricula that integrate learning in real-world and applied settings.

Much of this effort to encourage engaged research and pedagogy has been campus based, at the individual, departmental or institutional level. More is heard about creating engaged campuses than about engaged disciplines or disciplinary societies. Campus leaders, pressured by governing boards and legislatures to show a return on their investment in higher education, are embracing engagement as a means of creating visible contributions to their communities. Many disciplinary societies and their leaders, on the other hand, have remained more focused on providing publication outlets and meeting forums that advance their disciplines' status and knowledge base. This is particularly ironic because many of these academic societies were formed in the late 19th and early 20th centuries for the purpose of engaging the academy and faculty members more meaningfully in the public and its problems (Putnam, 2000).

Yet when asked about their profession, most faculty members will reply that they are a physicist, or a psychologist, or a historian, rather than a professor at a particular school. Their disciplines and professional/academic associations seem to define their identities, career ladders, and career choices. Consequently, any change in higher education depends on faculty change and disciplinary change. If we are to respond to mandates for greater engagement and increased partnerships, that change must involve faculty and the disciplinary societies with which faculty identify. Without the participation of both of these stakeholders, only those faculty who are willing or can afford to tie their futures to a particular institution that values engagement can be seriously expected to redefine their teaching and research. How, then, do we create disciplines and disciplinary societies populated by faculty with an interest in the scholarship of engagement? How do faculty and their disciplinary organizations collaborate to rediscover the soul of an academic citizen—the public intellectual? And what exemplars of engaged disciplines and disciplinary societies might we look to as models?

Step One: Define Engagement for the Discipline

Engaged research and teaching will need to take different forms in the arts, humanities, and social, physical, and biological sciences. Defining its disciplinary form requires simultaneously creating forums for discourse about engagement and providing concrete examples and highly visible projects to inform that discourse. National newsletters, international, national, regional, and state convention programs, and special publications should all be used. In some, if not many, cases, there may be a need to redefine and clarify the discipline's conception of engagement as it relates to basic and applied research. "Basic" researchers at research institutions often do not see the relevance of engagement to their work. Some may fear engagement means compromising academic integrity in service to the needs of other constituencies. These issues should be openly debated, and the arguments must address the relevance of engagement to research and teaching.

Disciplinary definition and adaptation must also take into account the reward structures of the campus cultures in which members reside. Opportunities to participate in national initiatives to create engaged teaching through service-learning will have greater meaning for members at teaching institutions. Efforts to link engagement to funded research projects and partnerships with highly respected foundations and agencies have more relevance on research-oriented campuses. The academic association most respected in the discipline can help in both areas—research and teaching—to enhance appreciation for the scholarship of engagement.

Step Two: Redefine Research in the Discipline

Disciplinary societies typically publish the journals and manage the appointment of the editorial boards of those journals. This is the coin of the realm for much of higher education. In addition, the societies play a key role in what kinds of work are valued at national, regional, and state association meetings so important to the early careers of faculty at almost every institution. The societies themselves must engage their departments and faculty in a meaningful dialogue about what high-quality engaged research and scholarship is, and they must value that scholarship in the publication and presentation outlets they provide. Only then will faculty develop a way of understanding and conducting quality research that is truly engaged and highly relevant to a more humane society. As part of this disciplinary dialogue, it is critical to note that this is not a rejection of the concepts of basic research but an expansion of what "counts" as valuable in a discipline's journals and at their conventions. Louis Pasteur provides insight here: "There is not pure science and applied science, but only science and the application of science" (qtd. in Stokes, 1997, p. 1). Additionally, the 1950 report of the panel on the McKay bequests to the president and fellows of Harvard College states, "A science is not the sum of two discrete parts, one pure and the other applied. It is an organic whole, with complex interrelationships throughout" (qtd. in Stokes, 1997, p. 1).

The distinction between basic and applied research has dominated higher education thinking about scholarship since the end of World War II and the creation of the National Science Foundation (Bush, 1945). For more than 50 years, faculty, disciplinary associations, universities, and funding agencies have embraced this simple linear continuum, with basic research assuming the more prestigious position. Embracing the notion of engaged scholarship will require rethinking this simplistic framework because the idea of engagement is typically linked to pedagogy and limited forms of action research. Yet engaged scholarship is relevant to our traditional research practices as well.

Stokes (1997) argues convincingly that our traditional conceptions of the role of research and the relation of basic and applied research are historically inaccurate and inadequate as a 21st-century approach to research. While acknowledging the value of basic and applied research as traditionally conceived (e.g., Bohr's work on atomic structure and Edison's applied research at Menlo Park respectively), Stokes documents a large tradition of research that offers another more complex arena for engaged scholarship that goes beyond applied or action research. He sees Louis Pasteur as the exemplar of this approach. Research in "Pasteur's quadrant" seeks to enhance basic understanding but is engaged in solving important problems. It is "use-inspired" basic research. As Stokes notes,

> Pasteur wanted to understand and to control the microbiological processes he discovered, Keynes wanted to understand and improve the working of modern economies. The physicists of the Manhattan Project wanted to understand and harness nuclear fission. . . . The molecular biologists have wanted to understand and alter the genetic codes in DNA material. (p. 80)

In short, the long tradition of research pursuing understanding and the improvement of lives and the solution to problems is another tradition of engaged scholarship that should drive the training of graduate students and the work of faculty in any institution in the business of research. Disciplinary societies must value such work in the context of their intellectual traditions. This is the kind of work being encouraged by those seeking to rethink doctoral education in America and create a new generation of faculty with a more complex understanding of the various ways their work can be engaged and how the intellectual capital they develop can be invested for the common good (Woodrow Wilson National Fellowship Foundation, 2000).

Specifically, disciplinary societies should increase the visibility of research in Pasteur's and Edison's quadrant, encouraging conversations that incorporate Stokes's more complex conceptualization into research and graduate education. This conversation should result in an engaged research agenda identifying those problems the discipline is best equipped to solve. Focusing on the connections between all forms of research will reduce the artificial isolation of basic research and encourage applied researchers to consider the implications of their work for basic research questions and problem-focused basic research. In this way engaged scholarship becomes an issue for the entire research community and not just the few relegated to secondary status in the discipline. The disciplinary societies can then play a role in connecting researchers as public intellectuals to the issues that affect our lives today and in setting our course for the future.

Step Three: Redefine Teaching and Learning in the Discipline

Disciplinary societies, here as in research, can play a powerful role and set the agenda for engaged teaching and learning. Examples of reconceptualizing pedagogy as an engaged activity can be drawn from higher education's recent past. Over the last decade, two prominent national initiatives on engaged teaching and learning took hold with faculty and on campuses, in large measure, by finding their voice and disseminating their message through academic associations.

The Carnegie Foundation's Academy for the Scholarship of Teaching and Learning awarded small seed grants to disciplinary societies to support advocacy activities and encourage faculty to examine their teaching in a scholarly manner. Most participating associations not only publicized the initiative but also created opportunities for reporting the results of studies at their conventions and in their journals. One society, the National Communication Association (NCA), established the scholarship of teaching and learning as a permanent theme of the organization's national convention and in the call for submissions to one of the association's leading scholarly journals. The result is the improvement of teaching practice in communication studies well beyond the individual classroom through shared experiences in peer-reviewed and well-respected publications. The Carnegie Foundation supported the work of NCA and 10 other associations through the foundation's publication of a monograph devoted to disciplinary styles in the scholarship of teaching and learning (Huber & Morreale, 2001).

Like the Carnegie Foundation, national advocates of service-learning provided grants to disciplinary societies over a three-year period to develop resources and advocate for this form of engaged teaching. Participating associations produced discipline-specific monographs that included general guidelines for service-learning in the discipline as well as models of its application in specific courses. They also provided opportunities to present the results of service-learning projects at national conventions and in their academic journals.

The result of this advocacy at an association level for the National Communication Association is a highly successful service-learning initiative, Communicating Common Ground, that is a joint project of NCA, Campus Compact, and the Southern Poverty Law Center (Applegate & Morreale, 2001). This course-based project teams faculty and students from college-level communication programs with P–12 schools and community groups to implement programs that foster respect for diversity and combat prejudice. College students and faculty lead younger students in learning activities designed to advance multicultural education and the creation of communities in which hate, hate speech, and hate crimes are not tolerated. Presently, NCA boasts about 75 Communicating Common Ground partnerships across the country, all of which trace their roots to the association's promotion of engaged pedagogy in the form of service-learning.

Redefining teaching and research in any discipline by providing engaged scholarship "space" in the journals and convention programs of the discipline is at the core of what disciplinary societies must do to advance the cause of engagement. However, some of the traditions embedded in doctoral programs and departments encourage the isolation of research and teaching from public needs and issues. So there is no guarantee that faculty will come if disciplinary societies build opportunities for engaged scholarship. Therefore, the associations also must engage in several other activities to build support for this work.

Step Four: Find Friends and Influential Supporters

Creating a critical mass of engaged scholars may be more difficult in some disciplines than in others and will require involving people from both inside and outside the discipline, collaborating within and across disciplines (Morreale & Howery, 2002). Experience suggests that government funding agencies, nonprofits, business/industry groups, and even other disciplinary associations are awash with programs and people who want to support engagement efforts.

Similarly, involving well-respected colleagues within the discipline is essential. Often a discipline has traditions in teaching or research that offer natural internal constituencies for engaged scholarship. Standing committees and boards, for example, need to be brought into the engagement fold. Senior faculty and department chairs are two disciplinary groups that hold promise as influential adopters of engagement efforts. Finding prominent senior scholars to lead engagement initiatives as part of their leadership roles in the organization may make all the difference in the association's ability to sustain a credible engagement effort.

Step Five: Celebrate Success

Professional associations have the power, if not the responsibility, to reward the engaged scholar's work. High-quality engaged scholarship must be promoted and rewarded at every turn if it is to survive and thrive. Presenting awards at national meetings and celebrating progress in large and small steps is crucial to advancing engaged scholarship. However, the focus must always be on high-quality work that significantly advances understanding of the discipline's key concepts, demonstrates the relevance of the work to society, and produces significant outcomes. To do otherwise runs the risk of damaging perceptions of engaged scholarship in much the same way as some early teaching award programs distorted the view of what it meant to be a scholarly teacher. Still, a disciplinary association can, on a large stage, recognize models and best practices of engagement that enhance the merit of the entire initiative in the discipline.

Step Six: Look to Disciplinary Exemplars

Seeing the scholarship of engagement with new eyes is no easy task. It will take pressure and support from internal and external constituencies, campus leadership altering tenure and reward structures, and a redefinition of the role of disciplinary associations. Some of the key elements to success are consistent commitment from associational leadership and involvement of more members (especially senior scholars) in visible engagement initiatives sponsored by the association. This approach is consistent with Gladwell's (2000) analysis about a "tipping point"—that broad change can be accomplished by a few people properly placed, promoting the idea of the scholarship of engagement. Some, if not many, disciplinary societies are moving in this direction and the network of Gladwellian change agents inside higher education is growing.

Disciplinary societies approach engagement with varying degrees of enthusiasm depending on whether they deem the substance of their fields as relevant to this initiative. Some disciplines, political science and communication, for example, have an impressive history of commitment to the scholarship of engagement. Here are several examples of academic associations that are highly engaged in engagement.

The American Political Science Association (APSA), according to its executive director, Michael Brintnall, has long played a role in civic education and engagement. Beyond maintaining a range of supporting resources for political scientists, APSA has established a permanent standing committee on civic education and engagement, as well as a specialized civic education web page, an actively managed listserv, and a collection of syllabi. According to Brintnall, "civic engagement must, as a necessity, move beyond the closeted halls of academia, and into the community" (personal communication, July 30, 2005). APSA accomplishes this by looking with new eyes at electoral practices, such as felony disenfranchisement and restrictive voter registration practices or the impact of inequalities of place and opportunity on a local or federal government's policy decisions. The goal is to provide practical recommendations to improve civic engagement and to move toward a stronger political science of citizenship. This association's latest publication on civic engagement is *Democracy at Risk: How Political Choices Undermine Citizen Participation, and What We Can Do About It* (Macedo, 2005).

The National Communication Association (NCA) realizes the relevance of the content of its discipline to the scholarship of engagement. Communication scholars research and teach in areas that naturally engage them in partnerships with external communities. They study and teach courses about intercultural communication and diversity and organizational, political, and health communication. They explore the role of communication in social change and link communication theory to debates on the First

Amendment, freedom of the press, and the nature of ethical communication in contemporary society and relationships.

The theme of a recent NCA national convention was Communication: An Engaged Discipline. At a more local level, the theme of the Georgia Communication Association's 2005 convention was Communication for the Common Good. NCA members also increasingly are involved in partnerships with multidisciplinary societies, such as the Consortium of Social Science Associations and the American Council of Learned Societies, and with national funding agencies. Through these partnerships, communication scholars frequently collaborate with speakers from other disciplines to present congressional briefings on timely topics of social interest such as international conflict resolution, communicating about risk, detecting deception, and privacy issues in the 21st century. NCA leaders and members also are integrating the engagement theme into their pedagogy and classroom instruction through involvement in the national service-learning and scholarship of teaching and learning initiatives. A recent engagement-focused publication by communication scholars sprang from an NCA-sponsored summer conference, *Communicating Politics: Engaging the Public in Democratic Life* (McKinney, Kaid, Bystrom, & Carlin, 2005).

The American Historical Association (AHA) also has done much to encourage historians to engage with public issues and needs, ranging from providing advice to corporations to serving as expert consultants for network news programming. For example, Columbia professor Eric Foner worked for the Chicago Historical Society and also with the Disney Corporation advising on exhibits. Cold war historian Philip Zelikow wrote much of the 9/11 Commission Report.

AHA Executive Director Arnita Jones presents a solid argument for history as an engaged discipline. "History as a discipline is very much a public concern and is slowly being redefined to fit the content of public issues and needs. Because interpretation of the past is so vital to democratic debate and civic life in the public realm, historians should enter public discourse so that their knowledge has an impact on the concerns and controversies of the present" (personal communication, July 30, 2005). Toward this end, thousands of historians have worked with public programming and with state humanities councils to give advice on museum exhibits, documentaries, and TV or cable specials. Like the political scientists, AHA has a Task Force on Public History that has made great efforts to reopen the discussion about what "counts" in the work of history faculty, with the goal of encouraging history departments to recognize a wide range of scholarly activities in hiring, tenure, and promotion decisions.

In addition to this exemplary work in the social and behavioral sciences, the Association of American Law Schools also is highly committed to engaged scholarship. Plenary sessions at their 2005 annual meeting bear witness to this commitment to engagement in a wide range of public arenas, for example, Law, Philosophy, and Foreign Affairs; Creating a New Field: The Evolution of Environmental Law; and Engaged Legal Theorizing. The association's president, Gerald Torres, said that questions about engagement such as these should command attention at the meeting: "What does it mean to do scholarship that bridges the 'purely academic' and the practical? How can scholarly projects that engage pressing questions of legal practice enhance the empirical breadth and theoretical sophistication of our work? What enables scholarship to be at once 'engaged' with questions of legal and political reform, and yet critical and probing?" According to Torres, "All of these questions are continuously alive in our discipline [the law]" (Torres quotes provided by C. Monk, personal communication, July 30, 2005).

Looking to the Future

In our effort to see higher education with Proust's new eyes, we are asking faculty and disciplinary societies to recognize that what we do matters to human problems and to teaching and learning that produces students committed to the public good. We do risk creating some conflict when we reenter the realm of the public intellectual and stand toe-to-toe with community partners whom we sometimes learn from and sometimes critique. Certainly there is value in talking and writing to and for disciplinary colleagues in our special disciplinary language. But if that is all we do and if we allow our disciplinary societies to be complicit in insulating us rather than connecting us to the public and its problems, then we should not be surprised when the public does not continue to support us for being the brilliant but irrelevant group we will have become.

References

Applegate, J. L., & Morreale, S. P. (2001, May). Creating engaged disciplines. *AAHE Bulletin, 53*(9), 7–9.

Boyer, E. L. (1990). *Scholarship reconsidered: Priorities of the professoriate.* Princeton, NJ: Carnegie Foundation for the Advancement of Teaching.

Bush, V. (1945). *Science—The endless frontier.* Washington, DC: U.S. Government Printing Office.

Gladwell, M. (2000). *The tipping point: How little things can make a big difference.* New York, NY: Little, Brown.

Huber, M. T., & Morreale, S. P. (Eds.). (2001). *Disciplinary styles in the scholarship of teaching and learning: A conversation.* Menlo, CA: Carnegie Foundation for the Advancement of Teaching.

Macedo, S. (2005). *Democracy at risk: How political choices undermine citizen participation, and what we can do about it.* Washington, DC: Brookings Institution Press.

McKinney, M. S., Kaid, L. L., Bystrom, D. G., & Carlin, D. B. (Eds.). (2005). *Communicating politics: Engaging the public in democratic life.* New York, NY: Peter Lang.

Morreale, S., & Howery, C. (2002). *Interdisciplinary collaboration: Down with the silos and up with engagement.* Washington, DC: American Association for Higher Education.

Putnam, R. D. (2000). *Bowling alone: The collapse and revival of American community*. New York, NY: Simon & Schuster.

Stokes, D. E. (1997). *Pasteur's quadrant: Basic science and technological innovation*. Washington, DC: Brookings Institution Press.

Woodrow Wilson National Fellowship Foundation. (2000). *The responsive PhD initiative*. Princeton, NJ: Author.

About the Authors

Sherwyn P. Morreale is a faculty member in the communication department at the University of Colorado, Colorado Springs and is engaged in research and teaching in organizational communication, communication theory, instructional communication, public speaking, and the assessment of communication competence. She received her undergraduate and master's degrees in communication from the University of Colorado and her Ph.D. from the University of Denver. She served as associate director of external affairs for the National Communication Association, the world's oldest and largest association of professors in the communication discipline. In this position, she was responsible for communication, instruction, research initiatives, and outreach on behalf of the communication discipline. She is the author of two communication textbooks and numerous monographs and articles in academic journals.

James L. Applegate is vice president for academic affairs at the Kentucky Council on Postsecondary Education. He previously served as president of the National Communication Association as well as professor of communication at the University of Kentucky and was chair of that department from 1984–1999. As a disciplinary leader he focused on creating research and teaching that were more engaged with the public needs. He was named as an American Council on Education Fellow, allowing him to study effective leadership in higher education. As chief academic officer in Kentucky, he has coordinated statewide research and teaching initiatives supporting institutional engagement in a public agenda for higher education.

18

The Engaged Department in the Context of Academic Change

Edward Zlotkowski, John Saltmarsh

The task of creating engaged departments is one of the most important and one of the most challenging facing the service-learning movement. Like other academic initiatives before it, the future of service-learning will depend to a large extent on its ability to access and win over the power at the heart of contemporary higher education: the academic department. We have, of course, always known that this day would come. While presidents have lined up to sign Campus Compact's *Presidents' Declaration on the Civic Responsibility of Higher Education* (Ehrlich & Hollander, 2000), while the percentage of faculty using community-based work in their teaching continues to increase, and while more and more institutions are moving to establish some kind of office to facilitate campus-community collaborations, one overriding question remains: Will individual faculty interest seeping up from below and administrative encouragement trickling down from above finally reach each other at the level of departmental culture or will they instead encounter an impermeable membrane?

That many keen observers of contemporary higher education recognize the pivotal importance of the academic department can be documented without great difficulty. As Kennedy (1995) observed:

... the action is all peripheral: it takes place at the level of departmental faculties. .... There is a powerful tradition of local control over most of the things that matter: disciplinary discretion, exercised through the choice of new faculty; curriculum; appointment and promotion criteria; and above all, the character of graduate study. .... Departments are the units in which the institution's strategy for academic development is formulated in practice. (p. 12)

Or, as Damrosch (1995) makes clear in *We Scholars: Changing the Culture of the University*, the "culture" he has in mind is largely generated at the department level.

We cannot address [the shape of the modern university] comprehensively by looking only at the local specifics of student life and work. ... Nor, on the other hand, should we go directly to the opposite extreme and attempt a global redefinition of the goals of education. ... It is at an intermediate level of academic life that this operational content can be found: in the *structuring* of courses and other forms of academic work, rather than in the specifics of individual offerings or in the generalities of academics' views of life as a whole... (p. 25)

Damrosch's central concern is that the culture of today's academy, grounded in and sustained by the culture that prevails in academic departments, has resulted in a scholarly ideal so individualistic it not only precludes the pleasures of genuine community, it also makes impossible many of the intellectual benefits that derive only from collaborative undertakings.

The most widely observed results of this shift toward the norm of the scholar as isolated individual have been the steady erosion of concern for teaching and the increasing rewards given to superstars.... A less visible but much more pervasive problem stemming from the ideal of scholarly isolation has been the attendant valuing of certain *kinds* of scholarship, and certain kinds of scholarly interaction generally, to the detriment of others. (pp. 87–88)

In short, it is not only a fact of academic life that the culture of academic departments largely sets the tone for academic culture in general, it is also a fact that departmental culture is, for the most part, relentlessly individualistic—so relentlessly individualistic that most academics have long since ceased to recognize just how all-pervasive that individualism is.

Thus, whatever obstacles may exist to the development of departments explicitly committed to a scholarship of engagement, they are, in the end, only "surplus" obstacles superimposed on a culture that makes interpersonal engagement—even strictly within the academy—unlikely. It is interesting, and perhaps illustrative, that Damrosch's (1995) text remains resolutely focused on the academy as an implicitly self-contained entity until the very final section of his final chapter, a section subtitled "Scholars in Society." Here he effectively brings his discussion back to that wider sense of social responsibility that prevailed some 100 years ago at the time when the modern university and its academic departments were first emerging. For it is a "process of overlay" between intellectuals working within and outside of the academy that

... creates the conditions for a dynamic interplay between public and academic concerns, a dynamism that was present at the turn of the century when academic life was achieving its modern form in dialogue with the society of its time. If we can create a contemporary academic culture that is as intellectually open as it is becoming socially varied, the next intellectuals can carry much further the interfusion of modes of inquiry, whatever their place of work. Academic and "public" intellectuals are already beginning to engage one another more closely ... (p. 211)

How ironic that Damrosch should wait until the very last moment to introduce the one factor that may hold the greatest promise in helping the academy reconfigure itself as a true *community* of scholars.

In other words, the significance of the engaged department as a concept is relevant not only to those who already appreciate the importance of community-based scholarship, but it also has important lessons for higher education reform in general. As Bender (1993) writes in the concluding essay of his book *Intellect and Public Life: Essays on the Social History of Academic Intellectuals in the United States,*

The integrity of academic intellect is not endangered by competing discourses of social inquiry [i.e., nonacademic modes of analysis and assessment]. The risk now is precisely the opposite. Academe is threatened by the twin dangers of fossilization and scholasticism.... The agenda for the next decade, at least as I see it, ought to be the opening up of the disciplines, the ventilating of professional communities that have come to share too much and that have become too self-referential. (p. 143)

To appropriate Bender's image, the academic department is itself a professional community whose future viability very much depends on its willingness to be "ventilated" by new interests, forces, and collaborations. Far from merely providing an opportunity for specific community-based projects and partnerships, such a ventilating can facilitate the development of more *internally* coherent, psychologically and intellectually satisfying forms of academic community. Bringing new voices to the table can help those already there learn new roles and new ways of working.

The attention that Campus Compact has directed toward the engaged department since the late 1990s clearly reflects this recognition of the role of service-learning and the department in larger efforts at reform in higher education. Specifically, with guidance and support from the Pew Charitable Trusts, Campus Compact's initiative on the engaged department emerged from the convergence of a number of developments in service-learning and higher education.

First, work focused on developing specific disciplinary materials in service-learning was based on an understanding of faculty culture and professional identity that postulated that faculty were more likely to adopt service-learning as a pedagogy if it were translated into the conceptual framework of their discipline. This strategic impulse, in turn, was driven by the assumption that faculty would embrace service-learning from within the context of their faculty role and disciplinary identity more readily than through an approach that expected service-learning itself to transform that role and sense of professional self as a condition of its acceptance.

Second, service-learning resonated within professional associations as the disciplines faced both pressure for public relevance and a need to capture and hold student interest through innovative pedagogies and active learning strategies. Disciplinary association interest in service-learning sent a strong message to faculty that it was a legitimate academic undertaking.

Third, there was the growing recognition, referred to earlier, that the department was the unit that controlled the curriculum and that set the standards for defining the roles and rewards of its faculty. At the same time, the department often appeared impervious to centralized campus-wide initiatives aimed at improving undergraduate teaching and learning. Few if any efforts were aimed at breaking through the unit most responsible for shaping faculty culture—the department.

These three developments led to an initiative begun in 1998 to focus attention on the department as a unit and to effect institutional change by developing strategies aimed at curricular coherence and faculty collaboration through service-learning and civic engagement. To mount this initiative, Campus Compact developed an Engaged Department Institute, a forum designed to bring together departmental teams that could develop strategic goals and specific action plans for incorporating service-learning and civic engagement into their departmental culture.

To lead this initiative, Campus Compact assembled an instructional team that worked together for three years developing and delivering national Engaged Department Institutes. Edward Zlotkowski, professor of English at Bentley College and a senior faculty fellow with Campus Compact, and John Saltmarsh, project director at Campus Compact, initially assembled the instructional team. Central to the team were Rick Battistoni, professor of political science at Providence College and an engaged scholar with Campus Compact specializing in civic engagement, and Sherril Gelmon, professor of public health at Portland State University and an engaged scholar with Campus Compact specializing in assessment and community partnerships. Finally, it was the compact's good fortune also to connect with Jon Wergin, then professor of education at Virginia Commonwealth University, whose book *The Collaborative Department* (1995) had just been published by the American Association for Higher Education. Wergin has devoted more time and energy than virtually anyone else in higher education to studying the department as a unit. (His most recent book, *Departments that Work,* 2003, includes a central chapter on "The Engaged Department.")

Many of the case studies gathered in the present book come from departments that were in some way connected to Campus Compact's Engaged Department Initiative, and all of them suggest the potential that a department-focused effort has for changing the culture of the academy. Take, for example, the statement made by the Department of Communication at the University of Massachusetts, Amherst.

CSL [Community service-learning] has been the basis around which many partnerships have formed among faculty within our own department and in interdisciplinary groups across the area. Participating faculty have reported renewed energy for teaching and community-based research and advocacy and better relationships with students and with community members.

Similarly, when the Department of Sociology and Anthropology at Georgetown University speaks of "set[ting] out intentionally to alter the culture of our department," their immediate focus may be accommodating community-based work, but their willingness to employ "a social movement model of social change, mobilizing and co-opting external resources as well as redirecting internal resources to achieve new ends" implies a far more comprehensive, transformative departmental undertaking.

In short, the process of becoming an engaged department mirrors the process of becoming a true *community* of scholars. This community takes joint responsibility for both its programs and its members. Like the Department of Chicana and Chicano Studies at the University of California, Los Angeles, it is willing to undertake "a comprehensive...curriculum review, especially of those requirements that did not work as smoothly as they could" and "sharing among faculty...individual efforts" vis-à-vis "off-campus course offerings and research/creative production." Like the Department of Art at Portland State University, it sees the collaborative process as necessarily reaching out to *all* department members, by making "department opportunities for grant money, faculty development, and dissemination [open] to all faculty including full-time, fixed-term, and part-time faculty" and increasing participation by mentoring individuals "through sharing syllabi, discussing and supporting projects, co-teaching, and teaching paralleled sections of the same course."

Indeed, essential to the self-renewal process of many of these departments is a new recognition of the importance of their students as members of the department. Again referencing Portland State's Department of Art, its "ability to facilitate and enhance the civic capacity of our students" has led to students' increased involvement in guiding the department: "Students have been polled to determine their interests, have worked on tandem research projects, have identified community partnerships, and been leaders in the classroom."

The Department of Communication at the University of Massachusetts, Amherst has discovered that

> Courses... that emphasize civic engagement are very well received. Students report (via course evaluations and project assessments) that they have better relationships with faculty, have learned and applied course material, will retain course material, and are more committed to doing community work in the future.

Samford University's Department of Communication Studies has made a similar discovery:

> Exit interviews indicate that our majors tend to be satisfied with their experiences in our department, and they have been effective recruiters for our program: in three years, we grew from 28 majors to 65, largely by student word-of-mouth advertising.

And, of course, as one would only expect, all these departments report a significant, new level of attention paid to interactions with their community partners. The Department of Chicana and Chicano Studies at UCLA has begun hosting a Community Partners Council, where partners are invited to meet with one another and with faculty to talk about the work of the partnership, ways the partnerships could be improved, and any other aspect of the administrative, programmatic, or curricular features of engagement.

Such mechanisms make it possible for those inside and outside the academy to begin working together more as true equals, sharing ideas related to design as well as operations, assuming greater shared responsibility for academic as well as social outcomes. With regard to social outcomes, we would do well to heed the warning of Ira Harkavy (2000), director of the Center for Community Partnerships at the University of Pennsylvania, that "In its 'classic' form, service-learning may function as a pedagogical equivalent of 'exploitative' community-based research" (p. 28). In other words, the fact that faculty mount community-based projects does not in and of itself guarantee that they deal with the community as a genuine partner. Surely the Department of Educational Psychology and Counseling a the California State University, Northridge is correct when it notes that

> Further study in service-learning must include a greater focus on community agency perspectives. Research that examines quantitative and qualitative responses by the community agencies must be included with discussions between academicians. Many of the same principles behind the early movement of service-learning, such as inclusion and diversity in thought, need to be re-examined to assure a much deeper and longer-lasting relationship between the engaged department and the community. (From unpublished chapter abstract)

Whether one focuses on the integrity, the sustainability, or the impact of academy-community partnerships, it is difficult to see how the national service-learning movement can realize its potential—or even reach the next logical step in its development—without the leadership of engaged departments.

Chapter 3 has outlined the elements that provide a necessary foundation for undertaking engaged department efforts. Chapter 15 has further addressed these elements based on research and ongoing work with 20 departments at Portland State University since 2002. It has also become clear, from the experience of many departments that have moved toward engagement, that there are some sustainability indicators for engaged departments. The success of engaged department initiatives appears to rest on a few key factors:

- *Leadership:* Support from the department chair (advocacy for faculty efforts/creating a supportive environment).
- *Collaboration:* Departmental curriculum designed and delivered in a collaborative way.
- *Curricula:* Civic engagement accepted as core academic work (faculty provide leadership for improved teaching, learning, and scholarship).
- *Reward:* Incentives for community-based teaching and scholarship (faculty roles and rewards are consistent with community-based teaching and scholarship).
- *Infrastructure:* Institutional mechanisms to support faculty in community-based teaching and learning (service-learning office, staff support).

Whether departments move productively toward engagement or whether they move ahead with difficultly will be determined in large part by these factors. While the case studies in this book reinforce the importance of these indicators—in particular, strong chair support, the academic credibility of community-based work, an institutional infrastructure to support departmental efforts—other case studies, where the engaged department efforts have shown less success, would reveal departments that undoubtedly have floundered due to deficits related to one or more of these indicators.

It is our belief, a belief strongly reinforced by the cases in this book, that the ability of service-learning to contribute to the renewal of American higher education will depend on its becoming an integral part of the core work of academic departments. Indeed, as we have already suggested, such work is the future of service-learning. While advances have been made over the last decade that address the concern raised by Harkavy (2000) and others that service-learning could be "reduced" from a vehicle of education for democratic participation to a merely pedagogical tool—advances in areas like community partnerships, civic engagement, and student academic leadership—it remains clear that for these advances to have lasting impact, they will need to be woven into the fabric of academic departments.

References

Bender, T. (1993). *Intellect and public life: Essays on the social history of academic intellectuals in the United States.* Baltimore, MD: Johns Hopkins University Press.

Benson, L., Harkavy, I., & Hartley, M. (2005). Integrating a commitment to the public good into the institutional fabric. In A. J. Kezar, T. C. Chambers, J. C. Burkhardt, & Associates, *Higher education for the public good: Emerging voices from a national movement* (pp. 185–216). San Francisco, CA: Jossey-Bass.

Damrosch, D. (1995). *We scholars: Changing the culture of the university.* Cambridge, MA: Harvard University Press.

Ehrlich, T., & Hollander, E. (2000). *Presidents' declaration on the civic responsibility of higher education.* Providence, RI: Campus Compact.

Harkavy, I. (2000). Service-learning, academically based community service, and the historic mission of the American urban research university. In I. Harkavy & B. M. Donovan (Eds.), *Connecting past and present: Concepts and models for service-learning in history* (pp. 27–41). Washington, DC: American Association for Higher Education.

Kennedy, D. (1995, May/June). Another century's end, another revolution for higher education. *Change, 27*(3), 8–15.

Wergin, J. F. (1995). *The collaborative department: How five campuses are inching toward cultures of collective responsibility.* Washington, DC: American Association for Higher Education.

Wergin, J. F. (2003). *Departments that work: Building and sustaining cultures of excellence in academic programs.* Bolton, MA: Anker.

About the Authors

Edward Zlotkowski received his Ph.D. in comparative literature from Yale University and is a professor of English at Bentley College. In 1990, he founded the Bentley College Service-Learning Project, an institution-wide program that involves all the college's undergraduate academic departments. As a senior faculty fellow at Campus Compact, he has lectured and written on a variety of service-learning topics. He is the general editor of the 20-volume monograph series *Service-Learning in the Disciplines,* originally published by the American Association for Higher Education.

John Saltmarsh is director of the New England Resource Center for Higher Education at the University of Massachusetts, Boston where he is a faculty member in the Department of Leadership in Education in the Graduate College of Education. From 1998–2005 he directed the Project on Integrating Service with Academic Study at Campus Compact. He holds a Ph.D. in American history from Boston University and taught for more than a decade at Northeastern University and as a Visiting Research Fellow at the Feinstein Institute for Public Service at Providence College. He is the author of numerous book chapters and articles on civic engagement, service-learning, and experiential education. His writings have appeared in *Liberal Education,* the *Michigan Journal for Community Service Learning, Academe,* the *Journal of Experiential Education,* the *National Society for Experiential Education Quarterly,* and the *Journal of Cooperative Education.*

Appendix A

Engaged Department Strategic Planning Matrix

Change Areas	What do you hope to achieve?	How will this be accomplished? (specific step)	Lead person? (name)	By when? (provide a date)
Course(s)				
Internal articulation				
External articulation				
Scholarship (of engagement and other forms)				
Partnerships and partner roles				
Student and student roles				
Other_____				
Other_____				

Note. Developed by Kevin Kecskes and Amy Spring, Center for Academic Excellence, Portland State University, 2004.

Appendix B

Connective Pathways for Engaged Departments

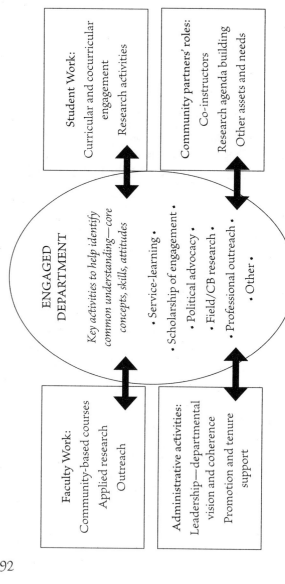

Source. Kecskes, K. (2006). Department-wide engagement: Creating and supporting durable structures for campus and community change. In S. G. Jones & J. L. Perry (Eds.), *Quick hits for educating citizens* (pp. 82–84). Bloomington, IN: Indiana University Press.

Appendix C

Engaged Department Resources

In 2003, the group of scholars who created the Campus Compact Engaged Department Institutes collected the materials from the institutes they had facilitated and created The Engaged Department Toolkit. This toolkit provides a contextual overview and background of the institutes and includes institute tools and worksheets on a CD-ROM. This is an important publication for campuses interested in promoting an engaged department initiative.

Resources that supplement The Engaged Department Toolkit include the following.

- *Introduction to Service-Learning Toolkit: Readings and Resources for Faculty.* Designed as a resource for faculty and others who are new to service-learning, this toolkit includes definitions, principles of good practice, a summary of service-learning research, bibliographies, and essential reading on theory, pedagogy, reflection, tenure and promotion, model programs, and more. It also includes a list of online service-learning resources. (Campus Compact, 2003, second edition)
- *Civic Engagement Across the Curriculum: A Resource Book for Service-Learning Faculty in All Disciplines.* This volume offers faculty in all disciplines rationales and resources for connecting their service-learning efforts to the broader goals of civic engagement. It provides concrete examples of course materials, exercises, and assignments that can be used in service-learning courses to develop students' civic capacities, regardless of disciplinary area. Richard Battistoni. (Campus Compact, 2002)

- *The Collaborative Department: How Five Campuses Are Inching Toward Cultures of Collective Responsibility.* This book contains five case studies of departments trying to act as "self-directed collectives working collaboratively toward goals derived from a well-articulated institutional mission," framed by an integrative essay. Jon F. Wergin. (American Association for Higher Education, 1995)

- *Assessing the Impact of Service-Learning and Civic Engagement: Principles and Techniques.* This toolkit provides an introduction to the assessment of service-learning and civic engagement programs. It offers guidelines for assessing program impact on faculty, students, communities, and institutions. Sherril B. Gelmon, Barbara A. Holland, Amy Driscoll, Amy Spring, Seanna Kerrigan. (Campus Compact, 2001, revised third edition)

- *Benchmarks for Campus/Community Partnerships.* This publication outlines the essential features of successful campus/community partnerships as defined by campus and community representatives at a 1998 Wingspread conference. It discusses partnerships in terms of three ongoing processes—designing partnerships, building relationships, and sustaining partnerships over time. (Campus Compact, 1999)

- *Service-Learning in the Disciplines.* Complementing all of the sessions that make up an Engaged Department Institute, this series features volumes that speak to the relevance of service-learning in almost every area of higher education, including the humanities, social sciences, natural sciences, health disciplines, business, engineering, education, and interdisciplinary studies. Edward Zlotkowski, editor. (American Association for Higher Education, 2004)

Index

academic reform, xix, xxiii
Agre-Kippenhan, Susan, 41, 89, 96, 97, 107, 221
American Association of Community Colleges (AACC), 78, 80
American Association of State Colleges and Universities, 4
American democracy, 8, 29
American Democracy Project (ADP), 4, 91
American Historical Association (AHA), xxi, 274–275
American Political Science Association (APSA), xxi, 273
analysis, 52–56, 68–69, 81–82, 94–97, 114–115, 131–133, 151–153, 163–165, 182–183, 200–203, 212–214
Applegate, James L., xiv, xvii, xxi, 264, 270, 277
assessment, 36–39, 41, 65, 67, 69–73, 146, 152–153, 165, 183, 188, 189, 212, 223, 227, 231, 234, 285, 294
Association of American Colleges and Universities, 91, 264
Association of American Law Schools, xxi, 264, 275

Barrio Service-Learning course, 192–193, 196, 199–202
Battistoni, Richard, xx, xxiii, 2, 5, 7, 11, 16, 18, 22, 26, 34, 40, 256
Bonner Office of Community Service, 127, 134
Bonner Scholars Program, 127, 135
Brammer, Charlotte, 63, 75

California State University (CSU) System, 207–208, 243–244, 261
California State University, Northridge (CSUN), 207–208, 211, 216, 217
Carnegie Foundation's Academy for the Scholarship of Teaching and Learning, 270
CASE in the Community, 153–154
Case Western Reserve University (CASE), 139–140, 144, 151, 153–154
Center for Academic Excellence (CAE), Portland State University, xviii, xxiii, 5–6, 93, 100, 104, 223–225, 227, 291
Center for Social Justice Research, Teaching and Service, 176, 177, 179, 183
Center for Social Work Education, 45–47, 49, 54
Chandler-Gilbert Community College (CGCC), 109–111
Characteristics of Engaged Departments: Four Perspectives (table), 6–7
Charman, Elisabeth, 89, 92, 100, 107
Chen, Yea-Jyh, 139, 152, 158
Chester Education Foundation, 49–50, 55, 59–60
Chile, 150, 172–174, 181
citizenship, 8, 12–13, 15–16, 18, 29, 31, 84, 273
citizenship, language of, 13–14
civic education, 13, 16, 31, 67, 234, 273

Civic Engagement (visual), 222
civic engagement, xiii, xvii, xviii, xx,
    6, 11–19, 22–24, 29–33, 35, 38–
    39, 49, 52–55, 58–60, 64, 67–68,
    91, 96–97, 100–101, 104, 106, 122,
    130–132, 137, 151, 185–188, 193,
    200–201, 208, 210, 220, 222, 224,
    227, 229, 273, 283, 285, 287, 288,
    293, 294
civic knowledge, xv, xx, 15–18, 19, 37
civic learning, xx, 14–15, 19, 22, 28,
    31, 37, 252, 254
civic mission, 11, 31, 33
civic skills, 16, 18, 38, 229, 236, 261
civic values, 18–19, 38
Communicating Common Ground,
    270–271
Community Engagement Through
    Service-Learning (CETSL), 142–
    143, 147–148, 150–155
community partnerships, 23, 35, 36,
    50, 53–55, 92, 140, 147, 151, 198,
    223, 231, 258, 259, 286
Community Research and Learning
    Network, 185
community voice, 23, 35, 94
Community-Campus Partnerships
    for Health (CCPH), 44, 264
community-university partnerships,
    40, 193, 222–223, 227, 231
Conceptual Frameworks From a
    Range of Disciplines (table),
    20–21
Conceptual Frameworks From the
    Social Sciences (table), 17
Connective Pathways for Engaged
    Departments (visual), 292
Cooks, Leda, 159, 171
CSU Board of Trustees, 244–245
CSU Chico, 255, 260

Davenport, Pam, 108, 113, 124
debate programs, 64, 67–69, 71

demographics, departmental, 46, 64,
    77–78, 90–92, 110, 129, 141, 161,
    194–197, 209–210
demographics, institutional, 46, 64,
    76–77, 90–92, 110, 129, 140,
    160–161, 194–197, 208–209
Department of Art, School of Fine
    and Performing Arts, Portland
    State University, 90–92, 100–101,
    285
Department of Chicana and Chi-
    cano Studies, University of
    California, Los Angeles, 192,
    193, 194, 195, 200, 202, 203,
    204, 284, 285
Department of Communication,
    University of Massachusetts,
    Amherst, 159, 283, 285
Department of Educational Psychol-
    ogy and Counseling, California
    State University, Northridge, 206,
    209
Department of English, Chandler-
    Gilbert Community College, 108,
    110, 115, 118
Department of Sociology, George-
    town University, 172, 178, 181,
    284
Dewey, John, 31, 136
Duffy, Evelyn, 139, 152, 158

Eckardt, Season, 243, 262
Engaged Department Institutes, xviii,
    5, 34, 202, 207, 212, 246, 247, 251,
    255, 283, 293, 294
Engaged Department Strategic
    Planning Matrix (table), 291
engaged learning, 28
environmentalists, 2
epistemological imperative, 30, 33,
    34
Examples of Roles of CETSL Stake-
    holders (table), 143

Frances Payne Bolton School of Nursing, Case Western Reserve University, 139, 140, 141, 150, 156
Fullerton College, 83

gateway course, 135, 179–180
Gelmon, Sherril, xiv, xx, xxiii, 2, 7, 22, 27, 34, 36, 40, 41, 44, 97, 227, 246
geographical information systems (GIS), 223
Georgetown University, 172, 174, 175, 176, 178, 179, 181, 187, 189, 284
Global Communication Initiative (GCI), 74
global communities, 1, 4, 74, 113, 122–123, 148, 179, 223, 240
global issues, 113, 123, 235

Harris III, James T., 53, 55, 56
Higher Education Research Institute (HERI), xxi, 248, 254, 256, 258–259, 263
Humboldt State University, 249, 251

Ickles, Harold L., 126
impacts, 56–59, 69–71, 82–84, 97–99, 115–118, 133–134, 153–154, 165–166, 183–186, 201–203, 214–216, 248–252
institutional renewal, 29

Jesuit, 174, 177
Jesuit institutions, 187
Judaism, 139–140

Kecskes, Kevin, xi, xiv, xix, xxi, 1, 7, 10, 219, 221, 224, 227, 238, 242, 291, 292
Kerr, C., 3
Kettering Foundation, 12
Kingwood College, 83

Kotter, J. P., 5, 8

Labor Center, University of California, Los Angeles, 195, 201
Laurent, Michael G., 205, 217
leadership, 6–7, 14, 36, 53, 54, 67, 80, 96–97, 104, 115, 118, 122, 125–127, 129, 152–154, 164, 182, 187, 197, 202–203, 228, 272, 287, 288
lessons learned, 59–60, 71–74, 84–87, 99–106, 118–122, 134–135, 154–157, 166–170, 186–188, 227–231, 252–260
Lindell, Deborah, 139, 148, 152, 156, 158
Lotas, Marilyn J., 139, 153, 158

Maas Weigert, Kathleen, 172, 191
Macías, Reynaldo F., 192, 204
Map of Key Components for Creating the Engaged Department (visual), 253
Marullo, Sam, 172, 191
Mason, Marybeth, 108, 114, 124
McIntosh, Judith J., 205, 217
Mean SWCS Interns and Non-SWCS Interns Practice Skills Score, 57 (table)
Media Literacy and Violence Prevention Program (MLVPP), 160, 162–163, 167
Michael D. Eisner College of Education, California State University, Northridge, 209
mission imperative, 30–31
Mitchell Family Counseling Clinic, 207, 212
Morehouse College, 126, 131
Morgan, Michael, 159, 171
Morreale, Sherwyn P., xiv, xvii, xxi, 66, 264, 270–271
Morrill Land Grant Act, 160

Narsavage, Georgia, 139, 148, 152, 158
National Association of Social Workers, 48
National Campus Compact, xviii, 4–5, 16, 44, 183
National Communication Association (NCA), xvii, 66, 70, 164, 270–271, 273–274
national disciplinary associations, xviii, xxi, 5
National Survey of Student Engagement (NSSE), 28–29
Newman, F., 14, 30–31
Nordhaus, T., 2, 3
Northwest Indian College, 83
nursing, xix, 65, 139–143, 146–158

O'Byrne, Kathy, 192, 204
Orange Coast College, xx, 76
Orange County Department of Education (OCDE), 83, 85–88
Oregon University System, 220

Palacios, Joseph, 172, 189, 191
Parker, Rhonda, 63, 75
Participating Departments in the Portland State University Service-Learning Grant Program (table), 226
pedagogical imperative, 30, 32–33
Percent Change in Student Learning Between Pre-Test and Post-Test Responses for Traditional Senior Seminar Compared to Project D.C. Students (table), 185
Pew Health Professions Commission, 141–142
Phases of Implementation of CETSL (table), 144–145
Portland International Initiative for Leadership in Ecology, Culture, and Learning (PIIECL), 226, 235–236

Portland State University (PSU), xiv, xviii, xxi, 5–7, 19, 89, 90–92, 97, 99–100, 104, 219, 220–225, 227, 231, 235, 237, 243, 283, 284, 285, 287
Portland State University's Development Model (table), 224
Poulin, John E., 45, 61
Presidents' Declaration on the Civic Responsibility of Higher Education, 4, 11–12, 31, 278
Prince George's Community College, 83
processes, 47–49, 64–68, 78–81, 92–94, 110–114, 130–131, 141–150, 161–163, 176–182, 197–200, 210–212
Putnam, R. D., 11, 265

Quantitative Analysis Before and After Service-Learning Projects: Summer 2001–Spring 2005 (table), 149

Randall, Erika F., 243, 262
retention, tenure, and promotion (RTP) policies, 255–258, 260
Rogers Mitchell, Rie, 205, 218

Saltmarsh, John, xiv, xviii, xx, xxii, xxiii, 2, 5, 14–15, 19, 27, 34, 43, 246, 278, 289
Samford University, 63–68, 74, 285
Savrin, Carol, 139, 152, 158
Scharrer, Erica, 159, 171
scholarship of engagement, xv, xix, xxi, 5, 40, 55, 140, 146, 151, 154, 156, 183, 202, 224, 264–269, 271–273, 275, 280
Schön, D. A., 4, 33–34
School of Dental Medicine, Case Western Reserve University, 147, 150, 154

School of Human Service Professions, 47, 50, 52, 59, 61
science, 78–88, 267
senior capstone, 22, 39, 40, 91, 97, 99, 135–136, 150, 170, 179–181, 184, 254
Shellenberger, M., 2, 3
Shepherd Poverty Alliance, 127, 131, 134
Silver, Paula T., 45, 61
social change, 3, 106, 125, 179, 182, 184, 188–189, 196, 212
Social Work Consultation Services (SWCS), 51–56, 58–60
Southern Poverty Law Center, 270
speech communication, 63–64
Spelman College, 125–127, 129–131, 134, 136–137
Spence, Cynthia Neal, 125, 138
Spring, Amy, xviii, xxi, xxiii, 219, 242, 291, 294
student voice, 23
SWCS Student Focus Group Themes: 2000–2004 (table), 58

theatre, 63–64, 68, 75
Transformational Learning Abilities (TLA), Samford University, 65–67, 69, 71–72, 74

University of California, Los Angeles (UCLA), 192–196, 199–200, 202–204, 285
University of Massachusetts, Amherst, 159–160, 283, 285
University Studies, Portland State University, 90, 97, 221, 226

vision, 60–61, 74–75, 87–88, 106–107, 122–123, 135–137, 170, 188–189, 203–204, 216–217, 260–262, 275–276
Vogelgesang, Lori J., 197, 243, 249, 263

Wallack, L., 3–4, 8
Walshok, M. L., 33–34
Wergin, Jon, xxiii, 2–3, 5, 7, 34, 246, 283, 294
White, Daryl, 125, 138
Widener University, xxi, 46–48, 52–54, 61
Wilhite, Stephen C., 45, 62

Yett, Jay R., 76, 88

Zlotkowski, Edward, xiv, xviii, xxii, xxiii, 2, 5, 34, 246, 278, 283, 289, 294